What People Are Saying about *Divorce-Proof Your Marriage*

"Gary and Barb, through their candid and contagious style, have an unflinching message for couples. And it's high time we all took notice. Through this pivotal book we pray that millions will catch the message and inoculate their relationships against the ravages of tough times. With uncompromising biblical standards and practical solutions for real-life problems, *Divorce-Proof Your Marriage* is bound to ignite within the church a movement that that will enable couples to safeguard their marriages and pass on an invaluable legacy to the next generation. We urge you to read this heartfelt book and begin building walls of protection around your marriage—starting today."

DRS. LES AND LESLIE PARROTT, Seattle Pacific University, authors of *Saving Your Marriage Before It Starts* and *When Bad Things Happen to Good Marriages*

"Whether or not your own marriage is in trouble, you need to read this book because the marriage of someone you know is at risk, moving toward emotional divorce. Intervene now—for the sake of your own marriage, for the sake of your neighbor's marriage, for the sake of the next generation."

DR. GARY SMALLEY, founder and chairman of the board of the Smalley Relationship Center, author of *One Flame*

"With penetrating compassion, conviction, and clarity the Rosbergs offer the solution for your marriage. Gary and Barb are indeed warriors for the family, and they offer proven answers to a needy generation. I applaud their campaign to 'take on divorce,' and I pray that they are successful in lowering the divorce rates. Read this book, and pass it on to a friend."

DENNIS RAINEY, executive director of FamilyLife, author of *Building Your Marriage*

"Divorce is a death that keeps on giving grief and heartache long after it is finished. When a bride and groom say their marriage vows, they never plan for their marriage to end up in divorce. But by simple neglect many good marriages slide toward dissolution without alarm. Gary and Barb Rosberg personally and practically offer a vision and a plan that could alter the American tragedy that eats away at the integrity of our culture. Their rare honesty will quicken your desire to walk a path that not only preserves your marriage but also grows your delight in the pleasure of love."

DR. DAN B. ALLENDER, president of Mars Hill Graduate School, author of *Intimate Allies*

"No couple in America is more dedicated to quality marriages than Gary and Barb Rosberg. Their approach is sophisticated, and their spirit is passionate and pure. In this new book they have taken a major step not only to help readers diagnose their marriage problems but also to divorce-proof those marriages. I am convinced that every marriage in America can grow substantially through the reading of these chapters. The material is lively and fast paced, highly intimate and illuminating, and the result is a powerful book that will profoundly change thousands of marriages for the better."

DR. NEIL CLARK WARREN, founder of eharmony, author of *Finding the Love of Your Life*

"What a pleasure for me to endorse this book. The Rosbergs are for real. Their passion for helping people in hurting marriages is very evident. Any couple who reads this book will say, 'We can do this. We can divorce-proof our marriage.' So if your marriage is slipping toward disconnection, you'll want to read every page of Gary and Barb's book. You won't be sorry you did. It's a great investment."

DR. KEVIN LEMAN, author of *Intimate Connections* and *Becoming a Couple of Promise*

"Helping to lower the divorce rate in America is no easy calling, and I applaud Gary and Barb Rosberg for accepting it. This book is a passionate primer on how we can protect our marriages from harm and reach for the very best God intends for us. Don't settle for less. Don't settle for divorce. Read this book!"

BILL MCCARTNEY, founder and president of Promise Keepers, author of *Sold Out: Two-Gether*

"With so many marriages in trouble today, couples need help. The Rosbergs' Marriage Map will help you assess where you are in your marriage, and the six facets of love will lead you on the path back to your dream marriage. You can't afford not to read this book. For the sake of your own marriage—as well as your children's marriages—study this book and make sure you are headed in the right direction: away from divorce and toward the dream you have of what your marriage should be."

DR. TIM AND JULIE CLINTON, president of the American Association of Christian Counselors, authors of *The Marriage You've Always Wanted*

"My wife, Karen, and I have known Gary and Barb Rosberg for almost twenty years. Their passion and calling have not wavered. They have given their lives to strengthening, rebuilding, and preserving marriages. *Divorce-Proof Your Marriage* is not only a call to enduring love and commitment but also a compelling manual that provides vision, hope, and practical help for building a marriage that will go the distance. This is Gary and Barb at their best."

DR. CRAWFORD W. LORITTS JR., associate director of Campus Crusade for Christ USA, author of *Lessons from a Life Coach*

"Gary and Barbara Rosberg take on one of the greatest scourges on the American family—but they do it with transparency, compassion, and grace. Their tender advice in *Divorce-Proof Your Marriage* gives couples who want to stay close and those who want to recover their lost dreams a plan that not only works but also rewards. You'll find a lot more than help and hope; you'll find two new friends to walk alongside you through the challenges of love. Gary and Barbara Rosberg are gentle sages of God's love and mercy—fresh voices for divorce-proofed marriages."

DR. TIM KIMMEL, executive director of Family Matters, author of *Basic Training for a Few Good Men*

"Gary and Barb love people, and they love God's Word. That's an unbeatable combination when it comes to the loaded issue of divorce. There is a fabulous balance that comes through time and time again from the Rosbergs—quite frankly, it's their joint ability to speak the truth in love."

DR. STEVE FARRAR, founder and chairman of Men's Leadership Ministries, author of *Point Man*

DIVORCE-PROOF *your* MARRIAGE

DR. GARY & BARBARA
ROSBERG

TYNDALE HOUSE PUBLISHERS, INC.
WHEATON, ILLINOIS

Visit Tyndale's exciting Web site at www.tyndale.com

Divorce-Proof Your Marriage

Copyright © 2002 by Gary and Barbara Rosberg. All rights reserved.

Cover photograph © by Mel Curtis/Getty Images. All rights reserved.

Authors' photos copyright © 2004 by Martha J. Dameron Photography. All rights reserved.

Interior heart illustrations copyright © 2002 by Mona Caron. All rights reserved.

Designed by Julie Chen

Edited by Lynn Vanderzalm

Published in association with the literary agency of Alive Communications, Inc., 7680 Goddard Street, Suite 200, Colorado Springs, CO 80920.

Some of the names and details in the illustrations used in this book have been changed to protect the privacy of the people who shared their stories with us.

Portions of part 2 were adapted from *Dr. Rosberg's Do-It-Yourself Relationship Mender*, copyright © 1992, 1995 by Dr. Gary Rosberg. Used by permission of Focus on the Family and Tyndale House Publishers, Inc., Wheaton, Illinois 60189. All rights reserved.

The diagrams in chapter 5 were adapted from *Dr. Rosberg's Do-It-Yourself Relationship Mender*, copyright © 1992, 1995 by Dr. Gary Rosberg. Used by permission of Focus on the Family and Tyndale House Publishers, Inc., Wheaton, Illinois 60189. All rights reserved.

Portions of part 3 were adapted from *The Five Love Needs of Men and Women*. Copyright © 2000 by Gary and Barbara Rosberg. Used by permission of Tyndale House Publishers, Inc., Wheaton, Illinois 60189. All rights reserved.

Portions of part 5 were adapted from *Guard Your Heart*. Copyright © 2001 by Gary Rosberg. Used by permission of Tyndale House Publishers, Inc., Wheaton, Illinois 60189. All rights reserved.

Unless otherwise indicated, all Scripture quotations are taken from the *Holy Bible*, New Living Translation, copyright © 1996. Used by permission of Tyndale House Publishers, Inc., Wheaton, Illinois 60189. All rights reserved.

Scripture quotations marked NIV are taken from the *Holy Bible*, New International Version®. NIV®. Copyright © 1973, 1978, 1984 by International Bible Society. Used by permission of Zondervan Publishing House. All rights reserved.

Library of Congress Cataloging-in-Publication Data

Rosberg, Gary, date.
 Divorce-proof your marriage / Gary and Barbara Rosberg.
  p. cm.
Includes bibliographical references.
 ISBN 0-8423-4995-2 (HC) — ISBN 0-8423-6577-X (SC)
 1. Marriage. 2. Marriage—Religious aspects—Christianity. 3. Love.
I. Rosberg, Barbara. II. Title.
 HQ734 .R7554 2002
  306.81—dc21   2002005966

Printed in the United States of America

08 07 06 05 04
 7   6   5   4

For the sake of our next generation—

Sarah, Scott, and Missy.

And for the sake of our future generations—

Mason.

We love you and promise to leave a godly legacy.

ACKNOWLEDGMENTS   IX

PART ONE—WHERE IS YOUR MARRIAGE?

1. When Our Dream Marriage Began to Fade 3

2. The Marriage Map 15

3. You Can Divorce-Proof Your Marriage 41

PART TWO—FORGIVING LOVE

4. The Rocky Road of Hurt and Anger 67

5. Closing the Loop 87

PART THREE—SERVING LOVE

6. In Honor of Your Spouse 111

7. Communicating Your Needs 131

PART FOUR—PERSEVERING LOVE

8. Love That Endures Tough Times 155

9. Weathering the Storms 171

PART FIVE—GUARDING LOVE

10. The Castle of Your Heart 191
11. Building Walls of Protection 205

PART SIX—CELEBRATING LOVE

12. Rekindle the Joy of Being Married 227
13. Building Spiritual Intimacy 249

PART SEVEN—RENEWING LOVE

14. A Love That Is Fresh Day after Day 273
15. Nurturing a Lifetime Marriage 289

APPENDIX A:
*Campaign Resources for Divorce-Proofing
America's Marriages 307*
APPENDIX B:
Marriage Map Self-Tests 315
APPENDIX C:
Discovering Your Top Five Needs 329
NOTES *331*
ABOUT THE AUTHORS *335*

Acknowledgments

$\mathcal{W}$e have had the opportunity to work on some great books with some wonderful publishing houses. We have tackled the topics of resolving conflict and forgiveness *(Dr. Rosberg's Do-It-Yourself Relationship Mender)*, moral purity *(Guard Your Heart)*, communication *(Improving Communication in Your Marriage)*, marital love needs *(The Five Love Needs of Men and Women)*, and dating your mate *(40 Unforgettable Dates with Your Mate)*. Barb has written a book about understanding women *(Life Notes: Understanding Women)*. Each book has had its demands, joys, and ministry impact. They were each written in different seasons of our lives and had significance in ministering to marriages and families for the glory of Jesus Christ.

This book, however, is different. It is more than a big idea. More than a project. More than a great topic. This book is the beginning of a movement, founded in our passion to use precious days in the history of America to challenge families and the church to capture the vision of restoring the Christian home.

We are committing our lives and ministry to equip America

to divorce-proof its marriages—for the sake of the next generation. We believe that if we don't do it now, we will lose a
whole generation of marriages. If we don't join hands in this
effort, then who will do it? We want to be faithful to do all
we can on our watch to deliver the message that marriages
can survive and thrive in the face of overwhelming pressures.
We have the passion and the heart to take this message to you,
your church, and this country that we love.

As was the case with each book we have written, we
couldn't have done this alone. In fact, never before in our
publishing endeavors has a book been more of a team effort.
We would like to honor our team:

First of all, thank you to Kevin Johnson. God raised you up
to help craft the initial drafts of our material. We are proud of
you, Kevin. You delivered. Thank you.

Second, we thank Ed Stewart, who polished the manuscript.
Welcome to the team, Ed. We appreciate you deeply. Thank
you.

Have you ever had God bring you a blessing that surprised
you in its significance? Dave Bellis is that blessing in our lives
and ministry. Dave has been raised up to take a book idea and
develop it into a campaign that will reach families all over the
country. He is the best guy in America at what he does, and we
are humbled to work with him. Thank you for fighting the good
fight with us, Dave. You are a joy.

We also want to thank Team Tyndale. Lynn Vanderzalm,
our senior editor, has honed her editing skills with some of the
world's best writers. It is such a joy to learn from you as you
coach us and shape our message, Lynn. You are the best! Ken
Petersen, you have been our consistent champion. Your keen
insight and advocacy are outmatched only by your friendship.
Thanks, Ken. And to Ron Beers, you are simply the best. We
love telling every author we talk to about our friendship and

partnership with you and Team Tyndale. You believe in us and have equipped us to carry out this exciting mission. Your support has exceeded anything we ever could have imagined. We just wish we lived closer together so we could hang out more often.

Also, thanks to Greg Johnson, our literary agent, for teaming us with Tyndale House. Your counsel was right on target, Greg.

This book and campaign will have incredible influence because God raised up our daily radio program to help equip us to expand the message. We would like to thank Jon and Peg Campbell, as well as our dear friend Evelyn Gibson at Ambassador Advertising, for launching our daily radio program. We love you, dear friends. We also celebrate God's expansion of our radio ministry through Greg Anderson and the Salem Radio Network. Thank you for teaming with us to send our message to America daily!

And on the home front, we thank Pastor Quintin Stieff of Valley Evangelical Free Church for shepherding us so well. We have the best pastor in America. To the team at America's Family Coaches, you serve us so well. Your labor, great hearts, and unity are being used by God to expand our borders. Stay the course.

And last, only because you are the closest to our hearts, we thank our family. Thanks to Jack and Colleen Bedford and Audrey Rosberg for being wonderful parents. Your modeling of covenant marriages has set the bar for us. And to Gary's dad, who is in heaven, your legacy is intact. I'm just writing what you taught me, Pop. Sarah, Scott, Missy, and Mason, we love you. It is such a joy to be your parents and grandparents. We are the most blessed family on earth. Love you!

Gary and Barbara Rosberg

Part One

WHERE IS YOUR MARRIAGE?

one

WHEN OUR
DREAM MARRIAGE
BEGAN TO FADE

Seven years into our marriage, my life was a blur. I was working hard at being a good provider for my wife, Barb, and our
two young daughters, Sarah and Missy. I had a full-time job as
the director of a correctional facility. At the same time, I was
working toward a doctoral degree in counseling, spending many
evenings each week studying at the university library.

Most of the time I felt stretched beyond my limits. As I
juggled family, work, studies, and church activities, I prayed
daily for strength and wisdom, longing for the day I could focus
full-time on counseling families. Even more important, I wanted
to free up more time to be with Barb, Sarah, and Missy—my
family, the love of my life. The job and doctoral dissertation
filled my schedule completely. I tried to eke out a little time
here and there to help Barb, but I was at best only a part-time
husband and father.

I honestly thought I was doing rather well in my role at that
time. Then one day I was sitting in my favorite chair, studying for
the final stages of my doctoral degree, when my five-year-old

Sarah announced herself in my presence with a question: "Daddy, do you want to see my family picture?"

I really felt stressed and pressed for time, with a week's worth of work to squeeze into a weekend. "Sarah, Daddy's busy. Come back in a little while, honey." Sarah obediently left me to my work.

Ten minutes later she swept back into the living room, "Daddy, let me show you my picture."

The heat went up around my collar. "Sarah, I said come back later. This is important."

Three minutes later she stormed into the living room, got three inches from my nose, and barked with all the power a five-year-old can muster, *"Do you want to see it, or don't you?"*

"No," I told her emphatically, *"I do not!"*

With that she zoomed out of the room and left me alone. And somehow, being alone at that moment wasn't as satisfying as I thought it would be. I felt like a jerk. So I got up and went to the front door. "Sarah," I called, "could you come back inside a minute, please? I would like to see your picture."

She obliged with no recriminations and hopped up onto my lap.

It was a great picture. She'd even given it a title. Across the top, in her best printing, she had inscribed: OUR FAMILY BEST.

"Tell me about it," I said.

"Here is Mommy [a stick figure with long yellow curly hair]. Here is me standing by Mommy [with a smiley face]. Here is Katie [our dog]. And here is Missy [her little sister was a stick figure lying in the street in front of the house, about three times bigger than anyone else]." It was a pretty good insight into how she saw our family.

"I love your picture, honey," I told her. "I'll hang it on the dining-room wall, and each night when I come home from work

and from class [which was usually around ten o'clock at night],
I'm going to look at it."

She took me at my word, beamed from ear to ear, and went
outside to play. I went back to my books. But for some reason
I kept reading the same paragraph over and over. Something
made me uneasy, something about Sarah's picture. Something
was missing.

I went to the front door again. "Sarah," I called, "could you
come back inside a minute, please? I want to look at your picture
again."

Sarah crawled back onto my lap. I can close my eyes right
now and see the way she looked. Cheeks rosy from playing
outside. Pigtails. Strawberry Shortcake tennis shoes. A Cabbage
Patch doll named Nellie tucked limply under her arm.

I asked my little girl a question, but I wasn't sure I wanted
to hear the answer. "Honey, I see Mommy and Sarah and Missy.
Katie the dog is in the picture, and the sun and the house and
squirrels and birdies. But Sarah, where is Daddy?"

"You're at the library," she said.

With that simple statement my little princess stopped time
for me. Lifting her gently off my lap, I sent her back to play in
the spring sunshine. I slumped back in my chair, dazed. Even
as I type these words, I can feel those sensations all over again.
She had nailed me, right between the eyes. I wasn't in her family
picture because I was at the library studying. I was too busy to
be her daddy at home.

Although I didn't remember Barb's having expressed those
thoughts, she had probably been trying to get through to me
for months. All of the cautions I had received from sermons,
books, and friends to keep a "balanced lifestyle"—God first,
family second, work third—had not penetrated my career-
bent brain. But Sarah's simple pronouncement got my attention big time.

A MARRIAGE FADING WITH TIME

Not long ago, I had an experience that helped me more fully understand what Sarah's picture really meant at that point in my life. I had pulled out some other pictures: my childhood family album. I flipped through old photos chronicling my life growing up. I stopped to examine a black-and-white photo of my mom and dad when they were newly married. I couldn't help smiling with pride at the images. Dad was one sharp-looking guy, reminding me of a movie idol from the 1940s. And Mom, I must say, was beautiful. I could see the sparkle in my parents' eyes, the look of love, their hope for a bright future.

Yet the photo itself wasn't as clear and sharp as it had been years ago. The crisp sheen that once caused this handsome couple to stand out on the page was now dull. Time had taken its toll on the old family album.

Decay is normal. In the natural process of aging, machinery wears out, buildings fall into disrepair, pictures fade, and our bodies lose their tone and strength. Scientists say, in fact, that everything in the universe is perpetually moving to greater and greater disorder—a state of entropy. You don't have to be a quantum physicist to know that even the most beautifully designed and well-built house will eventually crumble if left unattended. To keep anything fresh, alive, and in good order requires care, maintenance, and at times repair.

A marriage is no different. Unless a marriage is kept fresh and nurtured, it will fade like an old photograph. Marriage is a dynamic love relationship between a man and a woman, and at every moment that relationship is either growing deeper and richer or stagnating and decaying. And all deteriorating marriages are at least pointing down a dark and lonely road that can end in divorce.

When Sarah showed me the family picture with her daddy

missing, I realized (or at least admitted to myself for the first time) that I wasn't tuned in to the warning signs that my marriage and family life were in a state of entropy.

I WANT TO COME HOME

I mounted Sarah's drawing on the dining-room wall, just as I promised. And through those long, intense weeks preceding the oral defense of my dissertation, I stared at that revealing portrait. It happened late every night as I consumed my warmed-over dinners while my family slept. I didn't have the guts to broach the issue with Barb. And she had the incredible insight to let it rest until I was ready to deal with it.

I finally finished my degree program. I was "Dr. Rosberg," and I guess it should have been a big deal for me. But frankly, there wasn't much joy. It felt a little hollow.

One night after graduation, Barb and I were lying in bed together, and I found myself working up the nerve to ask her a question. Actually there were three questions. It was late, it was dark, and as I murmured my first question, I was praying Barb had already fallen asleep. "Barb, are you sleeping?"

"No."

Rats! I thought to myself. *Now I'm committed.*

Question number two: "Barb, you've obviously seen Sarah's picture taped on the dining-room wall. Why haven't you said anything?"

"Because I know how much it has wounded you, Gary."

Words from a wise woman, wise beyond her twenty-something years.

Next I asked the toughest question I've ever asked anyone in my entire life. "Barb, I want to come home. May I come home?"

Twenty seconds of silence followed. It seemed as if I held my breath for an hour. "Gary," Barb said, "the girls and I love you very much. We want you home. But you haven't been here. We don't know you anymore."

The words look cold in print, but she said them with restraint and tenderness. It was just the plain, unvarnished truth. My little girl had drawn the picture, and now her mom was speaking the words. I lay there in the dark, pretending to sleep. But I couldn't. Events raced through my mind. I remembered when Missy was two and refused to sit on my lap for more than a few seconds. Why? Because she didn't know her daddy. I recalled missed dinners with friends, evenings Barb waited for me to come home but I had to study just a little longer. I thought about the vacations we had canceled so I could finish a class. My life had been out of control, the people in my family were on automatic pilot, and I had a long road ahead of me if I wanted to win them back.

I didn't know at that time how God would heal the pain in our hearts. I just knew that I was at the end of myself and needed him like never before.

Maybe you have looked into the eyes of your spouse or your kids and known you were not connecting. Maybe you realized that your failure to connect heart-to-heart was mainly your fault. That's where I was that night. I was scared. It felt as if I were slipping down a mountainside, unable to grab onto something to stop the slide. I desperately hoped to regain my balance, but near terror was rising inside me. I was afraid I could never rebuild the family I loved.

After Barb's chilling words, I slipped out of bed and went downstairs to our living room. I pled with God that night for wisdom, perseverance, and faith. I begged him to restore my family. I was at risk of losing the security, joy, and direction I had dreamed of and expected from our marriage. Publicly, I appeared fine to our friends, coworkers, and even extended family. But privately, I could not fool the three people closest to me. I was a man "missing in action" in our family, and Barb, Sarah, and Missy knew it.

Deep down inside I knew that God is a God of second chances. He was capable of leading me through the restoration process with my family. But that night, as I poured out my heart to God in our living room, my hope for the future seemed buried under the avalanche of pain and discouragement in my heart.

And what about Barb? Would she offer me a second chance? I'll let her tell her side of the story in her own words.

FULL-TIME MOM, FULL-TIME PAIN

Gary wasn't the only one feeling terribly hurt over our marriage relationship and family life. I also was hurting. I was aware, though, that it takes two in every marriage to bear the fault. We were partners in the disconnected lifestyle we were living. We entered Gary's doctoral program in full agreement. We had decided that he would be a full-time breadwinner and doctoral student, and I would be a full-time, stay-at-home mom for our two little girls. We charged into this phase of our life together as most couples do, with optimism and our eyes wide open.

At the outset I worked hard at being my husband's greatest advocate and cheerleader. I was very proud of him and his desire to accomplish his goals and dreams. But over time, the stress, separation, and loneliness began to wear me down. Gary was constantly submerged in work and academic demands, distracting him from me and the girls. And I felt left out of his picture. In just a couple of years I went from being an optimistic wife to a woman who felt less and less understood. My resentment began to grow. I wanted to have family time together. At times I felt a bit like a single mom because Gary was absent so much.

I cried a lot. I felt isolated. I watched longingly at other young families who were doing so many fun things together, and I wanted that for us as a family as well.

Our marriage had been my dream come true. But during these stressful years it was hard to stay optimistic. Our marriage wasn't what I had expected it to be. Gary was my best friend, and I missed him. Most days he left home before seven o'clock in the morning, and many nights he didn't return until after ten o'clock. The girls hardly saw their daddy.

I loved my husband and was devoted to our marriage. The Lord comforted me, but it was still difficult. I was determined to keep my marriage vows to this man and to God, but I lived day in, day out needing more connection with Gary. I didn't understand at the time that God had created me with legitimate needs he intended to meet through my husband. And since Gary was so absorbed outside the home, many of these needs went unmet.

I came to the point where I quit talking to Gary about my thoughts and feelings of isolation. It seemed useless. And in some ways I stopped trying. I stopped expecting Gary to fight this enemy of workaholism that was undermining our marriage. I had made suggestions, tried new approaches, even pleaded. But nothing ever changed. I didn't know how to stop it.

One day a switch flipped on the inside, and I made the decision to give up. I never told Gary or anyone else, but I remember the moment I stood in the middle of our living room on the green shag carpet and made the decision to quit trying. I was protecting my heart from feeling the hurt, so I thought. But by building a wall of protection around myself, I was not only locking up my heart but unfortunately also locking Gary out. On the outside I continued to be respectful, even pleasant—but on the inside I knew the difference. There was less transparency and sharing between us and more formality and distance. We were committed to each other, and I never would have consciously thought about walking away from him. But I had emotionally disconnected from my husband.

I know now that we were in a very vulnerable position at that point. I know now that if our disconnection had lasted for six months or more, I could have become a statistic, a "walkaway" wife.

But God in his mercy intervened before that could happen. He began to answer my prayers once I got out of the way. Then he began to work in my husband's life.

God used our daughter's crayon drawing to break through to Gary. A child's simple picture was the tool. It became a nonthreatening voice to help a distracted man get refocused. When Gary asked that night if he could "come home," I had no doubts that he loved me. And my love was so deep and nonnegotiable that all I wanted was for him to come home. But would he? Could he really change? His doctorate was something we both wanted and worked for, but our marriage was suffering because of it. We didn't know how to nurture and tend to our marriage. I had become brittle and demanding. The distance had taken its toll, and we both knew it.

I sensed an emotional distance between Gary and me. When we were together, I didn't feel the same closeness and connection we once had. I desperately wanted Gary to come home, but in order for that to happen, something would have to change. Gary is going to share with you what that change would mean to him.

THE MISTRESS IN THE LIBRARY

In the weeks and months after I asked Barb if I could "come home," God showed me how I had been neglecting my family emotionally. At first I didn't want to admit that my affections had wandered from home. I had no intention of being lured away from my family, and I certainly had never contemplated divorcing my wife. Barb and our two girls were my treasures.

At the same time, I prided myself in pursuing a career in marriage-and-family counseling. And I was doing so for the sake of God's kingdom. Yet while my goal of becoming a counselor was legitimate, I allowed books and study to lure me away as a temptress. My scholastic endeavors captured my heart and became my treasure. The love of my life—my family—was slowly and insidiously being replaced with coursework and learning: a mistress in the university library dressed in pages of black and white.

I never dreamed it could happen. I never intended for it to happen. And I was unable to see or admit that it had happened until God used my innocent five-year-old daughter as a wake-up call. God showed me through my child's drawing that I had emotionally left my wife and family for the mistress in the library.

THE JOURNEY BACK HOME

Knowing how to remedy a deteriorating marriage is vital for keeping any marriage alive and well. Barb and I didn't know how to turn our relationship around, but as I finished my doctoral work, we agreed that something had to change. We committed ourselves to finding a solution to the emotional distance between us. Little did we know that our search would initiate a journey that has become the foundation for our ministry to married couples and families today. In the pages that follow we will share that journey with you.

Can you identify with the distance and deterioration Barb and I felt? How close are you to your wife or husband today? Have the stresses, demands, and disappointments of life created an emotional distance between you and your spouse? Do you know what to do to close the gap? If you are not growing closer together, you are drifting farther apart. Although you may never consider divorce, the road of a decaying marriage is always heading in that direction.

Is your marriage divorce-proof?

In our prayerful search to rebuild our marriage, Barb and I have discovered a marital road map that has led us back home together. We have shared this map with countless other couples—many with good marriages—and have seen their relationships revitalized and restored. The marriage map will enable you to identify where you are in your relationship, the first step in reversing relational distance and halting the slide into marital entropy. Understanding the map will help you fight negative tendencies, keep your love fresh and vibrant, and keep your relationship intimately connected and perpetually enriched.

We are not offering you a magic formula or a three-easy-steps program to marital bliss. Rather, we will describe a road traveled by thousands of couples we have encountered in the counseling office, in our conferences, or through our radio broadcasts. It is a road that leads toward home, not toward divorce. And it is a road Barb and I have traveled personally, though we have not always navigated it perfectly. It is a road rich with purpose, God's purpose. It is a biblical design that is guaranteed to deepen and enrich your relationship beyond your fondest dreams.

We cannot guarantee that walking on this road will be easy. But we can guarantee that following God's design will divorce-proof your marriage.

two

THE
MARRIAGE MAP

*J*ust for a moment, think back to your wedding day. Was the ceremony short and sweet or rich with detail and meaning? Did you speak your vows in a cathedral? a chapel? a cruise ship? a backyard gazebo? Were the tables at the reception spread with finger food or a sumptuous feast? Did you zoom away to your honeymoon in a sparkling limousine or putt-putt away in a four-door Rambler as Barb and I did?

One thing is certain: You and your spouse-to-be were drawn to that moment of marriage by the dream of spending the rest of your days with the love of your life. The mysterious and power-ful force of love so swept you away that you willingly pledged—before God, your family, and your friends—to stay together for better or for worse, for richer or for poorer, in sickness and in health, as long as you both shall live. Your hearts were filled with a hope, an expectation, a promise, and a dream that your marriage would be great and that your love would last forever.

When you uttered the words "I do," you no doubt believed firmly in that dream—the beauty and mystery and ecstasy of lifelong love. Your heart probably soared knowing that your special someone longed to know you intimately and promised to accept you unconditionally. Perhaps your soul was stirred at the realization that the two of you together could become what you could never be on your own. You anticipated the experience of wholeness, completion, security, and companionship that had eluded you before. You were never happier or more hopeful than on your wedding day.

And then, just like Barb and me, you entered the real world.

SHATTERED DREAMS, BROKEN MARRIAGES

As a married couple, you may still be living on the mountaintop of perpetual bliss. But more than likely, you and your spouse have lost your footing on that lofty peak and taken a tumble or two. Be honest now: It hasn't been as easy or magical as you expected, has it?

Regardless of where your marriage is, I think you will agree with Barb and me that, for most people today, living out the marital dream in the real world has become increasingly difficult. And all too often, a marriage relationship in difficulty ends in divorce. In our culture all marriages are under attack. As a nation we seem to have given up believing in the value of married love. America's divorce rate is double that of France or Germany and three times that of Japan—and these nations are generally less Christian than the United States. Only England has a divorce rate comparable to that of the United States, and it's been so only since 1996.[1]

Today in the United States an alarming 43 percent of all first marriages will end in divorce.[2] About 60 percent of remarriages will suffer the same fate.[3] Contrast that with 1952, when only one in 250 marriages, or .4 percent, ended in divorce.[4]

Do those statistics bother you? Sometimes we wonder if our culture has become so used to divorce that we just take it in stride. Have we become apathetic, thinking that divorce is here to stay and that we are helpless to do anything about it? Are we becoming immune?

We need to remember that divorce is more than statistics. It involves real people with real hopes and dreams—and real pain.

Let's get personal. Maybe some people in your immediate family—parents, children, siblings—have been divorced. Maybe you have. If that is the case, you are among the 70 percent of all Americans with firsthand knowledge of the tragedy of divorce.

Think a minute. How have those divorces affected your life? How have your relationships been marred by divorce—yours or someone else's? What has been the impact on the children involved?

Even if divorce hasn't touched your immediate family, you probably have friends, coworkers, or neighbors who have suffered the pain of family breakup. Our nation's divorce rate is anything but impersonal.

As we said, divorce is far more than population statistics and a social trend to be studied. Each divorce is really about the disconnected hearts of two human beings whose dreams of marital happiness and fulfillment have been shattered. The relationship that began blissfully in unity has been ripped apart, and the two are no longer one. Divorce is the death of a relationship between two people who had hoped to enjoy for a lifetime the safety, security, and happiness of emotional oneness. We are talking about the broken promises, shattered dreams, unfulfilled expectations, lost hopes, and damaged emotions of a husband and a wife.

The pain of divorce is not isolated to the couple involved.

More than one million children are hurt by their parents' divorce each year. Consider the emotional devastation in the lives of these children—the loss of security, the anger, the broken spirits, the disillusionment—all underscoring the tragedy in our divorce-ridden culture.

Barb and I witnessed this heartache again recently. We were in an airport restaurant, near a table where a little girl of about eight was eating a sandwich with her grandfather. Their conversation seemed strained and difficult. The grandfather was struggling to express himself. Choosing his words carefully, he said to the little redhead, "I'm sorry that your parents are not getting along."

The girl responded, "I wish they would at least talk to each other. They won't even answer each other's phone calls." Then she looked away and whispered more to herself than to Grandpa, "And now I don't get to see my dad anymore."

Doesn't that break your heart? If for no other reason, we must begin to divorce-proof America's marriages for the sake of the next generation.

LEGALLY MARRIED BUT EMOTIONALLY DIVORCED

Most couples accept the fact that there is more to a marriage relationship than the exhilaration and excitement they felt on their honeymoon. Most realize that being married in the real world includes plenty of relational ups and downs. If you and your spouse are not purposefully growing deeper in your relationship, you are in danger of losing your dream marriage and sliding down toward relational decay and marital entropy.

Disintegration in a relationship usually begins gradually, almost without notice. The ensuing emotional and physical separation do not occur suddenly either. A marriage in entropy almost always has suffered through a lengthy process of relational deterioration that has occurred over a period of months and even years.

You may say, "Our relationship is far from a dream marriage, but we're committed to each other. Divorce isn't even an option for us."

True, *physical* divorce may not enter your thinking. Yet if you and your spouse are not taking specific steps to avoid marital entropy, you are in fact sliding toward *emotional* divorce. One of you may not move out of the house physically, but without a focused effort at nurturing your relationship, you are in the process of leaving each other emotionally and relationally. Living under the same roof and sharing the same bed, you become strangers to each other and to your children.

SEVEN STOPS ON THE MARRIAGE MAP

Any long journey in the car, such as a trip across the country, involves a number of stops along the way. Each intermediate destination brings you closer to your final destination. So it is with the marriage map. It is a long journey from the marriage dream to divorce, but there are a number of in-between stops and telltale signs that will let you know if you are descending into emotional divorce.

We want to share with you seven stops on the marriage map. Each stop represents a stage on the slide from dream to divorce, from wholeness to disintegration. As we describe these steps, ask yourself if you have ever visited any of these destinations. Evaluate your marriage against the list of indicators provided in each section. Identifying where you are right now will help you determine what you need to do to reverse course and move back toward of the marriage dream you once held.

It's important that both you and your spouse read this section and evaluate your marriage. We suspect that the two of you will not always agree about where you are on the marriage map; most couples won't. But those differences of perspective are important as you try to understand each other. We've provided two blanks for every statement in the evaluative self-tests so that each of you can check the statements that apply to you: Husbands, put your responses in the *H* column; wives, use the *W* column. If it makes you feel too vulnerable to put your responses in the book, make two photocopies of the self-tests (see appendix B for copies of all of the self-tests) and record your responses separately. Be sure to discuss them later.

MARRIAGE MAP

1. Living the Dream

The "dream" is a real place on the marriage map, the place where

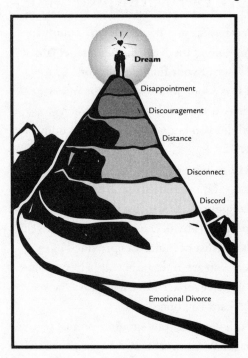

Barb and I want to live with each other, the place where you want to live with your spouse. The dream is the kind of marriage we all hope for and have tasted in our better moments together. It's the scintillating, fulfilling relationship that brought us to the altar in the first place and motivated us to pledge our lives to each other. It's the ultimate relationship between a husband and wife.

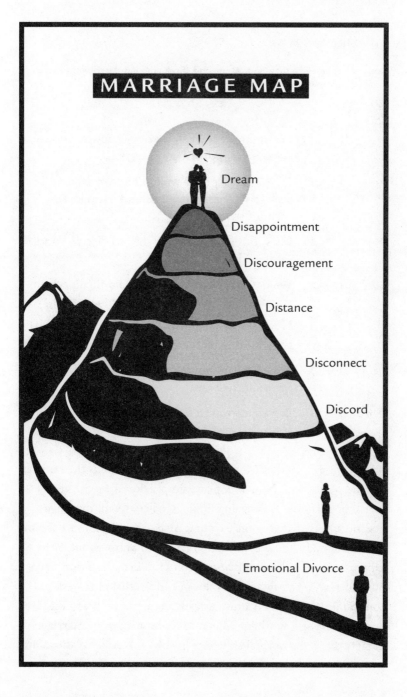

THE DREAM STOP

Compare yourself to these indicators, and check any that describe the current state of your marriage:

H   W

❑   ❑   I communicate freely with my spouse, and we keep no inappropriate secrets.

❑   ❑   I forgive my spouse when I am wronged and seek forgiveness when I offend. I am loved without strings.

❑   ❑   My spouse and I eagerly seek to discover and meet each other's needs.

❑   ❑   We have faced and conquered difficult circumstances that have undone other marriages.

❑   ❑   I consciously guard myself against threats and temptations that could pull our marriage apart.

❑   ❑   We enjoy ongoing emotional, physical, and spiritual closeness.

❑   ❑   We are committed to keeping our relationship fresh and alive "till death do us part."

We hope you don't think that living the dream is the same as marital perfection. Now *that* place simply doesn't exist in real-world marriages. Look again at our list. The dream marriage doesn't imply that we don't wound each other. It doesn't assume that we already know everything there is to know about each other. It doesn't pretend that difficult circumstances won't strike our marriage. And it certainly doesn't mean that closeness and communication happen automatically. You can be living the dream while still working diligently to improve your marriage. In fact, that's the normal state of a healthy marriage relationship!

Being married is like living on the San Andreas Fault. A

husband and wife are like two great land masses rubbing up against each other, trying to fit together. Throughout the course of the relationship, friction naturally occurs, and stress builds up. If there is no continuing effort to break loose the catch points of the relationship, all that pent-up pressure eventually releases— sometimes explosively. The ground rumbles. The earth quakes.

We are painfully naïve to assume that a dream marriage doesn't need constant work. Perhaps that's why so many couples are shocked to learn that their marriage is sometimes less than they dreamed it would be. We say things like, "I can't believe he did that" or "I can't believe she said that" or "I can't believe we let our marriage get to this point."

Friction and failing are normal in a marriage of two imper- fect people. Unwillingness to accept that fact and work on resolving marital tremors will eventually lead you to the next stop on the marriage map, which Barb will describe.

2. From Dream to Disappointment

Perhaps like you, I fell in love with and married my dream man, Gary Rosberg. My love largely blinded me to his faults and short- comings, just as Gary was blind to mine. But it didn't take us long to realize that neither of us got a perfect person. Can you relate to our experience?

Some people work hard at perpetuating the myth of perfection in their marriage. This was the case with Janelle and Steve. After their wedding, Janelle was intent on looking like an angel every morning. She awoke hours before Steve to "get beautiful," as she put it. She would tiptoe into the bathroom and spend a minimum of two hours on her hair and makeup. By the time Steve awoke, Janelle looked every bit as lovely as she did on their wedding day. And for the first three years of their marriage, Steve never saw Janelle at less than her fairy-tale-princess best. Imagine Steve's disappointment when that ended!

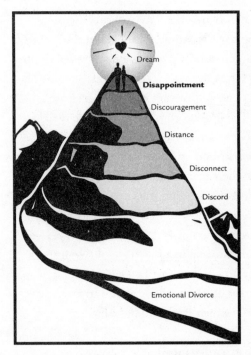

If you are like Gary and me or Steve and Janelle, your marriage dream has also been tainted by relational disappointment. Disappointment happens when you or your spouse fail to meet the other's expectations in some way.

Here is how disappointment played out early in our marriage. I fully supported and encouraged Gary's educational goals. I never questioned that he still loved me, even though he was absent from me so much of the time. But knowing that Gary loved me did not keep me from feeling disappointed in our relationship. The problem was that neither of us could bring resolution and closure to those ongoing disappointments.

Gary and I now understand that disappointments happen in every marriage relationship. We also know that if we had understood how to deal with our early disappointments, our relationship would not have deteriorated as it did. We were not alone in our ignorance. Many couples we talk to haven't learned how to quickly and effectively deal with the relational disappointments in marriage.

Whether you are the "disappointer" or the "disappointee," every disappointment needs a relational resolution. King Solomon understood the importance of acting quickly to resolve the little things. He urged, "Quick! Catch all the little foxes before they ruin the vineyard of your love" (Song of Songs 2:15).

THE DISAPPOINTMENT STOP

Compare yourself to these indicators, and check any that describe the current state of your marriage:

H   W

❑   ❑   I have difficulty expressing affirmation to or about my spouse.

❑   ❑   My spouse isn't the flawless person I thought I married.

❑   ❑   I feel surprised and let down when I notice an imperfection in my spouse.

❑   ❑   My spouse and I have caused each other to feel hurt and angry.

❑   ❑   My spouse and I have experienced conflict over personality differences, male-female wiring, or ways of doing things we learned from our families.

❑   ❑   I compare my spouse to other people.

❑   ❑   I have a mental list of things I wish I could change about my spouse.

Do any of these statements ring a bell with you? If you can see yourself in one or more of these descriptions, we want to assure you that you are normal. The key is knowing how to respond to and resolve your disappointment.

Unresolved disappointments that arise early in marriage often set the stage for further, deeper troubles. Gary sees this over and over in the struggling couples who come into his office for counseling. When the honeymoon ends and the glow

of the first year of marriage fades, husbands and wives begin
to rub each other the wrong way. They offend each other.
They hurt each other. These offenses blindside them; they
are not prepared for the conflict that inevitably enters every
marriage.

Marital disappointments are unavoidable because marriage
is the collision of two different perspectives and two ways of
living. Each partner brings into the union his or her own family
background and traditions, a unique personality, somewhat
different values, philosophies, and lifestyles, as well as a truck-
load of differing expectations. Add to this the fundamental
differences between men and women, and you have all the
makings for a lifetime of potential disappointments.

Is this where you are living on the marriage map? Can you
see how your relationship has been hindered by disappointment?
If you fail to address your disappointments as they occur, you
may find yourself descending to an even more painful stop on
the marriage map.

3. From Disappointment to Discouragement

Gary and I have learned from experience that disappointment
is not only unavoidable, it is also indispensable to enriching
and deepening our love life. In the process we have learned how
to make our disappointments a positive relationship builder in
our marriage. Unfortunately we didn't learn this soon enough
to keep us from the discouragement that results when marital
disappointment goes unresolved.

A teachable couple seeks out the skills to resolve these
normal conflicts. An unteachable couple allows disappointments to pile up, ushering in discouragement. This is the
place where I began to settle in when I didn't deal with the
letdown I felt in our marriage. I became discouraged from
Gary's lack of time spent with me, occasional lack of loving

responses to me, and lack of emotional investment in our marriage. As under-standing as Gary tried to be, he still didn't comprehend what I needed. And I didn't know how to explain my needs to him. The situation was zapping my cour-age.

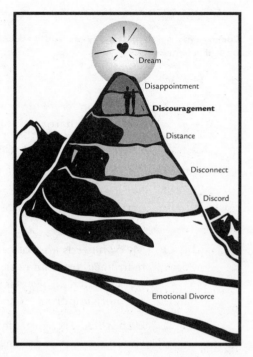

Many wives use the word *discouraged* to describe this piling up of relational problems with their husbands. Their "imperfect guy" is often what they talk about in those heart-to-heart chats with their moms or friends. Husbands, however, are more likely to stew silently about their dissatisfaction than to verbalize it to their wives or friends.

It's difficult to keep your relationship growing when the focus is primarily on the negative. You allow unhealed hurts to cloud your thinking. Your hopes for a better relationship begin to dim, your energy to work hard on behalf of your spouse gets depleted, and you lose heart. You find yourself shrinking back from time together, intimacy, and resolution of conflicts.

Couples living in discouragement find that their basic love needs are not met in the marriage. They may not be ready to file for divorce because of it, but they are living far from their marriage dream and what God has planned for them.

THE DISCOURAGEMENT STOP

Compare yourself to these indicators, and check any that describe the current state of your marriage:

H   W

❑   ❑   I often wonder if I am missing out on something in my marriage.

❑   ❑   I have a mental list of reasons why I am dissatisfied with my marriage.

❑   ❑   My spouse implies—or says—that I don't understand him or her or know how to meet his or her needs.

❑   ❑   My own needs are not being met in my marriage. I feel as if my spouse's friends, work, church involvement, and/or the kids are more important than I am.

❑   ❑   Even when I recognize my spouse's needs, I am not successful at meeting them.

❑   ❑   I have a difficult time expressing my needs in a way my spouse can understand and act on.

❑   ❑   I wonder if my choice of a spouse was a mistake.

That's the stuff of discouragement. You can be sure that the cracks in your marriage relationship have widened when you wonder if there isn't more to marriage than you have experienced or if other people are as unfulfilled in their marriages as you are in yours. You can also spot discouragement when you are preoccupied with a me-focused view of your marriage. Sure, we all desire to have our needs met. But a constant me-first attitude can lead you to complain, for example, that your spouse never spends time with you, even though some of us wives are equally busy—with the kids, volunteering at church, or spending time with our own friends. Self-centeredness can tempt you to think that things will

never get better, even when you know your spouse is trying
to change.

You may be among many couples today who are not tuned in
to the warning signs of discouragement. And when either spouse
doesn't adequately deal with discouragement in marriage, he or
she can easily slide to a place of relational distance. Gary will
describe this stop on the marriage map.

4. From Discouragement to Distance

Barb and I can easily spot couples who have reached a point of
emotional distance in their marriage. You have probably noticed
them too. You see them in restaurants—husbands and wives who
come in together, order and eat their meals, pay the bill and leave,
yet don't speak a word to each other the whole time. If you
followed these couples home, you would find that they are little
more than two strangers living under the same roof. They no
longer find each other exciting or even interesting. They are bored
with each other, even in bed.

Distanced husbands and wives find almost anything else more
exciting than pursuing a healthy, ever-deepening relationship with
their spouse. A husband might fill his time with building his career,
going on outings with the guys, participating in sports or other
hobbies, or doing a never-ending list of projects around the house.
A wife might busy herself with the children, a career, or volunteering while investing all of her emotional energy in female
friendships. Both partners use activities, possessions, and busyness
to fill the distance that has grown between them. These self-
centered distractions can destroy a marriage. Partners become
so preoccupied with their own "stuff" that they lose track of each
other and have no emotional energy left for each other.

God knew we needed togetherness as husband and wife.
After God had created the world and looked at what he had done,
he said, "It is not good for the man to be alone. I will make a

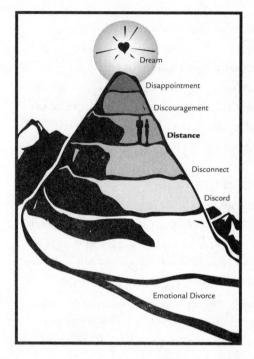

companion who will help him" (Genesis 2:18). God's primary solution to human aloneness is the oneness, companionship, and togetherness of having a spouse. When husbands and wives distance themselves from each other, they are fighting against God's plan for their marriage and missing out on the blessing of oneness that God designed for them.

Barb and I found in our own marriage that we slid easily into relational distancing. It was a natural by-product of two people who were very much in love with each other yet struggled with how to connect deeply in the midst of disappointment and discouragement. We were not purposely cool toward each other, but since we did not spend time on our relationship, we undermined the oneness we both wanted and needed.

THE DISTANCE STOP

Compare yourself to these indicators, and check any that describe the current state of your marriage:

H   W

❑   ❑   I could describe our relationship as "fair to partly cloudy, with no clearing in sight."

H   W

❑   ❑   I often fill my free time with activities that don't include my spouse.

❑   ❑   I have given up most of my expectations of my spouse.

❑   ❑   I wonder if my spouse ever feels excited about being married to me.

❑   ❑   My spouse sometimes seems like a stranger to me.

❑   ❑   I keep many of my thoughts and feelings from my spouse.

❑   ❑   I worry that we might someday face a problem bigger than our resolve to stay together.

Many couples accept a stale and distant relationship as the best they can do. It's as if they acknowledge that the honeymoon ended long ago and that a mediocre marriage relationship is typical. Interestingly, a majority of the couples Barb and I talk to actually *expect* to drift apart as their marriages age. It's not that people like the feeling of distance in their relationships. But most couples have resigned themselves to emotional distance without understanding how they got there or without believing that their dream for marriage can be recaptured. When disappointment and discouragement in the relationship are not addressed, you will find yourselves drifting apart and your dreams for marriage fading. And you will miss God's best for you.

If you find yourselves at a point of relational distance in your marriage, it is vital that you reverse course. Don't be satisfied with less than the intimacy and oneness God has designed for you. If relational distance is allowed to persist, you may find yourselves descending to the next stop on the marriage map: relational disconnect.

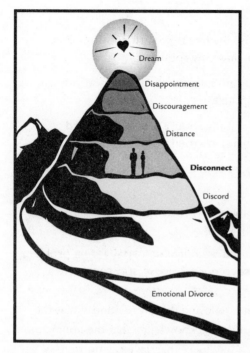

5. From Distance to Disconnect

God created each of us to be a relational being, and he wired into us a need to connect with other people on a deep emotional and spiritual level. The deepest human connection is reserved for the marriage relationship. In the intimacy and security of the marriage commitment a couple is free to share—and care about—each other's deepest hopes, desires, fears, struggles, and pain. God's plan is for Barb and me to enjoy this deep, fulfilling relational connection—and it's the same for you and your spouse. As this connection grows, we feel less and less alone, and we experience the rich intimacy and oneness God designed for marriage.

But when a husband and wife are distanced from one another and their lives are crowded with other activities and interests, there is little time to connect. And as the distance persists, there is even little interest in connecting. The relational pain from disappointment and discouragement is so great that one or both partners no longer trust the other with their deepest longings and needs. So they stop sharing at this level altogether. They disconnect relationally. The walls of self-protection are erected, and intimacy is rare.

In a disconnected marriage a husband and wife may live

together, but they are living virtually alone. The problem is, their wiring has not changed. They still have a need to connect with another person at a deep, intimate level. If that God-given need is not met legitimately through a spouse, it may find expression in another relationship. This is often how affairs get started.

A lonely husband receives the attention, sympathy, and caring he craves from a female coworker. A lonely wife pours out her pain to a compassionate male friend. These extramarital connections may not always result in adulterous affairs, but the vulnerability and temptation to sexual intimacy are very great. At the very least, inappropriate connections with a person other than your spouse may create an unhealthy emotional bond. As I learned during those long days in the library, we can be captured and drawn away from a vital connection with our spouse by something other than a person—from work to hobbies to overcommitment in good activities, even church activities.

THE DISCONNECT STOP

Compare yourself to these indicators, and check any that describe the current state of your marriage:

H W

❑ ❑   I sometimes feel lonely even when I'm with my spouse.

❑ ❑   It is difficult for me to "feel" that my spouse loves me. I may know it intellectually, but I don't sense an emotional connection.

❑ ❑   When we are together, we seldom have much to say to each other.

❑ ❑   When we do talk to each other, we often misunderstand and misinterpret each other.

H   W

❑   ❑   I prefer to devote my time, energy, and money to something or someone other than my spouse.

❑   ❑   I doubt that my marriage can grow or change for the better.

❑   ❑   I don't think my spouse is very interested in who I am or what I want to do.

Have you ever sensed that you and your spouse were no longer connecting relationally? If your marriage has suffered through unresolved disappointment, discouragement, and distance, you may be in the process of a painful disconnect. You may feel as if you and your spouse are no longer on the same team. And when you are no longer teammates, you can easily become adversaries, allowing your marriage to deteriorate into a state of discord.

6. From Disconnect to Discord

Couples living alienated and alone in relational disconnect are easy prey for disunity, division, dissension, and discord. Conflicts that were once suppressed now surface as open contention. Differing opinions escalate to defensive quarrels or arguments. Criticism and anger rule most verbal exchanges. Instead of simply hurting one another's feelings, you deeply wound each other's hearts.

Marriages in a state of discord run hot. Almost all married couples experience arguments, some of them loud and emotional. But couples in discord are at war most of the time. Their contempt for one another erupts like a volcano from a smoldering history of disappointment, discouragement, distance, and disconnect.

Relationships in discord can also run cold. Physical intimacy vanishes. Cuddling and sex are regarded as tantamount to sleeping with the enemy. Some couples in troubled marriages still enjoy a good sex life, but for most of those living in open conflict, the sexual flame has gone out.

Couples can reach a state of discord early in marriage, as evidenced by marriages that explode within weeks or months of the wedding day. But these "early exploders" are almost always living out problems established in their dating relationship.

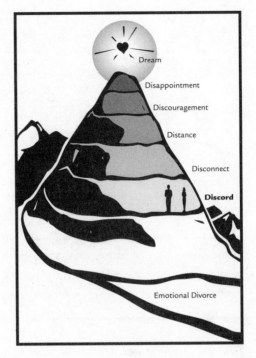

Dream
Disappointment
Discouragement
Distance
Disconnect
Discord
Emotional Divorce

THE DISCORD STOP

Compare yourself to these indicators, and check any that describe the current state of your marriage:

H   W

☐   ☐   Most of my thoughts about my spouse are negative.

☐   ☐   My spouse and I verbally lash out at each other, saying things that are hurtful.

☐   ☐   I often wonder what it would be like not to be married—or to be married to a different person.

☐   ☐   I daydream or fantasize about another person who would make a better spouse.

H W

❑ ❑ I feel as if my spouse and I are at war.

❑ ❑ True tenderness with my spouse is a faded
memory. We avoid sexual intimacy.

❑ ❑ Family and close friends notice that our
marriage is severely strained.

Couples living in marital discord seriously wonder if their lives would be better without their spouses. This looking-for-a-way-out attitude can undo a marriage quickly. William Doherty, director of the marriage-and-family-therapy program at the University of Minnesota, says, "The idea of a split slowly gains momentum over time. And a good marriage can be brought down in two years, by focusing on what you are not getting out of the relationship and how your partner fails to live up to your expectations."[5]

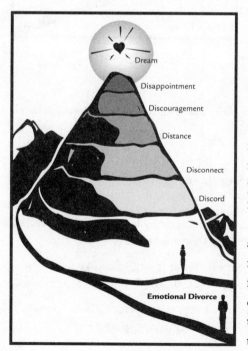

If a good marriage can be brought down in two years, how much nearer the precipice is a marriage that is in discord?

While discord in a marriage is not impossible to reverse, it is intensely dangerous. Unless the situation is defused and the combatants are disarmed, the dream of true love eventually dies, and emotional divorce is the result.

7. From Discord to Emotional Divorce

It is possible for a couple to be legally married and yet totally separated in heart. They live under a dark cloud of unresolved disappointment and discouragement. Their daily behavior is characterized by relational distance and discord. They may occupy the same house, but emotionally they live miles apart. Barb and I call this stop emotional divorce.

When a couple reaches the point of emotional divorce, the relationship has died. If they file for divorce, the court's paperwork simply serves as the death certificate for the marriage. But the relationship and the dream that gave it birth are already dead and buried. Still, some couples in a dead relationship refuse to file for divorce. They stay together for a number of reasons: the kids, finances, career image, or to avoid the "sin" of divorce. Trying to sustain a dead relationship because of guilt or to maintain appearances is pure torture.

THE EMOTIONAL DIVORCE STOP

Compare yourself to these indicators, and check any that describe the current state of your marriage:

H   W

❏   ❏   I am staying married for some reason other than love for my spouse.

❏   ❏   I have given up hope that my marriage could be better.

❏   ❏   I pretend I'm okay with my marriage to keep up appearances.

❏   ❏   My first goal in my marriage is to protect myself from further pain.

H   W

❑   ❑   My spouse and I have separated or considered separating.

❑   ❑   My heart is deeply attached to someone other than my spouse, even if I am not acting on that feeling.

❑   ❑   I know I have already walked away from my marriage emotionally.

So what's the difference between emotional divorce and legal divorce? In God's eyes, very little. Scripture teaches us that God is as interested in the attitudes of our hearts as in our outward actions. We can see this principle in Christ's sermon about adultery. In Matthew 5:27-28, Jesus points out that adultery isn't just the physical act of sleeping with someone other than your spouse. Adultery starts with an attitude of lust in the heart. Jesus tells us, "Anyone who even looks at a woman with lust in his eye has already committed adultery with her in his heart" (v. 28). Similarly, does God not view divorce in the heart—emotional divorce—the same as divorce that has been finalized by the court? Many Christians in dying marriages refuse to use the "*d* word." They know God hates divorce (see Malachi 2:16). They remember the line from the marriage ceremony: "Therefore what God has joined together, let man not separate" (Mark 10:9, NIV). So they shun any thought of filing for divorce. Since divorce is as much an attitude of the heart as a legal action, should they not just as ardently seek to reverse the pattern that has led to emotional divorce?

Is there still hope when a marriage has declined to the point of emotional divorce? Barb and I believe in a resurrected Christ, and we also believe that God can resurrect a dead marriage. We have seen numerous dead relationships brought back to life.

But that isn't the first place God wants to intervene in a marriage. It is, in fact, the last place he wants to get involved. God is willing and able to rescue a marriage and reestablish a loving relationship wherever couples may be on the marriage map. He wants to see us get back to living the dream of oneness and relational intimacy. And that's why Barb and I are committed to divorce-proofing America's marriages.

FOLLOWING THE MARRIAGE MAP BACK TO THE DREAM

When we talk about divorce-proofing America's marriages, we aren't just talking about helping couples avoid divorce court. Everyone reading this book is somewhere on the road between dream and divorce. And if you are not purposefully moving in the direction of the dream, you are moving—if ever so slowly—in the direction that ends in divorce. Divorce-proofing America's marriages is about turning couples in the right direction and equipping them for the journey of recapturing the dream.

So where are you on the marriage map? Do you see your marriage in any of the indicators we listed in this chapter? And which way are you headed? Are you moving toward the dream or toward emotional divorce? As you evaluate where you are, we trust that you have been challenged and encouraged to join us in the journey home.

As Barb and I have shared this marriage map in conferences across the country, we have yet to have a couple jump up and yell, "*Woo-hoo! We have it all together! We're living the dream every day!*" And that's not a claim Barb and I can make either. We are still on the day in, day out journey of divorce-proofing our marriage. Marriage takes work if it is going to grow. As difficult as it may be for you to admit that your marriage falls short of the dream, we hope you have been captivated by the reality that there is a path that leads back to the marriage you have always wanted.

Barb and I believe that the path back to the dream marriage is paved in love, but not just a generalized kind of love. We have identified six kinds of love that will divorce-proof your marriage and move you back to the dream. The remaining chapters of this book will unpack those six loves, which are rooted in God's Word.

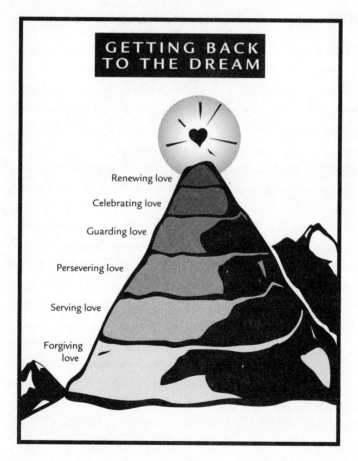

GETTING BACK TO THE DREAM

Renewing love

Celebrating love

Guarding love

Persevering love

Serving love

Forgiving love

three

YOU CAN DIVORCE-PROOF YOUR MARRIAGE

Seventeen-year-old Mike was a goal-oriented young man. He had noticed Cheryl around school and decided he wanted to get to know her, even though she already had a boyfriend. So when he found Cheryl working the counter at the local McDonald's that summer, Mike strolled up and asked if she would ever date someone other than her current boyfriend. Cheryl said, "Sure, sometime."

During a school football game that fall, Mike spotted an opportunity to make his move. While Cheryl's jock boyfriend was out on the field, Mike found her in the stands. She said yes to a date.

By the next summer, Mike had turned eighteen and graduated. Cheryl was seventeen, getting ready for her senior year.

And she was pregnant with Mike's baby.

The young couple's family and friends told them they were crazy to get married. Mike and Cheryl were also pressured to get an abortion. But they were in love and wanted to raise their baby together. So they married that summer, mere kids themselves about to raise a kid of their own.

Mike took on the situation as a challenge. He came from a successful family and knew he would probably be part of the family business some day. In the fall he started college full-time while working sixty-five hours a week delivering milk for the family's dairy.

Cheryl, a brand-new mother, stayed at home in their tiny house every day while Mike immersed himself in school and work. "It was a struggle from the beginning," she says. "I had no idea what my role was or what my commitment to Mike entailed. I made a lot of mistakes, bad choices. We had a new baby, but we didn't work on our relationship at all."

Because Mike and Cheryl were married and had a baby, they viewed themselves as adults. And since they were both above the state's legal drinking age of eighteen, they began living as they thought adults lived. They spent their nights and weekends drinking and partying with friends, running wild. Cheryl knew she wasn't bonding with either their son, Michael, or her husband the way she should. "I was just a little girl looking for love and having a good time. I didn't know how to be a mom."

"I wasn't an alcoholic back then," Mike insists, "but I was a heavy drinker. And when I was under the influence, my aggression and anger kicked in. I punched holes in walls, and I once smashed a kitchen chair on the floor. I also lashed out at Cheryl, not physically but verbally. We would stand on the front step of the house screaming profanities at each other. In just a short time, we had become enemies."

Mike's behavior was all too familiar to Cheryl. Having grown up in the home of an alcoholic, she had seen it before. What she saw in Mike scared her and made her question whether or not she wanted to deal with his drinking and rage the rest of her life. "Mike was never abusive with me," she says, "but I didn't feel safe around him."

As her relationship with Mike continued to deteriorate, Cheryl

agonized over what had become of their storybook romance.
"We were really miserable, so I decided to leave Mike. Our
divorce was finalized a few months later."

THE FRAGILITY OF MARRIAGE

Barb and I know that not all troubled marriages end so quickly—
or so explosively. But it's easy to spot the pitfalls of Mike and
Cheryl's relationship from the beginning. A teenage marriage.
A baby on board. Lack of support from family and friends.
Emotional immaturity. Financial stress. Alcohol.

We will come back to this young couple's story at the close
of this chapter. But for now, answer one question: Would you
judge your marriage to be as much at risk of divorce as Mike and
Cheryl's was?

"Us? With that much going against us? On the verge of
divorce?" you may reply. "Not at all." However, having located
your marriage on the marriage map, you may be ready to
acknowledge that your relationship is at greater risk of disconnect, distance, or emotional divorce than you once thought.
And you have likely observed that many marriages among your
extended family and friends live closer to emotional divorce
than to the dream.

If you get the idea that a marriage relationship—even
yours—is fragile and vulnerable to deterioration, you're right.
Barb and I talk to thousands of distressed couples every year
through our daily radio call-in program and our marriage conferences across the country. And I have counseled thousands
more in my twenty-plus years as a marriage-and-family therapist. Wherever we encounter married couples, we are confronted by this reality: *Without a plan for divorce-proofing, every
marriage is vulnerable to decay. And decay will ultimately result in
emotional and legal divorce.*

We have witnessed the implosion of too many marriages to think otherwise. Some couples faced obvious serious threats, such as Mike and Cheryl did. Other marriages appeared unassailable, at least on the surface. Yet again and again we have seen the devastation of divorce strike friends, family members, and acquaintances. And the fallen include Christian leaders and churchgoers as well as non-Christians.

We ache for couples who are unaware of how perilously close they are to emotional or legal divorce. Our hearts are heavy not only because every marriage is vulnerable but also because we are certain that every marriage can be safeguarded from entropy and divorce.

A CAUSE TO DIE FOR—AND LIVE FOR

Taking a stand *for* healthy, growing, lifetime marriages and *against* the looming threat of divorce is what Barb and I are called to do. It has been our ongoing commitment through my professional counseling career. It is the mission of America's Family Coaches, the ministry Barb and I share together. It is the focus of our radio ministry. And it is the creed of our own marriage. We are laying down our lives for America's marriages.

Why? We believe that if each one of us fails to address divorce now, the next generation of marriages will be lost. We must catch the vision for divorce-proof marriages and do all we can to push back the threat of divorce as far as our influence can reach. We want to join you not only in proactively protecting your own marriage but also in helping divorce-proof the marriage of every couple you know.

As we go to battle together for the cause of the Christian home, we will pay a price. We have a powerful enemy in this

endeavor. The apostle Peter warns, "Be careful! Watch out
for attacks from the Devil, your great enemy. He prowls
around like a roaring lion, looking for some victim to devour"
(1 Peter 5:8). You and your marriage are the devil's intended
victims. Since a divorce-proof marriage is high on God's priority list, you can know that such marriages are also at the top
of the enemy's hit list. Satan would like nothing better than
to discourage you, debilitate your marriage, and add another
crippled or broken family to his ledger. That is why we are
asserting that your marriage and family *are* your ministry.
They are the first line of defense that you can have a personal
impact on.

Let us proclaim together loudly and clearly: Divorce must
stop—and stop *now*. Starting in our home and in yours, let us
draw a line in the sand and tell anyone with ears to hear, "As
for me and my family, we will serve the Lord" (Joshua 24:15).
Let's agree to pull out all the stops in order to build biblical
homes—for the sake of our marriages, for the sake of the next
generation, and for the cause of Jesus Christ.

Why not become part of a movement of Christian families
who, through the power of the Holy Spirit, build their homes
on the rock of Christ Jesus and establish lifetime marriages
that enrich their lives and glorify Christ? Let us be as straight
with you as we can possibly be. If it doesn't happen in this
generation, in which young adults are choosing not to marry
because there are so few positive role models living out
successful, loving, and God-honoring marriages, when is it
going to happen?

If it doesn't start with us, who will take a stand?

When we see men and women feeling this fire in their
bellies, we see a land of marriages and families being taken back
for the glory of God. And that, dear friends, is a cause worth
living for.

A RICH LEGACY FOR
GENERATIONS TO COME

Barb and I are passionate about this cause because we believe families are at the center of God's heart. The family was his idea in the first place, his creation, his plan for humankind. He chose the family to exemplify the relationship between Jesus and the church. God does some of his best work among spouses, parents, and children: teaching us grace and forgiveness, showing us how to love with humility and servant hearts, and developing character. And in God's design, the family is the primary setting for children to know God and come to faith in Jesus Christ.

Divorce-proofing America's marriages is not just for us husbands and wives. It's for us *and* for our children—and grandchildren and generations beyond. The attention and effort you pour into your marriage today will leave a legacy for all who come after you in your family. As my best buddy Steve Farrar says, "We are not likely to know our great-grandchildren, but they will know us." Let your kids and grandkids know you as a man and a woman who took a stand for godly marriage in an ungodly culture. No matter how wealthy you may be, you cannot leave a richer inheritance to your offspring than to divorce-proof your marriage and live out the dream God has for you as a couple.

As we launch into this journey with you, this battle for America's marriages, Barb and I promise that we will not challenge you to take one step that we have not taken ourselves. We know what it means for our marriage and family to be at risk. We can remember the heat of the battle, the stench of the enemy's breath as he sought to devour the Rosberg family. We can remember crying out to the Lord Jesus again and again for wisdom, grace, and a second chance.

What we present in this book isn't merely an academic or

therapeutic exercise to us. This is our life story. Barb and I were vulnerable, and so was our family. We don't ever want to go there again. We want to warn others, including you, of the perils of failing to divorce-proof our hearts, our marriages, and our families. And we want to share with you the blessings that come to those who do.

DESTRUCTIVE LIES ABOUT MARRIAGE, DIVORCE, AND LOVE

Barb and I believe that divorce is a nationally acceptable alternative to marriage in America because our culture has swallowed three harmful lies about marriage, divorce, and love. These lies represent the consensus of our nation's attitude, shaping how we view life and lulling us into complacency to the real threat of divorce. Even if you and your spouse do not fully accept these misguided beliefs, you can be sure they are wholeheartedly endorsed by plenty of people in your immediate circle of family, friends, coworkers, and acquaintances.

Let's examine each of these lies, looking first at a commonly believed lie about marriage.

"Our Marriage Is Good Enough"

After twelve years together Dave and Libby have little in common beyond the marriage license that bears both of their names. But their relationship didn't start out this way. When they were first married, Dave and Libby couldn't get enough of each other. Their friends called them the "Klingons," partly because of Dave and Libby's fondness for the *Star Trek* TV series, but mostly because they were so "clingy." They did everything and went everywhere together, holding hands and touching each other.

Libby was only five months pregnant with their first child when she went into labor. Medication delayed delivery for another two months. Meanwhile Libby took an unpaid leave from work to rest in bed. She quit her job altogether when their son was born prematurely.

Saddled with the burdensome cost of caring for a high-need infant, Dave and Libby's happy life started to fizzle. Dave took on extra work to make up for Libby's lost income. It was difficult for him to come home to a fussy baby and a wife he now thought of as "whiny." He wouldn't admit it, but he resented that their son had come between them.

After a traumatic first pregnancy, the couple was relieved when Libby carried their second and third children to term without difficulty. But to Dave, more mouths to feed meant more hours at work. Even worse, he realized that Libby's preoccupation with the children left little of her time and attention for him.

Now, after a dozen years, Dave and Libby seem resigned to the idea that this is the best their marriage can be. It's not a great marriage, not even a very good marriage, but it's good enough. At the same time Dave is fending off thoughts about having a relationship with his attractive assistant at work. The young woman is eager, available, and devoted to her boss. For eight or nine hours a day she is at his side, just like Libby used to be. Dave wonders if he will ever be close to Libby again.

If somebody came up with a TV game show called *America's Perfect Couple,* none of us, including Dave and Libby, would expect to qualify for the grand prize. We readily admit that our marriages aren't perfect. But that's no excuse to settle for the status quo. A marriage that is merely "good enough" won't make it over the long haul. If you believe you can coast along indefinitely on a good-enough marriage, you are believing a big lie. The truth is that if your marriage isn't growing deeper, it is growing more vulnerable to disconnect, discord, and emotional divorce.

Remember: You are in a battle with God's archenemy over the vitality and success of your marriage. The forces arrayed against you are great. You must be on your guard because Satan is looking for an opportunity to bring your marriage down. Jesus said, "The thief's purpose is to steal and kill and destroy" (John 10:10). And the thief will wait as long as it takes to catch you with your guard down. "Good enough" isn't good enough when you are under constant attack.

You must not only be watchful, you must also take the offensive in this conflict. You must be proactive about nurturing your marriage relationship. Most doomed marriages don't end up in divorce overnight. Rather they atrophy over a period of years due to laziness and lack of effort. A marriage that looks healthy today can drift to the precipice of divorce in five or ten years if it is not constantly and purposefully reenergized.

Proverbs 24:30-34 paints a sad picture of the slumbering follower of God. It's a picture of our vulnerability to attack when we fail to tend to our marriages: "I walked by the field of a lazy person, the vineyard of one lacking sense. I saw that it was overgrown with thorns. It was covered with weeds, and its walls were broken down. Then, as I looked and thought about it, I learned this lesson: A little extra sleep, a little more slumber, a little folding of the hands to rest—and poverty will pounce on you like a bandit; scarcity will attack you like an armed robber."

Workers who coast through their jobs without industry or ambition cannot expect to enjoy the rewards and privileges of advancement. The slacker will eventually get fired. Christians who ignore spiritual disciplines such as Bible study, prayer, and fellowship with other believers cannot expect to be victorious over sin in their lives. Rather, they will always be easy prey to the tempter. And no couple drifting along in a good-enough, no-effort-invested marriage can expect to recapture the wedding-day dream. Instead, they are in danger of losing what little joy and intimacy they have.

No marriage is perfect, but neither should any marriage be regarded as good enough.

"Divorce Offers Me the Opportunity for a Better Life"

The divorce trend in our country is fueled by an erroneous perception about the outcome of divorce. While Barb and I don't know anyone who claims that divorce is painless, we have discovered that lots of people believe that divorce is the doorway to a fresh start and a happier life. These people reason, "If I could just get out of this dead-end marriage, if I could part company with my nagging spouse, I would finally be happy." And with divorce rates among Christians higher than they are among the general population, we may safely assume that many believers have swallowed this lie as well.

If you are sometimes tempted to believe that the grass is greener on the other side of the marital fence, forget it. It isn't true. Recent research followed a number of couples who had been unhappy in their marriages. Five years later these same couples rated their marriages as either "happy" or "very happy." What caused the difference? For one thing, time. If you just stay in a marriage and get past the stage of unhappiness, you are likely to find your marriage improving over time. Just think what could happen if we as Christians add to time the power of the Holy Spirit to *truly* give purpose to our marriages.

One of the great ironies of divorce is that people believe they are swapping their worn-out love relationship for something better. But in truth, marriage *is* the better thing. A review of more than 130 empirical studies from the 1930s to the present indicates that married people generally live longer, are more emotionally and physically healthy, are happier, and are

more likely to recover from cancer than unmarried people.[1]
Studies on marriages have found that married people live
longer, enjoy higher incomes and wealth, engage in less risky
behaviors, eat more healthily, and have fewer psychological
problems than unmarried people.[2]

Consider the following benefits of marriage over divorce:

1. *Health.* A married forty-eight-year-old woman has an
87 percent chance of living to age sixty-five, but a divorced
forty-eight-year-old woman's odds of reaching that age are
only 67 percent. A married forty-eight-year-old man has an
83 percent chance of living until age sixty-five, but a divorced
forty-eight-year-old man's chances of reaching that age are only
63 percent.[3]

2. *Wealth.* In 1994 married couples in their fifties averaged
net assets of $132,000. Divorced persons averaged $33,600,
never married persons $35,000, separated persons only $7,600.[4]

3. *Happiness.* Married persons are twice as likely as persons
who are single for any reason to say they are "very happy."
Thirty-eight percent of married couples say they are very
happy, compared to 14 percent of divorced men, 18 percent
of divorced women, 21 percent of never married persons, and
18 percent of separated persons.[5]

"Want to live long and prosper?" sums up Scott M. Stanley,
codirector of the University of Denver's Center for Marital
and Family Studies. "Take good care of your mate and your
marriage."

As great as the benefits of marriage are, the upside extends
far beyond the married couple to the next generation. Not only
are married people generally better off than divorced people,
but the children of married couples are also better off than the
children of divorced couples.

Judith Wallerstein has done groundbreaking, long-term
research on the effects of divorce on the next generation. In

her book *The Unexpected Legacy of Divorce,* this octogenarian researcher argues that the damage caused by divorce is graver and longer lasting than we have been led to believe.

Wallerstein finds that the children of divorce suffer in diverse, life-altering ways:

1. *Missing role models.* Adult children of divorce lack pictures of a healthy marriage partnership. Children from intact families take strength from their parents' marriages—even the choice to stay in an unhappy marriage. "Just because the adults are unhappy does not mean the children are," says Wallerstein.

2. *Prolonged adolescence.* When children of divorce provide emotional support to wounded parents, as they often do, bonds are harder to break.

3. *A diminished shot at life.* The fathers of 90 percent of children with intact families contribute to college expenses. Fewer than 30 percent of the children of divorce receive help from them.

4. *Rough stepfamily relations.* Remarriage shifts a parent's focus to pleasing a new spouse, at least at the start. Of the 67 percent of children in Wallerstein's study who grew up with divorce and remarriage of one or both parents, only a fraction bonded with all members of the blended families.

5. *More at-risk behavior.* The children of divorce use drugs and alcohol before age fourteen more often than do the children of intact families. Girls have earlier sexual experiences.

6. *Less social competence.* A reported 67 percent of the children of divorce rated above average in competence at work, but only 40 percent functioned well in social relationships. Another 33 percent went to therapists to work through their personal lives.[6]

You may think that your kids don't notice when there is distance or discord in your relationship. You may assume that your conflicts are out of their earshot. But Barb and I know from experience that kids are tuned in to their parents' relationship more than we want to admit.

In the process of writing my first book—on the subject of mending relationships, ironically—Barb and I were in our bedroom one evening having a conflict. The door was closed, so we were sure our two young daughters could not hear our heated discussion.

About ten o'clock we heard a knock on our door. I looked at Barb. "Who do you think it is?"

"I think it's one of the girls," she said. "You get it. You're the one who's barking."

I opened the door to find Sarah and Missy standing there in their pajamas. They were still very young. They looked at us and one of them asked, "Are you going to get a divorce?"

"What?" I asked. "Why would you ask that?"

"Well, my friend's parents have been arguing," answered Sarah, "and they're going to get a divorce."

Lord, help us, I groaned silently. Barb and I were so sad that our argument had caused our little girls pain. And we were shocked at how vulnerable they were to our conflict.

God intends us to divorce-proof our marriages not only for our good but for the good of our children.

"Our Love Makes Us Immune from the Threat of Divorce"

When Barb and I hear this statement, we begin to feel hopeful. Couples who buy into this lie are at least on the right track because the statement is half true. Love *is* the foundation for a thriving marriage. The critical question is, which definition of love are we talking about? In order to divorce-proof our marriages, just any old kind of love won't do. We need to understand and experience the kind of love God has provided to keep our marriages vital, growing, and safe from the threat of divorce.

We believe there are six key kinds of love needed to divorce-proof a marriage:

- ◆ forgiving love
- ◆ serving love
- ◆ persevering love
- ◆ guarding love
- ◆ celebrating love
- ◆ renewing love

These six expressions are the secret to an invincible, rock-solid marriage. As you begin to put these facets of love into practice by the grace of God, you will shield your marriage from the ravages of distance, disconnect, discord, and emotional divorce. We will spend the rest of this book exploring and applying these six vital expressions of love.

Forgiving love heals hurts and helps spouses feel accepted and connected.

Forgiving love offers a fresh start after you have offended and hurt each other. When you were first married, you felt important to your spouse, and you let your spouse know how important he or she was to you. But somewhere along the journey that feeling waned because of offenses ranging from minor disagreements to major blows of betrayal. Forgiving love equips you to communicate such a deep level of acceptance for one another that you can recover from the pain you occasionally inflict on one another and work through your offenses. Forgiving love helps you reconnect after you have hurt one another. It's the kind of love Paul described when he wrote, "Do your part to live in peace with everyone, as much as possible" (Romans 12:18).

Serving love discovers and meets needs
and helps spouses feel
honored and understood.

Serving love helps you discover and meet each other's deepest needs.
God created you and your spouse with physical, emotional,
and spiritual needs, and he wants you to be involved in meeting
those needs for each other. You may feel reluctant to express
your needs to your spouse, thinking you shouldn't be needy
or you should somehow be able to meet your own needs. Serving love is the process of identifying needs and taking steps
to meet them in each other. The apostle Paul wrote, "Honor
one another above yourselves" (Romans 12:10, NIV). You
honor one another when you serve each other, putting your
spouse's needs above your own. When we serve one another,
we are humbling ourselves just as Jesus did when he washed
the disciples' feet (see John 13).

Persevering love stays strong in tough times
and helps spouses feel
bonded—best friends for life.

Persevering love sustains you through the trials of life. Day-to-day
life is often hazardous. Accidents happen. Tragedies strike.
Losses occur. You need to love in ways that keep your marriage firmly grounded through the stormy trials and pains of
life. As you implement persevering love in your marriage,
you will bond with your spouse and enjoy a love that will last
through thick and thin. Enduring love is described in the New
Testament: "We can rejoice, too, when we run into problems
and trials, for we know that they are good for us—they help us

learn to endure. And endurance develops strength of character in us" (Romans 5:3-4).

Guarding love protects from threats and helps spouses feel safe and secure.

Guarding love protects your hearts from threats to your marriage. Marriages are threatened by many forces today: outside forces such as busyness, job stresses, sexual temptations, and worldly distractions, as well as internal forces such as competitiveness, worry, and high expectations fueled by the media and comparing ourselves to others. If you are not aware of the threats to your marriage or the potential havoc these forces can wreak on your relationship, then you are vulnerable. Maybe you have had some of these questions: Will I wake up someday to find that my spouse doesn't love me anymore? Am I playing second fiddle in my spouse's heart to a career, a hobby, a friend, or other distractions? Will I or my spouse fall prey to an extramarital affair? Guarding love is alert to the threats and does all it can to protect against destructive forces. The Bible reminds us, "Above all else, guard your heart, for it is the wellspring of life" (Proverbs 4:23, NIV).

Celebrating love rejoices in the marriage relationship and helps spouses feel cherished and captivated.

Celebrating love equips you to maintain a satisfying emotional, physical, and spiritual connection. Remember the spark and magic that characterized your first months of marriage? It may have been something like the excitement Solomon experienced when his wife enticed him: "Take me with you. Come, let's run! Bring me into your bedroom" (Song of Songs 1:4). Solomon returned her love by saying, "[I am] held captive in your queenly tresses. Oh, how delightful you are, my beloved; how pleasant for utter delight!" (7:5-6). King Solomon and his wife celebrated their love. They felt cherished and captivated by one another long after the honeymoon. Celebrating love keeps that spark alive, not only in the bedroom but also in all areas of the relationship. As you learn to celebrate your oneness, you will fall in love all over again.

Renewing love refreshes and supports the marriage bond and helps spouses feel confident and rooted.

Renewing love regards the marriage covenant as unbreakable. God's opinion of divorce is crystal clear in Scripture. Consider Malachi 2:14-16:

> You cry out, "Why has the Lord abandoned us?" I'll tell you why! Because the Lord witnessed the vows you and your wife made to each other on your wedding day when you were young. But you have been disloyal to her, though she remained your faithful companion, the wife of your marriage vows. Didn't the Lord make you one with your wife? In body and spirit you are his. And what does he want? Godly children from your union. So guard yourself; remain loyal to the wife of your youth. "For I hate divorce!" says the Lord, the God of Israel.

God hates divorce, yet marriages are dissolving around us every day, even the marriages of Christians. What guarantee do you have that your marriage will make it? Renewing love protects you from insecurity and provides you with confident assurance as you face your future with your spouse.

A VISION FOR DIVORCE-PROOFING YOUR MARRIAGE

As your marriage experiences these six key kinds of love in God's strength, you will be empowered to divorce-proof your marriage. Barb and I are not talking about merely gutting it out in a relationship that is a constant source of agony and unhappiness. That's no dream for marriage; it's a relational nightmare! Rather, we are talking about developing a marriage relationship that results in such a deepened love between you and your spouse that you discover a completeness that could never be attained alone.

Divorce-proofing is the greatest hedge of protection you can place around your family. It is within the boundary of protection that you can design the ultimate plan for a relationship in which you are known, understood, honored, protected, and esteemed to the point that your deepest love needs are fulfilled. It enables you to love one another in ways that will protect you from the fears, dangers, and threats that plague so many marriages. Living the marital dream by emotionally and spiritually divorce-proofing your marriage is a biblical way of truly loving your spouse. It is the path to the marriage of your dreams. Barb and I want to guide you down that path in the chapters ahead.

Consider what can happen when the applied principles for divorce-proofing marriages begin to strengthen your own relationship as well as other marriages in your church. Can you imagine the transformation when couples you know are

equipped to cherish their relationships and continually nurture
their dreams for marriage? Your church will be packed not only
with families who are free from the emotional pain of disconnected relationships but also with couples who have experienced
the joy of seeing their marriages healed. If you or your spouse
comes from a history of divorce, your family legacy will be one
that breaks the cycle of divorce. Your children, grandchildren,
and future generations will know you as a husband and wife who
embraced God's design for the permanence of marriage. Your
children will see a healthy marriage pattern that will equip them
to enjoy their own fulfilling marriages that will last a lifetime.

Furthermore, divorce-proof families will experience a joy
and unity so attractive and winsome that the outside world will
find them irresistible. It could spark a community-wide revival
of faith and marriage commitment as people discover the loving
God behind your transformed lives. Think about it: With so
many marriages healing and growing stronger, your town might
end up with the fewest number of marriage counselors and
divorce lawyers per capita in the entire nation!

Does this sound more like fantasyland in the Magic Kingdom than real life in the twenty-first century? It is far from a
fantasy; it is a potential reality. Divorce-proofing America's
marriages can happen one family, one church, and one community at a time.

And it can begin with you.

Right about now you may be saying that this is exactly what
your world needs. You may be thinking how much you want your
children to experience a divorce-proof marriage. You may be
pondering how divorce-proofing your own heart could bring a
deeper, richer marital experience to your relationship. Or you
may be wondering just how effective divorce-proofing is—will
it really work for you? Let us offer two important qualifiers for
our vision.

First, divorce-proofing a marriage isn't a once-and-for-all quick fix. You can't just read this book and consider the job done. Divorce-proofing is a process, a journey. The temptation to settle for less than God's dream for your marriage will always be with you. Therefore divorce-proofing must be a lifelong pursuit. It's not enough to simply agree with the principles; you must practice them and apply them consistently in your own relationships.

Second, as the old song says, it takes two to tango. Marriage is a relationship between *two* people, so divorce-proofing requires the cooperation of both partners. While you can read this book and apply its truth to your individual life, fully divorce-proofing your marriage takes the commitment and effort of both husband and wife.

You may have heard a despairing husband or wife say, "Our marriage is beyond saving." Perhaps you have thought the same about your marriage. That's another lie. Many marriages may be difficult and require months and years of prayerful work, but no marriage is beyond saving.

How do we know? Because Barb and I eventually reclaimed our dream after wandering carelessly down the path toward marital entropy. Two years after Sarah showed me her picture of the family with the missing father, our daughter Missy drew another picture. Only this time I showed up in the crayon drawing. That picture hangs in my office today as a testimony to God's faithfulness to Barb and me. While our marriage never reached the brink of legal divorce, it was headed in the wrong direction. But God in his mercy rescued us from the heartache and pain of ignoring his plan for us as a couple.

And we have watched other couples come back from the edge—couples who have wandered through disappointment, discouragement, distance, disconnect, discord, all the way to emotional divorce. As we share their stories throughout this book, you will learn that many husbands and wives have managed to overcome the same obstacles your marriage faces today.

In fact, we even know couples who have come back from *beyond* the brink of divorce. Remember Mike and Cheryl from the opening of this chapter, the teenagers who married, had a baby, and then divorced? We believe you will find the rest of their story a source of great encouragement.

THE REST OF THE STORY

After Mike and Cheryl were divorced, their relationship remained ugly. "I didn't want anything to do with Mike," Cheryl says. "I blamed him for everything that went wrong between us. We really weren't speaking at all. Our contact was limited to those times when we met to hand off our young son, Michael."

In the meantime, Mike had become a Christian, and Cheryl
was on her way back to the Lord. As God began changing
Mike's heart, he thought about the young family he had lost.
He made up his mind to try to win Cheryl back—and to do it
the right way this time.

Cheryl remembers being in the car one day as little Michael
sobbed. "Why can't we be with Daddy?" Soon after, Mike called
and asked if Cheryl would like to do something together. She
agreed. "After I talked with Mike for a while, I knew I would be
safe with him," Cheryl says. "He had a peace that wasn't there
before. He even sounded different. He must have noticed that
Christ was making a difference in my life too."

Following that first evening of being together with their
young son, Mike and Cheryl began reconstructing their relationship under the counsel of a wise pastor. They went back to
square one. Mike dated and courted his former wife. They had
no physical relationship during this time. They wanted to build
a love that would last, a love that was spiritual and emotional,
not just physical.

A year and a half after their divorce became final, Mike and
Cheryl were remarried in the presence of family and friends,
many of whom had bitterly taken sides when the couple split
up. The healing process in this family feud began that very day
when three-year-old Michael stood up during the ceremony and
yelled, "Hey, that's my mom and dad!" Hearts softened. Tears
flowed. Everyone realized they were witnessing a miracle in
the rebirth of Mike and Cheryl's marriage.

But the story doesn't end there. Mike and Cheryl recently
celebrated their twenty-first wedding anniversary. Barb could
not attend, but I was there. Their pastor led a service of celebration for a marriage that would not die. I had the joy of leading
the couple in reciting their marriage recommitment vows and
signing a marital covenant with them. When Mike and Cheryl

learned the truth about God's dream for marriage, the truth set them free, and they have a wonderful story of reconciliation to tell. Mike and Cheryl are living evidence that no marriage is beyond saving.

As Barb and I have followed God's design for divorce-proofing our marriage, God has fulfilled his promises to keep our relationship intimate and fresh. He has done the same for countless other couples. And he will do the same for you—he promises.

So let's begin the journey.

A SPECIAL NOTE ABOUT THE JOURNEY

Barb and I are utterly convinced that divorce-proofing America's marriages is possible. It has become a reality in our own marriage and in thousands of marriages across the country. We have seen emotionally distanced couples find the spark again, disconnected families reconnect, and broken hearts heal. That is why we are launching a national campaign called *Divorce-Proofing America's Marriages*. As a couple and as a ministry, we want to help by providing resources that will direct families and churches back to God's dream for marriage.

This book is the launch of our campaign. (See appendix A for ideas about how to launch your own church- and family-wide divorce-proofing campaign.) In the pages that follow, you will discover six ways of loving that will bring honor to God and provide joy, deep fulfillment, and lasting intimacy in your marriage relationship.

We are serious about assisting churches and families who are committed to divorce-proof marriages. We have created or are creating a book and workbook for each of the six facets of love covered in this book. We have also prepared a companion workbook to this book entitled *Divorce-Proof Your Marriage*

Workbook. These resources are designed to be used in a small group of married couples.

It is one thing to grasp with our minds what is needed to divorce-proof our marriages and keep marital love burning bright. But living out that concept in the day-to-day grind of life is another matter. These books and workbooks have been created so that experiencing these facets of love will become for you a pattern of the heart and a permanent part of your behavior. We also will be supporting this campaign through our daily syndicated call-in radio program, *America's Family Coaches . . . LIVE!* Check out our Web site at www.afclive.com to find a station near you. We encourage you to take advantage of every one of these helpful tools.

At the end of each section in this book, we will remind you of the availability of these resources. Our goal is to further equip you to move beyond *knowing* the right thing to do to actually *living it out.* Join a small group of couples or form a new group of your own. Discover how rewarding and vital it is to be part of an accountability group that has caught the vision for divorce-proofing America's marriages and families.

Part Two

FORGIVING LOVE

Forgiving love heals hurts

and helps spouses feel

accepted and connected

four

THE ROCKY ROAD OF HURT AND ANGER

I knew something was wrong with Mark, but I didn't know what it was," says his wife, Shannon. "He was distant from me and the kids, quite preoccupied. Most nights after dinner, he would hide out in the study, hunched over the computer, working on spreadsheets until after I went to bed. I called him 'The Zombie' because he just wasn't there for us. He was also detached from the rest of our family and friends."

Things were not going well at work for Mark either. The top salesperson in his division for years, Mark still moved products well enough to keep his bosses at bay. But his commission-based income had inexplicably plummeted, putting his family under severe financial strain.

The reason for Mark's distraction was revealed when he was fired for logging on to pornographic sites on his company computer. With his dark secret exposed, Mark also admitted to Shannon that he wasn't working on spreadsheets during his late-night sessions on the home computer. He tearfully confessed to her that he was addicted to Internet pornography.

Even after Mark sought help through counseling and a biblically based sexual-addiction support group, Shannon had difficulty
dealing with the impact of her husband's activities on her own life.
"Mark was out of work, so I had to take a job I hated in order to
pay our bills. Even worse, I felt as if I had lost Mark's heart to a
bunch of women on the Internet, women who didn't really exist.
I was furious. I wanted to rant at someone. I wanted to confront
a live person, someone whose head I could rip off. Instead, I just
stayed angry at Mark."

Eventually this hurting couple began a transformation, starting
with Shannon. "I gradually realized that in order to move ahead,
I had to forgive Mark for the hurt he had caused me. At the time I
thought forgiveness meant brushing aside what he had done, acting
as if it didn't matter or that he didn't need to change. But as Mark
and I began to study the topic of forgiveness in the Bible, I learned
that forgiveness isn't just a matter of saying 'I forgive you' and
trying to forget about it. We went through a long, tough process
of understanding and practicing forgiveness. Our relationship
still isn't perfect, but we both came through the process feeling
relieved and knowing God was restoring our hearts. Our marriage
has recaptured some of the freshness we lost a long time ago."

Four years after Mark's dark secret was exposed, Mark and
Shannon stood in front of their church and shared their story to
a hushed congregation. Within a few weeks, half a dozen men
contacted Mark to say they wanted to join the biblically based
sexual-addiction support group he was helping to lead. And Shannon has grown through the ordeal to the point that she is ready to
work with wives and girlfriends who have suffered as she has.

HOW DO YOU DEAL WITH THE HURT?

Have you ever been hurt by your spouse, burned in some way by
the husband or wife you trusted? If you can't answer yes to that

question, you either haven't been married long or you married the proverbial angel!

How has your spouse offended you? Have you been insulted? criticized? lied to? violated? mistreated? avoided? betrayed? How many of these offenses have you suffered in your marriage? How have you and your spouse failed to measure up to each other's expectations?

Couples won't get far in their marriage before tripping over at least a few relational transgressions. You already know about some of the pain Barb and I have caused each other. You have almost certainly felt let down by your spouse. You may have even been downright bewildered by his or her hurtful behavior. Or perhaps you suffer more in silence with a spouse who doesn't talk or doesn't care.

We have all been on the offending side of conflict, and we have all been on the receiving end, feeling the pain of hurt and disappointment. Whether you were hurt or caused the hurt, every offense in a marriage needs a resolution.

How do you and your spouse handle offenses? How do you deal with hurt and anger? Can you pinpoint the causes of friction between you? Can you think of a conflict you are facing right now, an issue that is bringing hurt to one or both of you?

Tragically most couples are without a clue about how to deal with offenses and regain the health of their relationships. Why? Because few have learned how to move past their disappointments. So rather than heal the hurt, they allow their hearts to harden. Frustrations and conflicts go unresolved.

Unresolved conflict was exactly what Barb and I were experiencing early in our marriage. Had we known how to deal with the disappointments we caused each other, our relationship would not have deteriorated as it did. But neither of us knew how to close the loop on our hurt, to bring resolution to our ongoing disappointments. So unconfessed and unforgiven offenses became an increasingly heavy burden to our struggling relationship.

We needed a love that would allow us to begin our relationship afresh after we hurt one another, a love that would enable us to move past offenses both large and small. We needed the forgiving love that heals hurts and helps spouses feel accepted and connected again.

A PATTERN THAT PRODUCES PAIN

As we have worked with couples over the years, we have noticed a painful pattern for dealing with offenses in marriage. You have likely lived out this scenario many times, just as we have. Barb will explain.

The Offense

It all starts when one spouse offends the other in some way. Offenses may be major, such as Shannon's being hurt by Mark's "affairs" with women he saw on a computer screen. Or they may be as minor as hanging the roll of toilet tissue the "wrong" way. Gary and I could supply a long list of ways we have offended each other over the years, but we are sure you have a list of your own.

It would be nice if all conflicts were as small as which way the toilet tissue is supposed to hang. But many offenses in marriage are far from trivial. Few couples escape the conflicts that result from differences in family backgrounds, personalities, gender preferences, or values. Couples squabble over where to spend the holidays, how to budget the money, and how to discipline the kids. Conflicts start with down-and-dirty personal sniping, such as cruel comments that set off a string of painful slights and slams. No matter how our marriages grow in maturity, we always seem to find ways of hurting one another, either intentionally or unintentionally. And with every offense comes pain.

The Hurt

Just as a physical wound brings pain and injury to tissue or
bone, so relational offenses traumatize our emotions. And it
hurts. Some offenses seem to sting no more than a pinprick.
Some of them pack a wallop that sends you reeling. At times
you are blindsided by an offense you never suffered before.
Then there is the constant bludgeoning you feel when the same
offense is repeated over a period of weeks, months, or years.

Regardless of the severity of the painful incident, if it is dealt
with quickly, it will have minimal consequences on the relationship. But many times the offender is unaware of the pain he or
she has inflicted or is in no hurry to correct the situation. This
leaves the offended spouse vulnerable to more hurt, just as a cut
or abrasion in the skin may become infected if it is not cleansed.
And the hurt only lingers or becomes worse until the offense is
resolved.

Hurt leaves us wide open, feeling as if our hearts have been
torn out, our tenderness brutalized, and our equilibrium upset.
Sometimes we don't recognize the inner pain right away. And
when we do, many of us try to hide it. We don't tell our spouses
when they have wounded us. We don't want to appear vulnerable. So we suppress the hurt and act as if nothing happened.

Early in our marriage, I developed a pattern of hiding my hurt
whenever Gary offended me in some way. We honeymooned in
San Francisco because Gary was in the final stages of securing a
great job there. Yet I felt the inner pain of being uprooted from
my home in Iowa, and I imagined being left alone in a strange
new city as he jetted around the country as a consultant. But I
said nothing to Gary, while quietly nursing my inner wound.

When the job fell through, we came home to Iowa to get our
old jobs back. But in that first year of marriage, Gary started to
work on his master's degree while we both worked full-time.
Again I felt hurt, and again I said nothing. Gary was ready to

conquer the world, and I just wanted to establish a home and a marriage. We didn't stop to work through our basic differences—how his calling and type A ambition clashed with my longing for security.

I stuffed all those things. I didn't know how to express my needs and my hurt, so I gave up and stopped talking about it. Gary will now tell you how unexpressed needs and pain lead to the next step of the pattern.

The Anger

When we feel hurt, it is because our emotions are sounding an alarm. The warning is telling us that we should stop immediately and resolve the situation. But, like most people, Barb and I didn't heed that alarm and deal with the pain in our marriage. As a result, the hurt turned to anger. When hurt is not addressed, anger develops, and anger often prevents conflicts from being resolved peacefully.

Anger is taboo in many Christian circles. We deny that we feel angry. In public we keep anger in check. But in the privacy of our homes, we often feel free to let it explode, and it does so with grim consequences.

One of the things Barb and I discovered when we went to God's Word is that God never said, "Don't be angry." He said, "In your anger do not sin" (Ephesians 4:26, NIV). Anger itself is not sin, but handling anger inappropriately may lead to sin— such as hurtful words, bitterness, or violence.

Just as it can be difficult for us to recognize hurt, it can be difficult to spot anger. As long as you deny that you feel angry over your unresolved disappointments and hurts, you won't deal with the problem. Barb and I guarantee it: Where there is an offense, there is hurt. And where there is unresolved hurt, there is anger.

When you are hurt, you may not be transformed from soft-

spoken spouses into red-in-the-face screamers. But everyone,
Christian or not, *does* experience anger. It is a God-given
emotion. In his book *Good 'n' Angry,* psychologist Les Carter
explains: "Anger per se is neither good nor bad. It is how people
use their anger that makes it positive or negative. Ideally, anger
was given to humans by God as a tool to help build relationships.
In its pure form, anger is an emotional signal that tells a person
something needs to be changed. It was intended to be a positive
motivator to be used in giving one another feedback about how
life can be lived more productively."[1]

It is crucial to admit that our anger exists. We need to be
open to what God can teach us whenever our emotions are
stirred so strongly. You may find it difficult to admit and work
through the hurt and anger caused by your spouse. But the
process is often necessary to restore the acceptance and connection that results when forgiving love is experienced in your
marriage.

In the normal process of the offense-hurt-anger pattern,
hurt comes before anger. But after a history of offenses, your
mind can learn to skip the hurt and go straight to the anger
stage. For example, your spouse has criticized the way you
dress so often that you explode at the first disparaging comment
he or she makes about your clothes.

The cause of anger can also be confusing. While most anger
is triggered by specific situations or events, anger can also be
displaced—sparked by one person or event but taken out on
someone else. For example, your spouse calls to say he or she
will be late for dinner—again. You hang up the phone and all
through dinner take your anger out on the kids, even though
they are not the cause of your hurt.

Anger can also be *leftover*—stemming from the past, sometimes so far back that the cause is even forgotten. For example,
your spouse fires off a volley of angry words at you for no

apparent reason. When you sit down to talk about it, you discover that he or she was hurt by something you did a month ago, something you barely remember.

Wherever the anger comes from, God has provided a biblical way to address it and disarm the offense-hurt-anger pattern that robs your relationship of intimacy and connection.

RESPONDING TO THE PATTERN: YOU HAVE TWO CHOICES

Whenever you experience the downward spiral of unresolved offenses, hurt, and anger, you have two options. First, you can simply ignore the offense and the hurt while allowing the anger to fester. But beware: This will take your marriage to a sad place you never dreamed you would go. You may continue to stuff your unresolved feelings deep inside, resulting in bitterness, resentment, and depression. You may explode, venting pent-up anger without regard for how it wounds and alienates your spouse. Either way, by failing to break the negative pattern, you continue to wear each other down. On the marriage map, you are moving farther from the dream and nearer to emotional divorce. The end result may be a relational earthquake that rattles your relationship to its foundation.

But you have a second option. It's called forgiving love. When you face hurt and anger, you can decide to resolve the conflict. That's the biblical way to deal with the offense-hurt-anger pattern. What we want to work toward—as individuals and as couples—is a commitment to address the pain and anger, to resolve the conflicts, to forgive the offender, and to renew the relationship. The goal is to bring the relationship to a place of healing, wholeness, and openness, helping you feel accepted and connected again.

In the next chapter we will introduce you to a process that will enable you to move past offenses, discover healing for your hurts, and find relief for your anger. What we need to understand first, however, is the power that makes this resolution possible. And we find that power in forgiving love.

WHAT IS FORGIVING LOVE?

Forgiving love safeguards your marriage by healing hurts and helping you feel accepted and connected. It's the love that brings you and your spouse back together when the inevitable offenses of a married relationship have pushed you apart. It's the first love every marriage needs in order to be divorce-proof. And it's a love that is securely rooted in God's love for us.

The New Testament uses several words for *forgive*. The root of the most common word means to "send away" or "dismiss." Another word sometimes translated as *forgive* means to "let loose" or "release." Yet another means to "bestow favor unconditionally." Practically speaking, biblical forgiveness means that we actively choose to give up our grudge despite the severity of the injustice done to us. It doesn't mean that we say or feel, "It didn't hurt me" or "It didn't really matter." Many disappointments wound us deeply. But after we recognize the hurt, we should choose to let it go. And when we cause the hurt, we seek that same release from those we offend.

The Bible says that our wrong behaviors alienate us from God and make us his enemies (see Colossians 1:21). But God's forgiveness, provided through our response of faith to Christ's sacrifice on the cross, opens the door to matchless benefits. When God forgives, he removes our transgressions "as far away from us as the east is from the west" (Psalm 103:12). But that's not all that happens. Along with forgiveness, Christ also

- rescues us from darkness (see Colossians 1:13)
- redeems us (see Colossians 1:14)
- reconciles us to God (see Colossians 1:22)
- makes us able to stand before God without blemish (see Colossians 1:22)
- clears us of all accusations (see Colossians 1:22)
- cleanses us from every wrong (see 1 John 1:9)

When we extend forgiving love to each other, we enjoy the same relationship-restoring experience. By offering forgiveness, we are offering the grace—the unmerited favor—that God has given us. We are following the Bible's wise command to "make allowance for each other's faults and forgive the person who offends you. Remember, the Lord forgave you, so you must forgive others" (Colossians 3:13).

When you exhibit the grace of forgiving love toward your spouse, you change the entire tone of your marriage. No longer are you like referees counting each other's fouls, ready to toss each other out of the game. Marriage becomes a safe place where you don't have to hide your foibles and your failings. Instead of feeling scrutinized and condemned for your shortcomings, you feel accepted and forgiven.

Think of a recent conflict between you and your spouse. Imagine what forgiving love can accomplish in this conflict and others. Forgiving love

- brings your relationship into the light
- sets free the offended—and the offender
- reconciles you to each other
- allows you to stand before your spouse without blemish
- clears you of guilt—and grudges
- cleanses you from every wrong

Forgiving love disposes of the wrongs done against you—and done by you. It allows you to see your spouse as if he or she has done nothing wrong. Can you imagine picking up your relationship as if the offensive behavior never happened? It's a divine makeover, a fresh chance to make the right choices. You are free to accept and connect with each other again.

Forgiving love restores a wounded relationship. It turns you back in the direction of the dream. When you practice forgiving love consistently, you protect your marriage from heading down the path to emotional or legal divorce.

THE COSTS AND BENEFITS OF FORGIVING LOVE

Forgiving love is often the most rewarding step in breaking through our relational disappointments. But it can also be the most difficult.

Gwen has an eye for antiques. She can list from memory the inventory of every antique store within fifty miles of her home near Des Moines. So when she has a free afternoon, she likes nothing better than discovering new shops, strolling aisle after aisle, store after store, digging for some fantastic find. Her favorite antiques are old ceramic dolls. Her collection isn't large, but it's beautiful. Occasionally she comes across a doll so unique and beautiful that she aches to add it to her collection. But as often as not, the price for such exquisite handiwork is far too high. So she walks away disappointed and empty-handed.

Forgiveness is like one of those china dolls. You may appreciate the value of forgiveness. You may discern the beauty of a marriage overflowing with forgiving love. You may wish you could bring this kind of godly grace home, enjoying the uninhibited connection with your spouse that only forgiving love provides. But you fear that you will have to give up too much to get it.

Yes, forgiveness can be costly. A major step in the process of forgiveness is releasing your offending spouse, giving up control of revenge and retribution and allowing God to work in his or her heart. It means letting your spouse off the hook, giving up your right to hold an offense over his or her head. And if you are the one who caused offense, forgiveness means surrendering your pride, admitting guilt, and seeking restoration. That's tough stuff.

But the benefits found in a renewed relationship are well worth the cost of forgiveness. In fact, the benefits of forgiveness are so overwhelming that if you cannot forgive for the sake of your spouse, you will want to forgive for how it will benefit you alone. Christian ethicist Lewis Smedes writes, "When you release the wrongdoer from the wrong, you cut a malignant tumor out of your inner life. You set a prisoner free, but you discover that the real prisoner was yourself."[2] Your choice is to let go of the wrongs done against you or to pay a heavy personal price.

When we forgive, we reap one-of-a-kind benefits. We are able to cast off the bondage of carrying an offense only God can bear. That's the supernatural power of forgiveness. Through it God allows us to start over. In fact, forgiving love allows a relationship to grow even deeper and more meaningful than before.

Both Mark and Shannon realized that the benefits of God's forgiving love were worth the high cost. Shannon says, "I grew up in an abusive home and knew well how to hide my feelings. But one day I cracked. Everything inside me came rushing out. I was able to tell Mark as a woman and as his wife how I felt about pornography. I told him about the fear he had caused in me by taking us to the brink of financial ruin. I confronted him with what I thought about his neglect of me and the kids.

"There's a verse that says that if we expect God to forgive us, we have to forgive others.[3] I realized I had become bitter over Mark's betrayal. Not only that, but I was taking my anger about my painful childhood out on him. Honestly, once Mark confessed his problem, he made rapid progress in breaking with his past habits. I was the one who took many months to make the slightest movement back toward Mark. I had to find God's way. And I discovered that God's grace toward me gave me the ability to forgive Mark."

Forgiveness is how we bring our relationship into the light. It's how we set free the offended and the offender, reconcile with each other after a conflict, stand before our spouse without blemish, cut loose the guilt and grudges, and are cleansed from every wrong.

DO YOU HAVE WHAT IT TAKES TO FORGIVE?

Can you remember your jitters as a little kid standing at the cash register of your favorite toy store? You had studied every possible toy before carrying your choice to the register. Trembling, you put your toy on the counter and handed the clerk your change. You had counted your dimes and nickels a dozen times. You were sure you had enough money—well, not totally sure. And sometimes you came up short. Not to worry. Standing behind you in the checkout line was your dad or your mom, checkbook ready.

At times you may be so deeply hurt by someone that when you reach into your heart to forgive, you don't know if you will find what it takes. In reality, you will never find enough in yourself.

On our own, we lack the limitless grace that can release the offender completely and forgive the offense. The good news is that God hasn't left us alone, fidgeting at the counter. He knows all about the cost of forgiveness. The Bible tells us that an innocent man, God's own Son, came to earth to fulfill the plans foretold in Scripture—to fulfill his Father's will. Jesus brought no one harm. He did not sin; he was perfect. He cared not for himself but for others. He taught about love, forgiveness, faith, hope. He did nothing wrong. Yet they crucified him. He didn't fight it. He turned the other cheek. God's Son was beaten, mocked, spit on. Then they nailed him to a tree. Pain. Agony. He went willingly. Why? Even though he was guiltless, he loved us enough to die the death of the guilty. He was our sacrifice for sin, the Perfect Lamb. And in the final moments, a cry. "Father, forgive these people" (Luke 23:34). Then death, darkness, silence.

That's what Jesus did for us. God chose the one way— a very costly way—to forgive sinful human beings. He gave us *grace,* favor we don't deserve.

God not only knows all about the cost of forgiveness but also is the Great Forgiver who wants to fill our hearts with what it takes to forgive our spouses. He has lavished on us this gift of forgiveness, amply supplying us with exactly what he wants us to give to others. God's command is that we forgive as he has forgiven us (see Colossians 3:13). The power to forgive in a marriage ultimately comes from God. All he asks is that we pass along his gift.

Remember Mike and Cheryl, the young couple from chapter 3? Cheryl told us that she was able to forgive Mike only after she came to understand that God had forgiven her. "One morning I was getting ready for work," she explains, "and there was a man preaching on TV. I know it sounds a little strange, but I broke down crying. I got on my knees in my little apartment, and I asked God to forgive me and change my heart. I was thinking, *Lord, how can you forgive me? I made such a mess of things. I have hurt so many people. No one has sinned the way I have sinned.* Right away I felt the warmth of his love. I felt his forgiveness.

"At that point, I just tried to get myself together. I didn't think about getting back with Mike at first. I just wanted to know God's peace, to be right with him, to do what was right for my son. But when Mike called that day, I realized my heart wasn't angry at him anymore. When I was able to accept God's forgiveness and let him put my life back together, a miraculous thing happened between Mike and me."

Forgiving love comes from God, and when God's forgiveness fills us, we have more than enough forgiving love to share with others, including our spouses.

DISPELLING THE MYTHS OF FORGIVENESS

Forgiving love is difficult and costly. But we often attach to forgiveness some costs that aren't even valid. These are the myths of forgiveness, false requirements many of us assume are true but are nothing more than obstacles to expressing God's forgiving love. These myths are popular in our society. We tend to believe them because we hear them so often. If you are to exercise forgiving love when you have been offended or hurt by your spouse, you need to make sure you don't believe these myths.

Myth #1: "When I forgive, I must also forget." The Bible says that God forgives and forgets: "I will forgive their wickedness and will never again remember their sins" (Jeremiah 31:34). But you are not God. He has the power to forget, but you don't. Actually Barb and I don't believe God intends for us to forget the pain we suffer. To the contrary, we are to remember it so we can value the lessons we learned. Remembering also helps to keep us from repeating the mistakes or needlessly placing ourselves back in a position where hurt happens.

Myth #2: "The hurt is too great. It is impossible for me to forgive." We have all endured situations so painful that we wonder if we can let go of the offense and forgive the offender. But forgiveness is always possible. God would never command us to do something that is impossible. Barb and I know husbands and wives who have forgiven each other for adultery. We have heard countless stories of heartbreak and betrayal in which a spouse forgave and walked through the pain because of his or her commitment to restoring the marriage. Spouses have been forgiven for

- ◆ secret spending: one spouse's spending that took the couple to bankruptcy;
- ◆ terrible wounds from in-laws: a husband who continually took his mother's side against his wife;
- ◆ scars from stepparenting: the biological mother sided with her own child against her new husband;
- ◆ pornography: a wife wondered if she had an authentic relationship with her husband when they were together.

Forgiveness can overcome the greatest of offenses, even offenses that threaten to drive couples to divorce. We have seen incredible peace come to people who have endured the most traumatic sins against them—victims of violence, men and women abused as children, husbands and wives betrayed by their spouses. They didn't dodge forgiveness. They walked through the eye of the storm to experience the pain necessary to later experience the healing they hoped for.

In our pain we experience God and his faithfulness. Author

C. S. Lewis understood this when he wrote, "God whispers to us in our pleasures, speaks in our conscience, and shouts in our pains; it is His megaphone to rouse a deaf world."[4] Countless hurting, offended couples have walked through the process of acknowledging their feelings of hurt and anger and then choosing to begin the process of forgiving the offending person. It is a peace-imparting, real-world process we will share with you in the next chapter.

Myth #3: "I don't feel like forgiving, so my forgiveness can't be genuine." When you have been offended, you often don't feel like forgiving the offender. But forgiveness really isn't about feelings. It's a choice, an act of the will. It's volitional. If you wait until you feel like forgiving, you are choosing to feed the monster of resentment and bitterness.

While the choice to forgive supersedes our feelings, it doesn't deny them. It embraces them and allows us to express them through effective communication, then resolve the conflict by entering the process of forgiveness. Even when we don't feel like forgiving, we need to ask God for strength to enter the process. He will direct us if we honestly seek him.

Myth #4: "I can't forgive until the other person asks for it." We may fantasize about receiving a groveling apology from an offender: "I was so wrong, and I'm so sorry I hurt you. Can you find it in your heart to forgive me?" But if you wait for that kind of response when your spouse hurts you, you may have to wait a long time. Besides, forgiveness is an act of grace. It's unmerited love. Your spouse doesn't have to jump through all the right hoops to earn it.

Our forgiveness of others must be patterned after God's forgiveness of us. When we forgive with no strings attached, we put into action the Bible's command, "Be kind to each other, tenderhearted, forgiving one another, just as God through Christ has forgiven you" (Ephesians 4:32). Did we earn God's forgiveness? Did Jesus die on the cross because we did something to merit such a sacrifice? No. God forgives us out of his grace. Forgiveness cannot be earned. So we must not offer forgiveness with any conditions, such as an apology or confession of wrong. Simply forgive as God does.

Myth #5: "In order to forgive, I must pretend that nothing bad happened." Forgiveness doesn't pretend that nothing happened or that the offense didn't hurt. Rather, true forgiveness acknowledges what really happened and how badly it hurt, then it chooses to let go of the offense. Forgiveness says, "I know what you did, and it really hurt. But in full view of this reality, I choose to forgive you. I do this because of the example and power of Christ, and because I want our relationship to be healed." Forgiveness never says that a hurt didn't happen, because if it didn't happen, there would be nothing to forgive.

Myth #6: "I must forgive right away, or it doesn't count." Often this myth is based on Paul's admonition, "Don't let the sun go down while you are still angry" (Ephesians 4:26). Barb and I have heard about couples who have stayed up all night trying to resolve a conflict because they honestly thought the Bible commanded them to do so. Often they ended up too tired to deal with the problem effectively, and the conflict worsened. If you want to apply this verse literally, you need to solve all your problems by sunset—not bedtime.

This verse isn't a formula for the amount of time it should take to grant forgiveness. It is a command that we should not let anger fester in our hearts. Since forgiveness is an act of the will, it may take you some time to come to the point where you are ready to forgive. If the offense was minor, the forgiving process may take less time. But if the offense was major, you may need to prepare for a longer healing process. The only mistake we make is in refusing to enter the process.

A BETTER WAY TO FORGIVE

Think about how our Christian culture deals with forgiveness. We know that the Bible commands us to forgive those we offend. So in our task-oriented efficiency, we occasionally make a list of people we have offended and either visit them, call them, or write them to ask for forgiveness. Or we make a list of those who have offended us, confront them, and await their apology. Having done our Christian duty, we check these people off our list.

This process can result in what Barb and I call "cheap forgiveness." For some of us, this is the only kind of forgiveness we know. We apply the formula, but we never come to a genuine resolution of the conflict. It's like painting over a crumbling wall instead of fixing it first. Cheap forgiveness gives rise to the myths of forgiveness we have just discussed. Cheap forgiveness does not reckon with the genuine costs of real forgiveness.

We think there's a better, more biblical way, a process we will share with you in the next chapter.

five

CLOSING
THE LOOP

$\mathscr{R}$yan and Jackie started out like two lovebirds settling nicely
into their cozy little marriage nest. Just past their one-year
anniversary, however, the couple began finding their nest to
be a little uncomfortable.

One day Ryan pulled up the footrest on his recliner and
flipped on the TV—while Jackie was talking to him. This had
happened a number of times in their first year together, and it
made Jackie furious. This time she turned, grabbed her purse,
and stormed toward the door. "I'm going shopping," she said.

"Don't spend any money," Ryan called over his shoulder,
his eyes glued to the TV screen.

On the way to the mall, Jackie dialed three friends on her
cell phone without finding one who could meet her there. Then
she called her mother.

Jackie had a couple of female friends who would listen
while she vented. Yet when she was really desperate, she
called her mom. Jackie was surprised to find herself asking for
relationship advice from her mom. Not that her mother ever

solved anything, but she didn't like Ryan much and was happy to hear Jackie's complaints.

What Jackie shared with her mom that day was nothing new. "I can't figure out where the Ryan I married has gone," she said. "He used to be so fun. He was the one who taught *me* how to lighten up. And now it's like his brain is somewhere out in space. He's always lying around. If I try to talk about bills or how work is going, he blows up. Then he stomps out to the garage to fuss with that stupid car of his. It's the only time he ever moves his sorry backside."

Back at the house, Ryan leaned back in the recliner and closed his eyes. He knew Jackie was bothered by something, but he couldn't figure her out at the moment. *I feel smothered,* he thought. *We never do anything I want to do. Jackie used to be interested in watching games and playing softball and hanging out with me in the garage. Now she acts like she's my mother.* Then he added something he would never say to anyone out loud: *And sex isn't all that I expected either.*

Both Ryan and Jackie buried their disappointment and hurt. Ryan withdrew. He went straight from work to hanging out with friends. When he did spend time around the house, he often lashed out at Jackie with unkind words. Jackie formed a habit of sneaking off to spend money on things she knew Ryan wouldn't approve of. She continued to complain about him to anyone who would listen.

Several years passed before something forced Ryan and Jackie to change the focus of their relationship. When Jackie was five months pregnant, they learned that complications might prevent the unborn baby from surviving to term. The difficult weeks that followed forced them to be honest with each other. Jackie told Ryan that she needed to know he was there for her. He couldn't be wandering off to who-knows-where at any time. As Ryan gazed into her pleading eyes, he realized again why he had married her. They both knew they had let the dream slip away.

Ryan and Jackie discovered that offenses and hurt are inevitable in a marriage relationship. Even before their first anniversary, Jackie felt the sting of Ryan's sharp tongue, and Ryan was burned by his young wife's temper. As the years passed, it got worse instead of better. Their close relationship before marriage—talks and long walks, nights out with friends, spontaneous fun—had deteriorated into a series of unresolved conflicts and unhealed hurts. They were well on their way to emotional and perhaps legal divorce.

But their threatened pregnancy brought them to a crossroads. Ryan and Jackie needed to clear the air between them. They needed to resolve the offenses and hurts, forgive each other, and find acceptance and connection once again. They knew they had to join together as a team to battle the problems they faced.

They now have begun the process of facing their conflicts and differences. But like other marriages riddled with offenses, hurt, and anger, they will survive and rediscover the dream only if they put forgiving love into action. Only forgiving love heals the hurts, resolves the conflict, and allows husbands and wives to feel accepted and connected again.

WHERE ARE YOU IN THE LOOP?

Barb and I often meet people like Ryan and Jackie through our radio program and marriage conferences. Couples trapped in the pattern of unresolved offense-hurt-anger with no idea of how to resolve their differences are caught in what we call an "open loop." The loop is a concept I developed while dealing with thousands of couples in my counseling practice. As I worked to understand the struggles of couple after couple, I saw that the pattern of offense-hurt-anger is just the beginning of a cycle of conflict that has two possible endings. The first outcome—an open loop—happens when conflict goes unaddressed and unresolved. See figure 1 for what this pattern looks like.

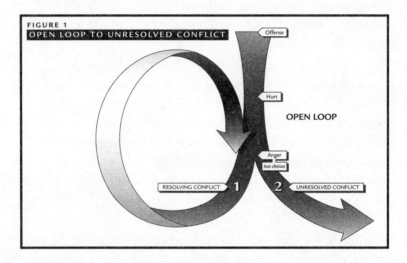

FIGURE 1
OPEN LOOP TO UNRESOLVED CONFLICT

Offense

Hurt

OPEN LOOP

Anger
two choices

RESOLVING CONFLICT   1   2   UNRESOLVED CONFLICT

Some marriages have dozens of open loops. For example, couples may live in ongoing conflict over how to discipline their children, who is responsible for taking out the garbage, who balances the checkbook, how often they have sex, etc. Some unresolved issues may be even more personal, such as wounds from criticism, insults, apathy, lack of love, etc. When loops are left open, conflicts accumulate and pile up on each other. Anger burns. The marriage bond is strained. Bitterness hardens hearts. And two people once very close and connected grow more and more isolated from each other.

But this bleak condition isn't couples' only option. They can choose to work through the process of "closing the loop" through forgiveness. Only forgiveness enables couples to rebuild trust and enjoy a fully restored relationship. This is the outcome we are aiming for in our ministry to couples. Examine this outcome and the steps to closing the loop in figure 2.

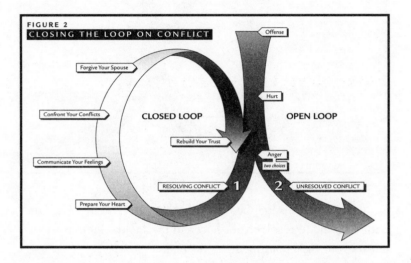

FIGURE 2
CLOSING THE LOOP ON CONFLICT

Suppose an offense happened just this morning between you and your spouse. Not just any offense, but one that happens so often that you are both weary of dealing with it. You hate the flash of anger it ignites within you. For the first hour after you went your separate ways for the day, you replayed the conflict in your mind, thinking of all the nasty comments you could have shot back. By midmorning your fury has started to cool, but you dread the next round when you meet at the end of the day.

You have a choice. What will you do? Every conflict with your spouse brings you to a fork in the road. After the offense has led to hurt and the hurt has turned to anger, you are faced with the choice of how to handle the situation: Will you work to resolve the conflict and close the loop? Or will you let it pass and leave the loop open to collect the debris of more hurtful conflicts? Figure 3 shows what that choice looks like.

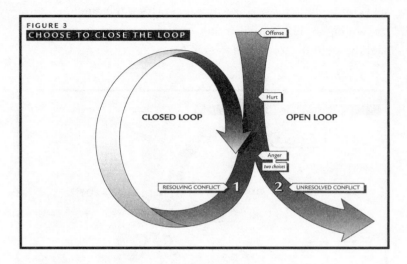

One path—closing the loop—leads to restoration. The other path—failing to resolve your hurt and leaving the loop open—allows your disappointments to deepen.

Have you ever been at that fork in the road? Do you recognize what we're talking about? Can you identify some current situations where you stand at that point of choosing whether or not to work toward closing the loop?

At first thought, it sure seems easier to ignore the problem, to shove aside the wrong you suffered—or the wrong you inflicted. But that quick fix won't last. It takes courage to restore and rebuild a relationship, regardless of which side of the offense you're on. It takes time, patience, trust, and maybe even some tears. But if Barb and I could sit down with you and your spouse, we would look you in the eye and assure you that whatever conflicts you face right now, the benefits of a restored relationship far outweigh the effort of closing the loop.

Closing the loop is forgiving love in action. This is the biblical pathway to confronting offenses, resolving conflicts, and healing hurts. This is God's way to restore mutual acceptance and intimacy in the wake of misunderstanding and pain. Closing the loop through forgiving love is a vital component in divorce-proofing your marriage.

CLOSING THE LOOP STEP-BY-STEP

Couples often ask Barb and me how long it will take for their relationship to "get better." In other words, how long does it take to close all the loops? We wish we could tell you the process is easy. We wish we could offer you a few platitudes that might make you feel better. But good feelings don't lead to lasting change. Many people approach us with hurts that take time to sort out and heal. We encourage you to take a head-on approach to dealing with conflicts and hurts in your relationship. Don't bury them. Don't beat around the bush. Just face them, and close the loop, no matter how long it takes.

We want to coach you on five biblical steps for sharing forgiving love with your spouse and closing the loop of offense and hurt. We know the process works because it is God's way of healing hurts and restoring relationships.

Step 1: Prepare Your Heart

Ryan and Jackie's hearts were broken the day they learned about the complications with their unborn child. Confusion overtook them as they were asked to make decisions regarding medical procedures they had never heard of. Worse yet, they both realized that this new stress was piling up on top of all the hurts they had caused each other, making it doubly difficult to focus on closing the loop.

The couple wisely sought their pastor's help in working through the necessary medical decisions. As their unborn child's condition stabilized, Ryan and Jackie began dealing with the backlog of unresolved offenses.

Like Ryan and Jackie, some couples are motivated by a crisis to decide to resolve their differences. Other couples take much longer to deal with the clutter of unhealed offenses, hurts, and anger. Either way, healing begins only when one or both partners choose to engage in the necessary heart work that clears the way for closing the loop. Here are several elements in the process of heart preparation:

Humble yourself and pray. Step back, go to God, confess your sin, and pray! "God," you can say, "give me the humility to resolve this issue in a way that honors you. Help me to be gracious to my spouse and sensitive to his [or her] perspective. Help us talk things through. Help us to close the loop and rekindle our love for each other." You can also pray the words of one of the psalms of David, a man who created deep hurt through his offenses. "Search me, O God, and know my heart; test me and know my thoughts. Point out anything in me that offends you" (Psalm 139:23-24).

Prayer softens our hearts. Prayer helps us reprioritize. While you're talking to God, tell him that you are committed to love, humility, and obedience. You can pray through Philippians 2:3-5, which describes how to close the loop in a Christlike manner: "Don't be selfish; don't live to make a good impression on others. Be humble, thinking of others as better than yourself. Don't think only about your own affairs, but be interested in others, too, and what they are doing. Your attitude should be the same that Christ Jesus had."

Look for the underlying cause of the conflict. Sort through the surface stuff, and look for the *real* source of the hurt. Is your anger really about the offense, or did something else set you off? Try some of these ideas to help you dig deeper:

- ◆ Look for external forces—such as pressure at work or finances—that cause stress in the relationship.

◆ Decide what really matters. Is the basic issue of your conflict a nonnegotiable, or is it a matter of personal preference, like the proverbial difference about how to squeeze the toothpaste tube? Is the issue a "hill to die on" or a minor irritation?

◆ Brainstorm about ways to set aside stresses on your marriage, even temporarily, so you can focus on the relationship. Consider going away for a day or enjoying a night out or a quiet evening at home without the kids.

◆ Try to understand and accept how your spouse deals with conflict.

◆ Be realistic. Don't expect everything to be done the way your mother—or your spouse's mother, for that matter— did it.

Commit to making your relationship the top priority. One of the greatest saboteurs of healthy relationships is the tendency to put them on the back burner. When we're stretched and stressed and living in the fast lane, sometimes the people closest to us are the ones who get hurt the most.

In their book *Fit to Be Tied,* Pastor Bill Hybels and his wife, Lynne, write about "crisis mode living," which they define as "spending every moment of every day trying to figure out how to keep all your balls in the air and all your plates spinning." The implication of crisis mode living is that relationships suffer. As Pastor Hybels writes, "Your bond with your spouse that used to be strong and intimate becomes increasingly weak and distant. You hope he or she doesn't have a serious need because you don't have the energy to deal with it."[1]

God intends your relationship with your spouse to be a safe place to resolve conflicts. It becomes that kind of haven as you commit to God and to each other to keep the relationship alive no matter what.

Involve a trusted accountability partner. The more deeply rooted the conflict and hurt, the more important it is that you involve a trustworthy third party who will hold you accountable for closing the loop. It should be someone who loves and respects both you and your spouse equally—instead of "my friend" or "your friend"—and who will guard your relationship with the utmost confidentiality. Find a pastor, Christian counselor, accountability group, or mature mentoring couple to keep you focused on forgiving love. Invite this person(s) to hold you accountable by periodically asking you questions like these as you work through the process of closing the loop:

- ◆ Are you maintaining a high value on your relationship?
- ◆ Are you valuing and respecting both yourself and your spouse?
- ◆ Are you facing your conflict head-on?
- ◆ Are you shrinking back or avoiding conflict?
- ◆ Are you resisting tendencies to control or manipulate?
- ◆ Are you working hard at reconciliation?

These are tough questions to answer, but they will help keep the process of forgiving love on track.

Step 2: Communicate Your Feelings

Communication is often called the number one problem in marriages. Why? Maybe it's because communication breakdowns lead to breakdowns in so many other areas. When we stop communicating, conflicts flare up, tension builds, and intimacy cools.

Communication in the context of closing the loop involves honestly describing your thoughts and feelings about the offense you suffered. This is where you become transparent and vulnerable with your spouse by sharing what impact the conflict has had on you.

By the time Ryan and Jackie could take a breather and con-
structively talk together about their disappointments, they each
had compiled a laundry list of grievances. Their complaints were
filled with language such as "I expected . . ." and "I thought . . ."
Jackie felt abandoned. Ryan felt manipulated. Jackie couldn't tell
if Ryan even liked her anymore. Ryan was frustrated at having
to answer to Jackie for "every minute of every day" with no time
to let down. Jackie felt controlled by Ryan for every penny she
spent, even though they both earned good salaries.

It was a painful, tearful exchange, but Ryan and Jackie bared
their souls to each other and aired their hurts. In the process,
they gained new insights into each other's feelings. Accusations
of "You're never . . ." and "You're so . . ." turned to "I didn't
realize I hurt you when I . . ." and "I had no idea you thought that
. . ." Their honest communication helped them reach a better
understanding of their conflicts; they began to see the issues
through the other's eyes.

We recommend a number of crucial strategies for effectively
communicating your feelings to your spouse:

Think ahead about what you want to say. Make a list, or write a
paragraph on each issue so you will be able to state your grievances and pain simply and clearly.

Recognize gender differences in communication. Men sometimes
zoom straight to the point, omitting details. That's not the
warmest approach for a woman. Women sometimes meander
through every detail, clouding the bottom line. Men want to
hear the bottom line; women want to have a context for the
bottom line.

Get a referee. When the issues are too big or too painful to
deal with on your own, find an objective, trustworthy third
party to help you talk them out.

Deliver your whole message. Speak kindly and calmly, but say all
that you have come to say. A whole message consists of thoughts,

feelings, and needs. Share your thoughts, which include your perception, values, and attitudes about the conflict. Then share how you "feel" about it. Do you feel fearful? anxious? disappointed? hopeful? optimistic? Then move to completing the whole message by sharing what you need from your spouse. Do you need an answer? a hug? space for a few hours? another viewpoint?

Commit to listening. As you listen to your spouse describe the offense and hurt, resist the urge to defend yourself or prove him or her wrong. Instead, listen first, asking questions that lead to clarification and understanding. The Bible reminds us, "My dear brothers and sisters, be quick to listen, slow to speak, and slow to get angry" (James 1:19).

Focus on the positive. Affirm positive traits or habits. Say things such as, "I appreciate . . ." or "I am so grateful that . . ." or "You are so good at . . ."

Avoid the silent treatment. Sometimes—especially when spouses are angry—they clam up and give each other the silent treatment, thinking that the silence will communicate their perspective. Don't mistake silence for communication. In fact, it often is only manipulative. The goal is to open communication, not play games.

Say what you mean. Don't say, "I hate football" if what you really mean is, "I wish we could spend some quality time together on Saturday afternoons." Before you speak, think carefully about what really upsets you.

Don't use generalizations. Avoid statements like "You *never* take out the garbage like you're supposed to" or "You are *always* talking to your mother on the phone." They are usually exaggerations, and they are certainly not helpful.

Use I-messages. "I sometimes feel ignored and lonely" goes down a lot easier than "You never pay any attention to me." Focus on your thoughts and feelings rather than harp on your spouse's failures. Invariably generalizations will lead to a defen-

sive response from your spouse because he or she will feel the
need to set the record straight.

Agree on a plan for handling conflicts. Answer this question
with your spouse: How do we want talk to each other when
a conflict arises?

When you are in a conflict, it is imperative that you communicate openly and honestly. Failure to share your feelings and
talk through your differences will stifle any efforts to clear the
air and restore intimacy.

Step 3: Confront Your Conflicts

Barb and I teach regularly at FamilyLife conferences around
the country. At one point during each of these "Weekend to
Remember" conferences, we instruct husbands and wives to look
each other in the eye and repeat a statement that we hope will
burn into their memories: "My spouse is not my enemy." Don't
you love that thought? So often in the midst of a conflict, husband and wife view each other as adversaries to be defeated.
Instead of working toward resolution, we aim darts at each
other's heart. But the essential truth is that we are on the same
team. We should be working together to find a solution.

However, even in the atmosphere of team spirit and honest
communication, certain conflict issues must be confronted and
resolved. For example: Are we going to hang the toilet tissue
your way, my way, or alternate with each roll? Or more seriously: Will we spend Christmas morning with your parents, my
parents, or at home with our kids? How many nights a week shall
we commit to being home together? Who will pay the bills? Will
it be you, me, or both of us together? If you don't make necessary decisions on how to proceed, the conflict won't go away.

We would like to offer you a starting point that virtually
guarantees success. It's a four-word phrase that may surprise
your spouse, but it will also help disarm the conflict and set the

stage for the decision-making discussion. The starting point is this: "Let's pray together first."

Prayer makes a positive impact on the resolution of conflict. Prayer takes two people on opposite sides of an issue and welcomes into the debate a third person—Jesus. Bringing Jesus into your debate means deciding together to play by his rules.

Once you have prayed, the most practical way to make Jesus part of this decision-making step is by going to the Bible to find solutions. What does the Bible say about your situation? Are there clear commands you need to obey? Are there biblical principles that apply to this issue? When you look to God's Word, you level the playing field by welcoming God's solution.

During their difficult heart-to-heart talk, Ryan and Jackie expressed some honest hurts and disappointments. They vented their anger. It felt better to have the issues out in the open, but they still needed to come to some conclusions: Just how much time should Ryan spend with friends? How could Jackie make Ryan feel more relaxed at home? How was Jackie going to put a stop to her backbiting? What was going to change about how the couple handled money? And how were they going to stop the war of words?

The first thing Ryan and Jackie agreed on was to make time to connect after work. Ryan, who arrived home first, got a few minutes in his recliner to settle his brain after a long day. But as soon as Jackie got home, it was talk time.

On the financial side, they agreed to discuss any purchases above a certain amount—fifty dollars felt reasonable to them as long as they were both working. They decided the best way to put a lid on Jackie's complaining—especially to her mother—was to get together as a couple with Jackie's parents. No one-on-ones with her mom until Jackie felt that she had some nice things to say about Ryan. And they decided that doing these things and keeping open lines of healthy communication would be the fastest way to keep their conversations from degenerating into shouting matches.

Can you see how Ryan and Jackie found middle ground that respected both of their needs? That's a prime goal of confrontation. Here are some other ideas for loving confrontation:

Choose an appropriate time and setting. Do you and your spouse really need to solve an issue moments before two dozen guests arrive for a dinner party? Select a time and place that minimize distractions and guarantee privacy from the children.

Ask permission to address the conflict. For example: "Are you ready to talk about our disagreement over how to discipline the children?" or "I'm ready to confront our money problems. Are you okay with that?" Make sure your spouse is ready to face the issue before you bring it up.

Avoid statements that assign blame. I-statements encourage discussion; you-statements shut it down. Start your sentences with "I feel . . ." or "I think . . ." rather than "You are . . ." or "You should . . ."

Step 4: Forgive Your Spouse

After Ryan and Jackie agreed on the issues that had been undermining their marriage, they experienced an even more significant breakthrough in their relationship. "The biggest thing we've learned is to forgive," Jackie says. "We know now how to say, 'I was wrong,' and we are learning to ask for and grant forgiveness. We can't think of a more important skill for our marriage."

The core of forgiving love is the act of forgiveness. This stage is very difficult for many people, yet it brings the greatest amount of healing for hurts and conflict. Barb and I believe that forgiveness brings us closer to God than anything else we can do. Relationships demand it. Jesus modeled it. Our hearts need it. It all begins in your marriage when you and your spouse agree to let each other off the hook.

Have you made the decision to forgive? Are you ready to experience "whole forgiveness" together? As you will see, whole forgiveness takes two people—one seeking forgiveness and one granting it—and the heartfelt statements described below.

REQUESTING FORGIVENESS   Think of a conflict you have experienced recently with your spouse, and imagine how it could be resolved by making the following statements:

"I was wrong." When you need forgiveness, it's not enough to say, "Okay, if you think I did something wrong, let's talk about it." It's also not appropriate to say, "I don't think what I did was such a big deal, but if you think it was, let's talk." We need to confront the wrong for what it is. Here are some ways to say it: "I was wrong"; "What I did/said to you was wrong"; "I did something wrong, and I need to talk to you about what I did to offend you."

"I'm sorry." How often have you sought forgiveness and said "I was wrong," thinking that would take care of the problem? Perhaps the offended person appeared confused, leading you to think, *Well, I said I was wrong. Shouldn't that be enough?*

Admitting wrong behavior is vitally important, but there is more. You need to express your sorrow over the hurt your wrong behavior caused: "I was wrong, and I'm so sorry that I hurt you." It takes both elements for your offended spouse to sense your sincerity. By expressing your sorrow, you demonstrate empathy for the other person. "I'm sorry" helps restore the relationship by diminishing the resistance between two hurting people, allowing communication to open up and self-protection to be put aside.

"I don't ever want to hurt you like this again." This is a statement of repentance and is different from the first two statements.

"I was wrong" is a statement of confession. "I'm sorry" is a statement of contrition or sorrow. They should be followed by a statement of repentance, your desire to change and to turn from your hurtful ways. Confession and contrition without repentance leave forgiveness incomplete. "I don't want to hurt you again" is a way of saying the hurt you caused—and may cause in the future—is unintentional and distressing to you. Repentance swings wide open the door to deep healing.

"Will you forgive me?" At this point you demonstrate the ultimate in humility in the process of seeking forgiveness. When you sincerely ask, "Will you forgive me?" you place yourself at the feet of your spouse, taking the servant's position. This question brings the process of forgiveness to a crescendo. It is forgiving love at its best.

Let's review those four critical steps again:

1. Confession—"I was wrong."
2. Sorrow—"I'm sorry."
3. Repentance—"I don't ever want to hurt you like this again."
4. Request—"Will you forgive me?"

If you leave any of the four elements out of your request for forgiveness, you risk leaving the conflict unresolved. Too often we leap to the request for forgiveness without acknowledging our wrong, expressing our remorse, or offering repentance. This is cheap forgiveness, leaving the offended person with the pain of the wrong suffered.

GRANTING FORGIVENESS The spouse from whom forgiveness has been requested must respond in two ways: grant forgiveness *graciously* and grant it *specifically.*

"I forgive you and close the loop on this issue." Forgiving graciously means letting go of the offense and welcoming your

spouse back into your heart. This is the way God forgives us when we confess in sorrow and repent. God's forgiveness is free. It's undeserved. It can't be earned or bargained for. He won't ever rescind it. Forgiveness is a no-strings-attached gift in response to our humble confession of sin. You must graciously forgive your spouse because God has graciously forgiven you.

"I forgive you for . . ." Forgiving *specifically* means stating the wrong for which your spouse has asked you to forgive him or her. You fill in the blank: critical words, insincerity, lying, wasteful spending, not meeting your needs, infidelity, insensitivity, ignoring you, belittling you, etc. By naming the issue, you assure your spouse how complete and inclusive your forgiveness is. It doesn't leave the offense hanging in the air. Rather, it dispels any questions in your spouse's mind: *Did he or she understand what I was asking forgiveness for? Did he or she really forgive me for what I did?*

Forgiveness—the ability to let go of past hurts—is perhaps the single most important relationship skill we can develop in marriage. Keeping your spouse on the hook for past offenses may give you a gratifying sense of power, but it always occurs at the expense of the relationship. It may feel good at the time because of the momentary relief it provides you from the resentment and hurt still seething within you. But the *only* way to restore harmony in the relationship is to permanently remove those negative feelings. No relationship can recover from serious disappointments and grow in intimacy if one or both partners cannot let go of the bitterness. You cannot enjoy trust, acceptance, or connectedness while you are secretly— or openly—resentful of your spouse.

Once forgiveness happens, you can work for something more: reconciliation. Family counselor David Stoop writes, "Forgiveness is unilateral. It is something we can do all by ourselves. Reconciliation requires the participation of another person. We cannot 'make it happen,' no matter how hard we try."[2] Reconciliation—the true healing and coming together of two people who had been in conflict—can occur only when both spouses want it and are willing to work for it: to confront the offense, the hurt, and the anger, and choose to communicate.

True reconciliation cannot occur unless both spouses are willing to participate. It may *look* like reconciliation as two people reopen the lines of communication, but something will be missing: genuine forgiveness. And that lack will be a gaping hole in the foundation of the relationship.

So, are you stuck forever if one of you refuses to complete the reconciliation? Not fully. You can forgive your spouse even if he or she will not complete the process. While one-sided forgiveness is not the ideal, it is the only way some people can close the loop with spouses who are either unwilling to confess wrong or who are no longer living. In such cases, you can grant unrequested forgiveness and feel released and free of resentment.

Step 5: Rebuild Your Trust

What would it take for Ryan and Jackie to feel that they have finally moved past their conflicts and pain? They have exercised forgiving love by communicating feelings, confronting issues, and forgiving each other. Wouldn't it be great if all the worries and fears that went along with those hurts would disappear? Wouldn't it be freeing for Ryan to know that Jackie is no longer criticizing him and for Jackie to come home each night to a husband who is ready and willing to talk to her? Don't you think such a change of heart and behavior would propel their marriage back toward the dream?

This is what happens during the last step in closing the loop: rebuilding trust. In some conflicts and hurts, trust may not need much repair. But when the wounds are deep and trust has been eroded, it is essential.

If you have hurt your spouse deeply or repeatedly, he or she may be willing to forgive you. But that doesn't mean that the relationship is completely healed, that you can go on as if nothing happened. For true restoration to occur, you must be willing to work at rebuilding your spouse's trust over a period of time. You need to prove to your spouse over the long haul that your confession, contrition, and repentance are genuine.

Trust isn't rebuilt overnight. If you have been unfaithful to your spouse, it may take long months of single-minded devotion before a foundation of trust is reestablished. If your spouse has endured years of unjust criticism from you, you have a long road of affirmation and appreciation ahead of you. The sanctity and peace of your relationship may be in ruins at your feet. But through the power of Christ's redeeming love, your marriage can be transformed from rubble to restoration. Begin that healing process today. Begin to rebuild trust today. Be faithful and patient, and you will experience the restoration you seek.

Throughout your marriage, you will frequently find yourself at the familiar fork in the road, the choice between ignoring hurt and deciding to close the loop. No marriage completely escapes the pattern of offense-hurt-anger. But every time you choose the healing process of closing the loop, you will experience the healing power of forgiving love. And you will be one step closer to divorce-proofing your marriage and recapturing the dream you left at the altar.

A SPECIAL NOTE ABOUT THE JOURNEY

Are you aware of some open loops in your relationship with your spouse? Loops can be closed. What does it take? You must be willing to humble yourself and let go of your pride in order to reach out to your spouse. You need to engage in the process of forgiveness and reconciliation God created for us. It takes courage! It also takes practice. Forgiving love doesn't come naturally. It is something we learn through experience.

This is why we have created a separate book and workbook on forgiving love. We call it *Healing the Hurt in Your Marriage: Beyond Conflict to Forgiveness.* There is much more to understand and apply to make forgiveness a consistent fixture in your marriage. The book and workbook will help you make giving and receiving forgiveness an established pattern that will result in a deepened intimacy in your relationship. And in the process, you will divorce-proof your marriage. (See appendix A for more details on this book and workbook and how you can form your own couples group to launch a Divorce-Proof Your Marriage emphasis in your church.)

Part Three

SERVING LOVE

Serving love discovers and meets needs

and helps spouses feel

honored and understood

six

IN HONOR OF
YOUR SPOUSE

𝒯he first time Gary spoke at a Promise Keepers stadium event,
I went along to support him and pray for him. Gary stood before
a vast sea of men—about sixty thousand of them—and preached
with fire and passion about the importance of godly marriages.
I sat behind the stage, watching the monitor, praying, and beaming with pride.

Toward the end of Gary's message, I was stunned to hear
him mention my name. "I'm going to ask my wife, Barbara,
to join me on the platform," he said. "She doesn't know I am
going to ask her to do this."

As his surprising invitation swirled inside my head, someone led me up the metal steps to the massive stage. Just when
I thought my knees would give way from fear, a man guided
me to a chair. I didn't dare look at the crowd, thinking I
would surely faint at the overwhelming sight of sixty thousand
men.

So I focused my attention on Gary, waiting for some hint
of what he was about to say or do. In mild panic, I flashed him

a silent question with my eyes: *What now?* His return glance
communicated all I needed to know: *Trust me.*

Gary stood before me with Bible in hand. As he began to
read from Scripture, I realized he had turned to the Gospel of
John: "'No,' Peter protested, 'you will never wash my feet!'"
(John 13:8).

Fear engulfed me. *Feet? Whose feet? Oh no, nobody's washing
my feet—not in front of sixty thousand men!*

All I could do was trust Gary, my soul mate, my best friend.
So I watched and waited. Gary had a bottle of water and his
hankie in his hands. He knelt in front of me, removed my shoes,
and began washing my feet. Tears rolled down his cheeks as he
demonstrated the depth of his love for me, serving me as Christ
had humbly served his disciples. My tears flowed too. In those
solemn moments, I felt as if Gary and I were the only two people
in the stadium.

When he finished, Gary stood again before the awestruck
crowd of men. Forcefully and compassionately, he challenged
them to go to the next level of love for their wives. He invited
them to kneel while he prayed. Across the stadium, men
dropped to their knees, committing publicly to return home
and love their wives with a servant's heart.

Do you have any idea how I feel living with a man like
Gary? No, I don't mean the kind of man who calls me up in
front of sixty thousand men without warning. I mean a man
who unashamedly kneels to serve me in front of sixty thousand
men. A man who is the same man in public that he is in private,
inside the walls of our home. I'm talking about a husband who
strives to discover my needs and meet them, who showers me
with a love that causes me to feel understood and honored.

I value what Gary did on the platform that day because it
matches how he lives with me day in, day out. Don't get me
wrong; Gary's not perfect. I'm not blind to his mistakes and

tendencies to get distracted. But over the long haul of our more than twenty-seven years together, Gary has been a consistent model of serving love. There's no need too small for him to notice, such as bringing me a cup of coffee in the morning, tossing in a load of laundry, or washing the dishes. He prays for and with me, and he's been known to e-mail three hundred strangers to pray for me. When I had surgery, Gary slept at the hospital and suffered through the same bland food I had to eat. His heart is totally wired into my needs.

Gary's willingness to serve me—as he demonstrated not only in that dramatic moment at a Promise Keepers rally but also in the everyday moments of our marriage—convinces me on the deepest level that no matter what comes our way, no matter what flaws I have, no matter what I might do to disappoint him, he cares for me and is committed to meeting my needs.

Gary and I call this *serving love.* Are you connecting with your spouse at this level? Serving love means honoring your spouse to the degree that you purposefully seek to discover and meet his or her needs, even placing those needs before your own. Serving your spouse in this way helps him or her feel honored and understood. Serving love is a key component to divorce-proofing your marriage.

SERVING LOVE: JESUS' KIND OF LOVE

When you said "I do," a large part of your marriage dream, whether conscious or subconscious, was probably that your new soul mate would meet your needs. You wanted a spouse who understood your basic human needs: physical, emotional, relational, spiritual. You wanted someone who was sensitive to your gender needs as a woman or man and to your unique personality needs as an individual. And you probably expected that your understanding spouse would devote his or her life to meeting those needs.

Have those expectations been realized? Are you experiencing serving, need-meeting love? If your answer is "no" or "not very often," you may wonder if it is really possible for spouses to serve each other with such deep understanding and willingness. You may even wonder if such serving love really exists.

Yes, it does exist. It is an expression of biblical love that is clearly seen in Jesus. That day in the stadium when Gary washed my feet, he was reenacting an amazing biblical scene that illustrated Jesus' serving love for his disciples.

The Bible tells us that on the night before he was crucified, Jesus devised a way to demonstrate to his disciples "the full extent of his love" (John 13:1). At supper Jesus "got up from the table, took off his robe, wrapped a towel around his waist, and poured water into a basin. Then he began to wash the disciples' feet and to wipe them with the towel he had around him" (John 13:4-5).

Now you have to understand the customs in Bible times to grasp the significance of this picture. You had a dozen men who had been trudging the dusty roads all day in leather sandals. It was common courtesy for a host—more likely, the host's servants—to wash the feet of his guests. So Jesus wasn't acting out of sentimentality. He wasn't merely creating a symbol or coming up with what would be a touching Bible story. He was actually performing a customary act of service for his disciples. Consider what was happening when Jesus took off his robe, grabbed a towel, and washed his followers' feet:

Jesus met a genuine need through an act of servanthood. Jesus took the job that usually fell to the lowest servant in a household. Foot washing soothed and cleansed the guests' dirty, tired feet.

At least one disciple felt uncomfortable being on the receiving end of Jesus' serving act. Peter pulled away when Jesus approached him to wash his feet. Why? It could have been pride or self-sufficiency. Perhaps it was discomfort at the thought of Jesus' taking on a dirty task that Peter wouldn't dare touch himself. Or maybe Peter feared that if he accepted the Lord's serving ministry, he might have to do the same for someone else.

Jesus demonstrated that even the greatest among us is to be a servant of all. Jesus, the teacher who took a lowly servant's role, would soon elevate serving love to infinite heights by dying for the sins of humanity.

We dare not miss Jesus' words that tell us the value and importance of serving love:

> You call me "Teacher" and "Lord," and you are right, because it is true. And since I, the Lord and Teacher, have washed your feet, you ought to wash each other's feet. I have given you an example to follow. Do as I have done to you. How true it is that a servant is not greater than the master. Nor are messengers more important than the one who sends them. You know these things—now do them! That is the path of blessing. (John 13:13-17)

None of us is greater than our master, Jesus. None of us is above serving. None of us can shirk his example. Furthermore, none of us can afford to miss out on the blessing Jesus promised to those who minister to others through serving love. And those couples who desire to divorce-proof their marriages must practice serving love.

Gary and I realize that serving love is countercultural. It's not human nature to be other-centered, to purposely take a lower place to honor another, to willingly get dirty so someone else can be clean. Wives, you may think that serving love puts you at the mercy of a Fred Flintstone type who hollers, "Wilma, where's my supper?" Who wants to be barked at and bossed around? Husbands, you may fear that serving love means signing up to be nagged and henpecked.

We need to be clear that servanthood doesn't mean the bondage of slavery. As Jesus put on the towel and served his disciples, he proved to us conclusively that God's kind of serving love flows from choice not coercion, from strength not weakness, from gladness not guilt. It's positively liberating.

THE MYTH OF THE 50/50 MARRIAGE

One of the biggest problems among the couples Gary and I talk to is husbands and wives who measure out their need-meeting service for each other in reciprocal portions. The best many marriages ever do is operate according to the popular "50/50 plan," the I'll-meet-your-needs-if-you-meet-mine philosophy. In this plan, marriage becomes an issue of trade-offs and compromises, with spouses keeping score so one person never gets or gives more than the other. The goal is to meet each other halfway.

To be fair, some couples who live by this rule are generous to each other and even moderately happy. But apportioning love usually doesn't result in the spouses' feeling honored and understood. The problem, writes Dennis Rainey in his book *Staying Close,* is that "it is impossible to determine if your spouse has met you halfway. Because neither of you can agree on where 'halfway' is, each is left to scrutinize the other's performance from his or her own jaded perspective."[1]

Ben and Carrie both grew up watching their mothers get trampled by their demanding fathers. So when Ben and Carrie married, they vowed that they would evenly divide all tasks and responsibilities between them. Household work would be split down the middle. They insisted that their 50/50 relationship would be 100 percent fair.

Instead of creating a fair and stable environment, Ben and Carrie have created a monster. They argue about who washed the dishes last—or who did the laundry or who cooked. Carrie's weekend with her college roommates is matched minute-for-minute and dollar-for-dollar by Ben's hunting trip with his buddies. They track their child-care duties as if they have a stopwatch ticking in their heads. When Ben comes home from work, Carrie knows she is off duty. They also keep track of the money they each earn, the running totals clearly distinguished in separate bank accounts. A friend of ours calls people like Ben and Carrie "ledger people."

Since the highest goal of Ben and Carrie's marriage is keeping everything even, their marriage is more about grabbing for self than giving to the other. Even in things as simple as pouring sodas to enjoy in front of the TV, they wait for the other to give in and serve first. By striving to be fair, Ben and Carrie cultivate a me-first attitude. And they miss out on the blessings Jesus promised to those who follow his example to serve one another selflessly.

In a 50/50 marriage, serving and submitting to one another is often replaced by a strong emphasis on getting what is rightfully yours. Someone is missing in this kind of relationship, the person who desires to live right in the middle of a marriage, the one who makes the rules and mediates between your needs and your spouse's needs. That person is Jesus Christ, who provides not only the example but also the power of serving love through the Word of God and the Holy Spirit.

THE JOY OF A 100/100 MARRIAGE

Let's face it: We all love to have our needs met. We all desire the understanding and honor that result when someone cares enough to serve us without expecting anything in return. That's why I felt so special the day Gary washed my feet and why I continue to feel that way because of his continual desire to love me with a serving love.

The problems come when we focus on being served—even in a 50/50 arrangement—instead of serving. A me-first attitude can get us complaining, for example, that our spouse never spends time with us, even though we are constantly busy with the kids, volunteering at church, or spending time with our friends.

There's a better way. It's the 100/100 marriage, as illustrated by Robert and Nancy's story. Robert says, "Nancy and I dated for four years before finishing school, settling into our first jobs, and getting married. We were both professionals, driven to do well in our careers. We had it all, as they say, but we were restless in our relationship."

But this couple was not about to settle for second best in their marriage. Robert continues, "It took us a while to grasp the problem. As assertive as Nancy was in her work, I realized that in our marriage she hadn't been up-front with me about her needs. She was so eager to please me that when it came to any decision—like picking a restaurant or choosing where to spend a holiday or even where to live—she almost always responded with, 'Whatever you want, honey.' Or she parroted back what she knew I wanted. But Nancy was feeling trampled. I was frustrated because I truly wanted to honor her desires, but she wouldn't let me know what they were."

Nancy admits that when her unmet needs and desires started coming to the surface, they boiled over as anger. "For a couple of years I trampled on whatever Robert wanted," she says. "Everything had to go *my* way. He was the one saying, 'Whatever you want, honey.' I didn't like the imbalance in that way of doing marriage, and it certainly left Robert unsatisfied. When we stopped and looked at what was happening to our marriage, we admitted that we were not only dealing with a desire to control one another but also missing out on God's design for a husband and a wife. A friend encouraged us to study what the Bible had to say about a husband and wife's role in marriage. Over time we discovered that we were missing what God intended for us. As we studied the apostle Paul's words in Ephesians 5, we learned that a husband's love for his wife is to be like Christ's love for the church, a sacrificial kind of love. Listen to what Paul said: 'Husbands, love your wives, just as Christ loved the church and gave himself up for her to make her holy' (Ephesians 5:25-26, NIV).

"When a husband 'gives himself up for his wife,' he chooses to serve her because of his desire to be obedient to God's design for him. He is stirred not only by pleasing her but also by pleasing God."

As Robert began to get his arms around this biblical truth, he realized that by loving Nancy sacrificially, she would in turn respond to him with serving love. As they began to live this out, the issue of control diminished. Nancy began to trust Robert in a way she never would have imagined in the past. And as she trusted him, she realized that her ultimate trust was in the work God was doing in her life as well as in her husband's.

Nancy and Robert now say, "Our goal is to outdo the other. Our marriage is a 100 percent commitment to serving God and each other."

Deep inside each of us is a longing to understand and be understood, to honor and be honored. When a marriage lacks that kind of need-discovering, need-meeting love, feelings of disappointment give way to frustration and conflict. Perhaps you have experienced these bitter verbal clashes in your own marriage—the ones that spill out when your spouse says you don't meet his or her needs. Or instead of an open fight, you may have each launched into "guerrilla warfare," quietly undermining each other or avoiding each other. A lack of serving love leaves needs unmet and keeps you far from the dream God has planned for you.

Serving love is the alternative. Gary will now share how much better even a good marriage can get.

THE BENEFITS OF SERVING LOVE

Barb and I have a good marriage. In fact we have a *really* good marriage. There are times when we think we have the best marriage on the planet. We'll look each other in the eye and say, "What we have couldn't get any better." Then there are other times when we know we haven't arrived yet. But armed with our love for each other and the necessary tools, we keep working to make our marriage the best it can be. We want a *great* marriage, and that's our desire for you too.

We have already admitted our marriage isn't perfect. When I allowed my heart to be drawn away by my doctoral program, Barb was past disappointed. She was discouraged by my lack of attention. I was too busy to discover her needs and lovingly meet them. She didn't feel honored and understood because I was distracted in my career and schooling. The result was a distance and discord that we never expected and never want to experience again. And, of course, that was not the only time we have done things that headed us in the wrong direction.

We have both found that when we forget that our marriage is a marriage of three, with Jesus Christ in his rightful place, we act out of our natural selfishness. God's sanctification and his moving us toward maturity continually cause us to have to confront our own tendency to "go our own way." We still have a lot of growing to do, but we know we are on the right path.

Does this sound painfully familiar? Is the sense of mutual honor and understanding infrequent in your marriage or missing altogether? Serving love, the love that selflessly gives to meet needs, is the answer. Here's why.

Serving love allows you both to feel honored and understood. If you want to feel understood, if you want to feel satisfied, if you want to feel honored, then build a marriage overflowing with serving love. If each of you is committed 100 percent to understanding and meeting the other's needs, then both of you will enjoy 100 percent honor and 100 percent understanding that result from that mutual commitment.

For Barb and me, our individual lives and our source of fulfillment originate in our relationship with Christ. He meets our deepest needs, and we each enjoy the overflow of God's blessing in our individual lives. I benefit from the overflow of Barb's relationship with Jesus on a daily basis, and Barb tells me that she enjoys the same benefit from my walk with Christ. Through each other we have gained completeness that otherwise wouldn't be there. And we have gained a personal fulfillment I have found in no other human relationship.

When you become what your spouse needs, you are God's instrument of serving love. You complete your spouse. In the world's eyes that's codependency; in God's eyes it is a true interdependence—a marriage of three: Jesus, husband, and wife. It is God's design. If you serve each other without meeting needs, your serving means little and leaves you both frustrated. But when you genuinely meet each other's needs out of the abundance of Christ's love in you, you become fulfilled persons.

Barb and I are not ashamed to admit that we have a deep

desire in us to push our lives and influence for the kingdom of God to the uttermost. But, next to serving Christ, our greatest ambition is to be the best husband and wife that we can be. That means doing everything possible to discover and meet each other's deepest needs, thus lavishing each other with honor and understanding. And since we share the same goal, our dream is becoming a reality. Our marriage doesn't hold us back from our dreams; it has been the *reason* for our dreams.

Serving love allows you to live out your vows to each other. When you got married, you promised to love and cherish each other, to face good times and bad, hand in hand. Those wedding vows were all about meeting each other's needs. When you serve each other in love, you meet the needs of your spouse and fulfill your marriage vows.

When you focus on discovering and meeting your spouse's needs, you are doing what God has called you to do in marriage. As a husband sets the pace by initiating serving love, he often finds that his wife becomes increasingly secure in responding to his serving heart. And when husband and wife do this mutually and wholeheartedly, the relationship is doubly strengthened. The results are a fulfilling, lasting marriage that only gets better with time.

Some of the New Testament's most powerful verses call us to sacrificial, serving love. Jesus said, "The greatest love is shown when people lay down their lives for their friends" (John 15:13). And the apostle Paul admonished, "Don't just pretend that you love others. Really love them. Hate what is wrong. Stand on the side of the good. Love each other with genuine affection, and take delight in honoring each other" (Romans 12:9-10).

God wants us to consider the needs of our spouses as more important than our own. When you meet your spouse's needs sacrificially, you are being "God with skin on," a phrase we use

to describe the privilege we have of reflecting Christ's love
to each other.

Serving love helps divorce-proof your marriage. Failing to meet
your spouse's deepest needs could ultimately cost you your
marriage. How many times have you heard a divorced person
lament, "He didn't meet my needs," or, "I needed more from
her"? Perhaps the bottom-line reason for meeting your spouse's
needs is that if you don't, you could lose him or her to someone—or something—who will meet those needs.

You would never think of ignoring your husband's or wife's
need for food and water. He or she would die without these
essentials. Yet your spouse's emotional, relational, and spiritual
needs are just as vital. If they go unmet, your marriage will
begin to die. It's that simple. When you generously minister
serving love to your husband or wife, you guard your marriage
against temptation and decay.

Tim and Grace enjoyed most of the trappings of material
success. As a young, dual-income, childless couple, they
devoted most of their time and attention to their careers—
to the detriment of their marriage. But as Tim became more
and more successful in his business, the person he longed to
impress—Grace—seemed totally involved in her own world.
Neither of them guarded the boundaries of their relationship,
and Tim eventually found himself opening his heart to a
coworker at the office. Kathy was always there, friendly,
helpful, praising his accomplishments and listening sympatheti-
cally to his needs. Months later in my counseling office, Tim
confessed to Grace that his heart was being drawn to another
woman.

When asked how and why this happened, Tim said, "Grace
was rarely there for me. She was so caught up in her own things
that I got tired of trying to get her attention. Kathy seemed
interested in what I did. She would ask me how my projects

were going. She affirmed me a lot. She seemed to value who I am. Kathy encouraged me when I was struggling."

Grace sat there stunned at first, pain etched on her face. Then the questions came fast and furiously. "Tim, did it get physical? Did she kiss you? Did you touch her?"

"Grace, nothing physical ever happened," Tim assured. "We just talked. Remember how we used to do that? I just needed affirmation from someone. I am sorry I have hurt you this way. I let down my guard and let her in. I know it wasn't right. And I want you, not Kathy. But I really need you to support me, to encourage me, and to let me know that you think I'm a good guy."

Both Tim and Grace heeded this clear wake-up call and thankfully made it safely through the depths of betrayal and pain.

Your situation as husband and wife is probably different from that of Tim and Grace, and we hope you haven't experienced the pain they did. Yet your spouse has needs, and you are wise if you seek to discover those needs and meet them. As you do, you will be exercising serving love and taking a major step toward divorce-proofing your marriage.

A DECISION TO HONOR YOUR SPOUSE

How important is serving love in our relationships, including our marriages? The Bible calls us to the same serving love Jesus has shown for others. Here's what we are taught in Philippians 2:1-7:

> Is there any encouragement from belonging to Christ? Any comfort from his love? Any fellowship together in the Spirit? Are your hearts tender and sympathetic? Then make me truly happy by agreeing wholeheartedly with each other, loving one another, and working together with one heart and purpose.

Don't be selfish; don't live to make a good impression
on others. Be humble, thinking of others as better
than yourself. Don't think only about your own affairs,
but be interested in others, too, and what they are
doing.
Your attitude should be the same that Christ Jesus
had. Though he was God, he did not demand and cling
to his rights as God. He made himself nothing; he took
the humble position of a slave and appeared in human
form.

After reading these lines, you may feel that you could never
manage the level of serving love Jesus demonstrated. If so,
you're right! Serving love starts with the strength of Jesus—
in the encouragement, comfort, and fellowship of a personal
relationship with him. And if you are growing in these qualities,
you are beginning to imitate his servant heart.

Do you want a great marriage? Do you want a relationship
characterized by intimate understanding and mutual honor?
When you meet the needs of your spouse, you build the foundation for a great marriage. And without serving love, you won't
experience honor or understanding.

How can it happen in your relationship? It all begins with
honoring your spouse. Barb will kick off this section.

IDEAS FOR HONORING YOUR SPOUSE

One of the most valuable gifts Gary gives to me is honor. If you
were to eavesdrop on our conversation most mornings, you
would hear him affirm who I am and what I do. He generously
voices his appreciation for me with an attitude of honor. Once he
gets focused for work, he doesn't say as much. The work mode

has a way of changing the whole focus of a man. Then hours later we can be seated in a team meeting, and Gary will begin talking about his "wonderful wife" and something she said that was strong, wise, and relevant. Sometimes when he does this, he catches me so off guard that I lean forward on the boardroom table thinking, *I wish I could meet this woman.* Gary makes me sound far better than I am, and I'm honored by it.

Your spouse is your best teacher in how to meet his or her needs. In the next chapter we will talk about how you as a couple can begin to discover and communicate those needs. The goal of this section is to help you lift up and honor your spouse. We suggest that you select two or three things to do or new habits you want to put into action in your relationship. Don't announce them. Don't make a big deal about your intention of honoring your spouse. Just quietly start doing it.

For Husbands Only

It's easy for men to get caught up in work and providing for the family. Sure, they appreciate all their wives do, but sometimes they forget to communicate appreciation in a way that conveys honor. Men often assume that their wives already know how they feel. All we women really want is to see those feelings demonstrated.

A lot of women talk to me about how they wish their husbands would treat them. So, men, let me share with you what I hear. Gary will share a similar list of suggestions with wives in the next section.

1. Ask her how you can help her, or dive in and help without being asked. It sounds like this: "Where do you need more of my help?" In a word: initiate!
2. When you disagree, immediately acknowledge her position. You don't have to understand or agree. Just

acknowledge that she has the right to her thoughts and feelings. It may sound like this: "I respect the fact that you feel strongly about this issue, and I always want to listen to your feedback. I need you to listen to my perspective as well."

3. Never humiliate her. If she does something embarrassing in front of others, don't make it worse. Regardless of the details or even if she's at fault, don't do it.

4. Share with others how important she is to you. Keep pictures of her in your wallet and on your desk. Talk about her to your friends and coworkers. Let her over-hear you bragging about her—it does wonders for the relationship!

5. Support her in front of the children. Whether or not you agree with a decision she makes, back her up, then discuss your differences later in private. Tell the kids how much you love their mom and how much you appreciate all her gifts.

6. Never remind her of her mistakes, especially in front of others. Learn to forgive and work through concerns privately with her. This builds confidence in the marriage.

7. Remember special dates! Obviously, her birthday and your anniversary are key. But you should also commemo-rate dates such as the anniversary of the death of a parent or another loved one. Send her a note and comfort her on those days.

8. Never compare her to other women. This includes your mother, previous girlfriends, women friends, or coworkers. Don't even compare her to other women in a positive way.

9. Eat together. Don't start eating the meal until she sits down, and don't leave the table until she's finished. And don't leave her to eat in front of the TV!

10. Talk over decisions with her *before* they are made—even the minor ones.

11. Set family goals so your wife doesn't feel as if she is bearing the whole load. Be specific about what each family member must do to get the work done.

12. Share with her what you're reading. Tell her about the key points you're getting out of a book. Spark discussion with her on current events.

13. Ask her about her childhood. Work to understand her heritage and why she is the way she is. (Just steer clear of mother-in-law jokes!)

14. Compliment her cooking. Make special requests!

For Wives Only

Just as Barb can speak with authority on how a wife likes to be honored by her husband, I think I can share several helpful tips with you women. I know it's easy for you to get caught up in the busyness of everyday life, whether it's working outside or inside the home, keeping up with household responsibilities, caring for children, spending time with your family and friends. You see your husband as your partner in getting things done, but he is also your partner in marriage. It's important to keep your husband's wants and needs in front of you. How are you honoring him and communicating that you really appreciate him?

Here are some simple acts of serving love that will make a huge difference.

1. Make time alone with him a priority. In this busy world, other things become more important than husband-and-wife time. Learn to say no in order to love, honor, and cherish your husband above all else.

2. Honor his favorite things. Make a list of his favorites— such as favorite dinner, dessert, date activity, TV

program, etc.——and make sure he gets to enjoy those things occasionally.

3. Celebrate his birthday. Make his birthday a big deal even if he says he doesn't want you to.

4. Say please and thank you.

5. Tell him what you need. He can't read your mind——at least not always!

6. Lift a burden. Ask him, "If I could take something off your to-do list today, what could I do for you?"

7. Allow him to be himself. Don't assume that your husband is going to think, feel, or behave as you do or as "the ideal husband" does. He will make mistakes. Allow him that freedom.

8. Affirm your husband's maleness by showing interest in his hobbies. Attend a sporting event or watch a ball game with him occasionally. If he participates in sports, be there to cheer him on.

9. Be more curious of your husband than critical. What interesting things does he do? Don't judge him. Investigate and ask questions about why he does the things he does.

10. Appreciate his hard work. Thank him for working hard for you and your family. Let him know that you notice and admire his work.

11. Praise him to your children. Tell the kids how hard he works and what a good man he is. Tell them how much you love him and how important he is to you.

12. Compliment his efforts to be sensitive. If he makes special attempts to understand, listen, or comfort you, let him know how meaningful they are to you. Be specific about what you particularly like.

The suggestions we have offered in this chapter will help you demonstrate serving love in a general way. But even though your spouse shares many similarities with others of the same gender, he or she is also unique. Your spouse has a number of specific needs, and your efforts to discover those needs and lovingly meet them is an even higher expression of serving love than the ideas just presented. In the next chapter, we will equip you to identify and communicate your deepest needs so that mutual understanding and honor will grow even deeper.

seven

COMMUNICATING
YOUR NEEDS

*W*hen Robertson McQuilkin's wife of forty years was diagnosed with Alzheimer's disease, he was president of Columbia Bible College and Seminary (now Columbia International University) in Columbia, South Carolina. He soon resigned his prestigious position to care for his ill wife full-time. At that moment his world of widespread Christian leadership and global ministry shrank to a life of meeting Muriel's every need, including feeding her, bathing her, grooming her, and taking her to the bathroom.

A friend wrote to Dr. McQuilkin, saying that Muriel should be institutionalized. "Muriel doesn't know you anymore," the man said, "doesn't know anything, really, so it's time to put her in a nursing home and get on with life."

But Muriel needed him, McQuilkin protested, and he needed her. "Do you realize," he wrote to his friend, "how lonely I would be without her?"

When McQuilkin left his job to care for Muriel, he was living out a choice he had made four decades earlier. In his book *A Promise Kept,* Dr. McQuilkin writes, "The decision was made, in a way, 42 years ago when I promised to care for Muriel 'in sickness and in health . . . till death do us part.'. . . I love Muriel. She is a delight to me—her childlike dependence and confidence in me. . . . I don't *have* to care for her. I *get* to! It is a high honor to care for so wonderful a person."[1] McQuilkin regards meeting Muriel's needs as just a small return on the care she gave him for more than forty years.

Twenty years after the onset of Muriel's illness, Robertson McQuilkin is still entering into Muriel's world to understand and meet her most basic needs. He sees himself not as a co-victim of Alzheimer's but as the recipient of Muriel's love. "In her silent world Muriel is so content, so lovable, I sometimes pray, 'Please, Lord, could you let me keep her a little longer?' If Jesus took her home, how I would miss her gentle, sweet presence. Oh yes, there are times I get irritated, but not often. It doesn't make sense. And besides, I love to care for her. She's my precious."[2]

One of the most poignant insights from McQuilkin's testimony is how he has continued to grow in understanding Muriel's needs even though she is unable to communicate with him. Years ago she lost her ability to speak, and not much later she lost the ability to communicate altogether when first one hand, then the other went limp. "That right hand was the last way she had to communicate," McQuilkin writes. "She would reach out to hold hands, pat me on the back when I hugged her, push me away when she didn't like what I was doing. I missed her hand."[3] Today, even without a word or gesture from Muriel, Robertson McQuilkin keenly discerns and meets his wife's every need on a daily basis.

The ministry of serving love involves discovering and meeting needs. Being *committed* to serving love is one thing; *knowing how to discover and meet those needs* is quite another thing. Robertson McQuilkin is a shining example of both deep commitment to serving love and dogged persistence in meeting his wife's needs. And he continues his ministry to her without the benefit of a vital key to discovering and meeting needs in marriage: communication.

COMMUNICATION: KEY TO DISCOVERING AND MEETING NEEDS

Barb and I believe that communication is indispensable to the ministry of serving love in marriage. Let's face it: None of us is a mind reader. If Barb doesn't communicate her needs to me, my chances of meeting those needs are mighty slim. And if I don't communicate my needs to her, she's flying blind when it comes to serving me. In a marriage relationship, discovering and meeting needs in an atmosphere of serving love presupposes that husband and wife are willing to talk. It is in the process of communication that needs are shared or discovered.

When I was growing up, I witnessed firsthand a couple's commitment to enter each other's world and to discover and meet each other's needs through serving love. Those people were my parents. Every evening when we kids heard Dad drive into the garage after work, we yelled, "Dad's home!" We rushed to meet him at the back door, and he greeted us by ruffling our hair or hugging us. But then, for the next sixty minutes, the four Rosberg kids disappeared (most of the time) while Dad and Mom sat and talked. Sixty minutes!

Barb and I have carried that tradition into our own home. Within minutes of greeting each other at the end of the day, we are sitting in two mauve-colored chairs and talking—just the two of us. We talk about the kids, we review Barb's day and mine, we celebrate each other's highs, and we mourn each other's lows. We talk about everything! Sometimes our discussions are deep and serious; other times they are just newsy, connecting chats.

During this time, as we listen intently to each other's heart, we notice what brings joy or tears. And we discern needs. Most significant, we walk away from our chat with a better idea of the struggles we face individually and as a couple. We know better how we can meet each other's needs in the midst of our trials. In our talking, we discover exactly where to apply serving love. Barb learns how to help me; I learn how to help her.

Barb and I hate to imagine what would happen if we didn't have this daily connecting time. Actually, we don't have to imagine it, because we encounter the grim results in our ministry all the time. Nearly every day during our call-in radio broadcast, a love-starved husband or wife laments to us the pain of a marriage lacking in communication. When couples do not share their lives and hearts with each other consistently, the atmosphere in the home can get colder than an arctic winter. Without communication we fall out of sync and disconnect, leaving plenty of room for chilly distance and selfishness to grow.

Communication is the process of sharing yourself verbally and nonverbally in such a way that your spouse both understands and accepts—though not necessarily agrees with—what you are sharing. Studies show that couples who communicate frequently have a more satisfying relationship. And couples who achieve deep levels of communication enjoy the most satisfaction of all.

So what does "deep communication" look like? Here are five levels of communication, each one deeper and more enriching than the previous one:[4]

1. Sharing general information. We speak largely in clichés: "How are you today?" or "I'm fine, how are you?" or "Lovely weather we're having" or "How about that team of ours!"

2. Sharing facts. We discuss people and events, but nothing personal: "What did you do today?" or "I took Susie to the dentist and Brett to soccer practice" or "I had lunch with the sales manager" or "There was a terrible wreck on the expressway."

3. *Sharing opinions and beliefs.* We share personal information, but nothing too risky: "Brett is turning into a very good soccer player" or "I think the coach is a jerk!" or "I really want that job in the sales department" or "Wrecks like that wouldn't happen if they lowered the speed limit."

4. *Sharing feelings and emotions.* We begin to open our hearts: "I'm worried that Susie is going to need braces" or "If they promote Frank over me, I'm going to quit!" or "I'm so glad it wasn't you who was hurt in the accident. I would feel so sad."

5. *Sharing needs, intimate concerns, hopes, and fears.* We vulnerably share our heart of hearts: "If you lose your job, what are we going to do? We have bills to pay" or "If I can't make it in sales, I'm washed up, finished!" or "I love you and need you. I don't know what I would do without you."

Can you guess what kinds of communication promote serving love? Of course, those further down the list: sharing opinions and beliefs, sharing feelings and emotions, and especially sharing needs, intimate concerns, hopes, and fears. The more we share our hearts with one another, the better prepared we will be to discern and meet each other's deepest needs.

GOING DEEP: GETTING INSIDE YOUR SPOUSE'S HEART

When we urge you to communicate your needs to one another as husbands and wives, we know we are coaching you to go deep, to unveil the deepest parts of your souls. But it is the only way to gain the crucial insight Proverbs 24:3 talks about: "By wisdom a house is built, and through understanding it is established" (NIV). If you want to build a solid, divorce-proof home, you must understand each other. And to understand each other, you must share your hearts with each other.

Hardly a husband and wife on earth would say they have no need for further growth in deep communication. If Barb and I walked into your church on Sunday morning and asked all the married people to raise a hand if they needed to work on communication, we would expect to see a room full of flailing arms. Some people would have both hands raised. Some wives would be raising their husbands' hands—and vice versa! Everyone has room for improvement in the area of communication.

Understanding and meeting your spouse's needs through communication is kind of like exploring a cave. We don't mean a little hole in the side of a hill like the one you may have played in as a kid. We're talking about a *real* cave—one with a vast labyrinth of underground caverns someone could spend a lifetime exploring.

When you were first married and just learning about each other, you felt your way through the dark, unexplored cave of your relationship hand in hand. In the dim light, you could make out features common in many caves—the stalactites and stalagmites of the human soul, the kind of stuff you already knew about some of your best friends.

The deeper you go into a cave, the more you are surprised and awed by what you find: rushing underground rivers, rare rock formations that glisten like buttered popcorn, precious gems and minerals you never expected. You may squeeze through a small crack in the rock wall to find a cavern as breathtakingly beautiful as any cathedral. At times you may stumble on a pile of rock debris you must clear away before you can go any farther. But every step, every turn in the labyrinth, every new day of exploration yields surprises and challenges too good to miss.

Similarly, the further you venture into your marriage relationship together, the more you will appreciate its uniqueness. The more you explore the heart of your spouse through honest, vulnerable sharing, the more fulfilling your marital journey becomes. Your discoveries will take your breath away—sometimes in fear, sometimes in excitement. Surprises await around every corner. You will discover new wonders daily—if you dare to enter in and keep exploring.

OVERCOMING OBSTACLES TO DEEP SHARING AND MEETING NEEDS

Barb and I want to coach you in the skill of exploring your hearts and communicating your needs. Unfortunately, it won't be easy. Remember: We're comparing this journey to the rigors and dangers of cave exploration, not a ride on a merry-go-round. Communication isn't automatic for any of us. There are many obstacles to overcome. But it is a skill every couple can learn. Communication is a cornerstone of serving love.

The first step to communicating needs is getting rid of those inner barriers that keep us from talking about our needs. Some of these obstacles are rooted in our attitudes about serving and being served, our reluctance to reveal our neediness, and past hurts that block us from sharing. Are any of the following obstacles keeping you and your spouse from sharing your deep heart and meeting each other's needs?

"My spouse doesn't care about my needs." We have heard countless husbands say something such as, "She devotes all her time and attention to the kids. Don't get me wrong, I love my kids. But what about me?" This isn't the poor-me tune of a self-centered whiner. Wives, you need to know this is the heart cry of a man who feels neglected and in need of his wife's attention.

We have also heard wives complain, "I feel as if I am last on my husband's list. All I want is a night away from the kids occasionally, a time when we talk about something other than bills."

Husbands, this is a woman who wants to connect with you. Our experience has shown that when you step out and take care of your mate's needs, your own needs will be met as well.

"After what my spouse did, I'm not interested in meeting his [or her] needs." This spouse is saying, "You hurt me, so I'm not sure I want to open my heart to you again." This is deep stuff that must be worked through with forgiving love. Are there times when you have ignored your mate's needs in the past? Are there other ways you have hurt your spouse? Start by going through the process of closing the loop on your own offenses. As you do, you will find opportunities to communicate ways your spouse has let *you* down.

"If I admit I have needs, I'll feel as if I'm begging." We know wives who are reluctant to ask their husbands to take a walk with them just to talk. We know of husbands who rein in their sexual urges, thinking that they are asking too much of their wives. We also know that God has put your spouse in your life to meet your legitimate needs, whatever they are. If your spouse has somehow caused you to feel that your needs are unimportant, make that a point to talk about. But start with "I feel like . . ." rather than "You never . . ."

"If I share my needs, I'll be mocked for being weak." This spouse is saying, "I'm not supposed to have needs." That's a societal myth, a lie. Yet many husbands fail to share their needs with their wives because they see it as a sign of weakness on par with reading the instructions, stopping for directions, or admitting they need help in any form. And many women don't share their needs because, after all, who wants to be known as a clinging, needy wife? Both of these attitudes ignore the truth that God has created us with needs.

"If I give an inch, my spouse will take a mile." One husband remarked, "When you talk about serving love, all I can hear is the sucking sound as my wife drains all my energy!" The goal of serving love is not to enable controlling or demanding behavior in your spouse. Rather, you are striving to be God with skin on, serving

him or her selflessly as Christ has served us. In our experience, when one spouse begins to consciously apply God-powered serving love, it is usually reciprocated.

But it rarely starts with a cognitive decision to "serve" each other. It typically comes through pain. It may be loss or fear of loss, but it likely is rooted in a family's response to difficulty and pain. We have repeatedly found that as God works through the brokenness of our lives, serving love becomes increasingly apparent. And invariably it starts with the brokenness of the husband. When a husband and dad reaches the end of himself and trusts God deeply, he sets a pace for the entire family. A wife and mother, as well as kids living in a home where a husband and father is sold out to Christ, will feel the security and protection of a servant leader.

"Why bother? My spouse won't notice if I do something nice." It will be difficult for your spouse to ignore your efforts to discover and meet his or her genuine needs. It will be even harder for your spouse to resist being asked about his or her needs. If you think your spouse is reluctant to be served, assert your desire to love him or her with a servant love. Show kindness the way your spouse wants it shown, not how you think it should be shown.

Some of you may be saying, "Every one of these obstacles exists in our marriage." These misunderstandings, conflicts, and hurts must be addressed by closing the loop through forgiving love. Barb and I encourage you to make that a priority. As you do, you will be clearing the path for the rich and exciting experience of deeper heart exploration.

For most couples, serving love is lacking simply because of inattention. Or perhaps the two of you have fallen into a pattern of petty selfishness: "I won't meet your need until you meet mine first." Someone needs to take the initiative and start serving regardless of the obstacles. Even better, why don't you both agree to serve the other in spite of your fears and reservations.

Serving is the fastest way to break into new behaviors. We are asking you to put your selfish attitudes aside and serve your imperfect spouse. Ask God to open your heart so you can serve freely with the attitude of Jesus.

DISCOVERING EACH OTHER'S NEEDS

In order to serve each other meaningfully, you must have an idea of what the other needs. One of the most fruitless and potentially damaging assumptions Barb and I have heard relates to needs. It goes something like this: "If I treat my spouse the way I would like him or her to treat me, I will be meeting his or her needs." This statement is rarely true. When it comes to needs, the Golden Rule *does not* always apply.

Why? Because a man's needs often differ from a woman's needs. Take intimacy, for example. Typically, a woman's need for intimacy is met with deep, intimate conversations. Because these chats fulfill a woman's needs, she assumes they meet her husband's needs as well. However, a man's need for intimacy is often met through sexual intercourse. But his need is often greater than his wife's. If he thinks having sex with her several times a week fully meets her needs simply because it meets his needs, he is mistaken. A couple practicing serving love will ensure that each partner's unique needs are being met.

Your spouse is your best coach and resource in helping you meet his or her needs. That's where communicating needs comes in. But what do you communicate *about?* This is where we may be able to coach you both as you explore each other's love needs. We want to give you something concrete to talk about.

Barb and I surveyed more than seven hundred couples (fourteen hundred people) to discover the top needs for men and women. We presented each person with a list of twenty basic

love needs. Then we asked people to rank in order of importance (1) what they needed most from their spouse and (2) what
they thought their spouse needed from them.

Before reading our findings, you may want to complete this
exercise yourself. Turn to appendix C and read through the list
of needs. Then rank your top five needs.

The chart below summarizes the results of our extensive
survey. Here is how the husbands and wives ranked their needs.

HUSBANDS' TOP FIVE LOVE NEEDS	WIVES' TOP FIVE LOVE NEEDS
1. Unconditional Love and Acceptance	1. Unconditional Love and Acceptance
2. Sexual Intimacy	2. Emotional Intimacy and Communication
3. Companionship	3. Spiritual Intimacy
4. Encouragement and Affirmation	4. Encouragement and Affirmation
5. Spiritual Intimacy	5. Companionship

Because each of these is so important, we have devoted an
entire book, *The Five Love Needs of Men and Women,* to discussing
what the needs look like in husbands and wives and how those
needs can be met.[5] Here we include only a brief snapshot of each:

A Husband's Needs

Most husbands' top five needs included these:

1. Unconditional love and acceptance. This reflects the deep desire
to be accepted and loved just the way we are, no matter what.

2. Sexual intimacy. Much of a man's masculinity is rooted in
his sexuality, a part of his maleness he cannot erase. As most
couples discover, men spell intimacy S-E-X.

3. Companionship. Husbands need a place to let down and be

themselves, a place where they do not have to perform. This is
a need for friendship.

4. *Encouragement and affirmation.* A husband needs to hear two
primary voices cheering him on: his wife's and God's. The more
encouragement and affirmation he receives from his wife, the
easier it will be for him to discern God's voice.

5. *Spiritual intimacy.* Husbands need a spiritual connection—
with God, with their wife, and with other believers. Wise wives
will help their husband discover pathways to spiritual growth.

A Wife's Needs

Most wives' top five needs included these:

1. *Unconditional love and acceptance.* In a world where women
often compare themselves to each other and come up short,
wives need a husband who is totally accepting.

2. *Emotional intimacy and communication.* Wives spell intimacy
T-A-L-K. For many women, conversation is the primary way
they process thoughts, feelings, ideas, and problems.

3. *Spiritual intimacy.* Wives find no greater comfort or security than in knowing that their husband walks closely with God
and supports the family's spiritual growth. They need a husband
to pray for them and with them.

4. *Encouragement and affirmation.* Wives need daily doses of
support. They value comfort and understanding through their
problems more than advice on how to fix them.

5. *Companionship.* Wives need a place to let down, where
they don't feel as if they are valued only for what they do, and
to be themselves. This is the need for friendship.

How do the top love needs from our survey compare with your
own list? In what ways are they similar? dissimilar? Does the rank-
ing of needs in our survey surprise you? Does your spouse's rank-
ing of needs surprise you? Does your list surprise him or her?

You now have something to talk about, something that will start you down the path to understanding and meeting your spouse's top needs. "Talk about needs?" you may object. "Hey, Gary and Barb, we don't have enough time to talk about family finances, the kids' education, and what's for dinner tonight, let alone our top love needs."

We hear you. And if it's any consolation, most couples are in the same boat. One of the biggest enemies to discovering needs is time: time to reflect, time to talk, time to pray together. Yet you are wise to spend your most precious resource—your time—on your most precious possession—your marriage. You can have all the communication skills down pat, but if you don't schedule time to exercise them, what good can be accomplished? To help create the atmosphere in which you can discuss and meet each other's needs, we have written *40 Unforgettable Dates with Your Mate,* a book that gives date ideas—twenty for husbands and twenty for wives—that will help you meet your spouse's top five needs.[6] The book also includes dozens of reflection and discussion questions that will help you discover and understand each other's needs.

Your marriage is a living organism. It thrives with attention. So take some time over the next few days to discuss your top love needs with your spouse. Take the initiative; don't wait for your spouse to do it. Here is a suggestion for working through this discussion. If necessary, consult the list of twenty needs presented in appendix C.

1. Make a list of what you think are your spouse's top five needs.
2. At the same time make a list of your own top five needs.
3. Sit down with your spouse, and say something like, "I want to learn what your needs are so I can meet them more fully. I have made a list of what I think are your top

five needs, and I want to discuss the list with you. But even more important to me is what *you* think are your top needs. I am committed to honoring you by meeting your needs." Then begin to discuss your spouse's needs.

4. If your spouse asks you what your love needs are, you will have your list ready.

5. Read the two books we described above to help you grow in your awareness of and ability to meet your spouse's needs.[7]

This is only the beginning. Our hope is that you are motivated to continue the process of healthy, ongoing communication about your needs, desires, and dreams. Barb and I want to help you with this. Let us coach you on a few key skills for good communication.

CONNECTING THROUGH GOOD COMMUNICATION

What do you think of when we say *communication?* Talking, to be sure. But just because someone's mouth is moving doesn't mean communication is taking place. Communication is sharing yourself verbally and nonverbally in a way that your spouse both accepts and understands. If the message is spoken but not understood, it's not clear communication.

In addition to talking—or what we call *expressing*—there are two other vital elements to communication: *listening* and *responding.* We have a responsibility when we communicate not merely to unload what is on our minds but to ensure that our message is understood. Expressing, listening, and responding are all part of the communication process. We want to explain these three components and coach you on how you can use them to improve your communication as husband and wife.

Expressing

As the youngest child in a family of five verbally aggressive siblings, Marita got the feeling that nobody really cared what she thought. By adulthood she had developed the habit of waiting to be asked before expressing her opinion. To her husband, Rich, it was like playing a frustrating game of twenty questions. Marita rarely expressed her thoughts and feelings voluntarily. And if Rich didn't ask the right question, he was seldom rewarded with the information he sought. Rich longed to explore his wife's heart, but it was locked, and he had no key.

Some of us express ourselves naturally and easily. But for others, expression is a skill to be learned. If you want to communicate clearly with your spouse, you must begin with deliberate expression. When you have something to share with your spouse, sort what you want to say into three categories—what you *think,* what you *feel,* and what you *need.* Then start talking. Give details. Don't be put off if your spouse asks you clarifying questions. And don't expect the other person to read your mind or fill in blanks.

Expressing openly and in detail doesn't mean expressing carelessly. As Proverbs 18:21 points out, your words can be dangerous: "The tongue can kill or nourish life." Be careful about what you say.

Try these three rules for effective expressing.

1. Take one issue at a time. A full day's worth of news and experiences and troubles can be overwhelming. Pouring everything out at once seldom gives your spouse much information about anything. It's one way we tend to skim over our issues and never get to the core of them.

You can help your spouse stay on track with a few helpful phrases: "Tell me more about . . ." or "What were you saying about . . . ?" or "That sounds like another issue. Let's talk about the other one first and come back to this one later." If your spouse needs reassurance that the issue won't be brushed aside, write it down in front of him or her.

2. Allow one person to speak at a time. When you are communicating with your spouse, keep him or her in the spotlight. When your spouse is expressing, give him or her room for full expression—no interruptions, no feedback. If you both fight to be heard at the same time, communication is bound to break down.

3. Be specific and to the point. Barb and I communicate kind of like we trim a Christmas tree. Our styles are reflective of basic male-female differences. I like to start at the top. The most important thing—the star—goes up first, then I work my way down from there. When Barb trims the tree, she takes out each ornament, rotates it slowly in her hand, and recites the ornament's history to anyone within earshot. Eventually all the ornaments make it on the tree.

Similarly, when I express, I start at the top—the main point—and go from there. To Barb, this approach sometimes feels rushed and even a little rough. She would rather talk around the topic and eventually arrive at the main point. To me, that's like filling in the background before you draw attention to what you really want to say.

Wives, you will likely be more successful at expressing if you accommodate your husband's need to hear the bottom line up front. And husbands, you will make communication more enjoyable for your wife if you include plenty of detail with your main point.

Listening

If you are like most couples, the biggest single step you can take to improve communication in your marriage is to improve listening in your marriage. My dad always said that we have two ears and one mouth for a reason. Even though he didn't become a Christian until late in life, he had a good handle on James 1:19:

"My dear brothers and sisters, be quick to listen, slow to speak, and slow to get angry." Dad knew that one of the secrets to great communication was to listen attentively.

When Natalie didn't have Jerry's attention during their conversations, she was tempted to use the technique her three-year-old daughter used when her daddy wasn't listening—except Natalie knew it was a childish way to express herself. Whenever Tabitha noticed that her daddy wasn't totally focused on her, she grabbed his chin and put her face nose-to-nose with his.

So as Natalie worked at communicating her needs to Jerry, one of the first things she said was, "Sometimes I feel as if I don't have your attention when we talk." But instead of citing the hard evidence of his frequent attention lapses, she shared a personal confession. "When you are excited to tell me something, I know I have a habit of cutting you off. When I am focused on doing something, I don't exactly encourage you to talk."

Then Natalie asked Jerry what *he* thought got in the way of their communication. At first he hesitated. Then he said sheepishly, "We talk a lot less since I bought a TV for the bedroom." Natalie nodded in agreement.

By the time Natalie and Jerry finished talking, they had closed the loop on this issue—and reinvigorated their listening habits.

If you want your spouse to freely share his or her heart with you, you must convey with absolute certainty that he or she has your undivided attention. Listening attentively isn't easy. Maintaining eye contact may be unnerving to you. Jumping in with a solution may be hard to resist. But listening is the key to understanding your spouse's needs.

Responding

At some point in a discussion, it is appropriate to move beyond listening to join the conversation. The point is not to introduce your own agenda but to clarify and fully understand what your spouse is expressing. This communication skill is called responding. We can get into trouble at this point if we fail to look out for our spouse's best interest. Proverbs 18:13 says, "What a shame, what folly, to give advice before listening to the facts!"

Typically, men and women have different ways of responding. Men tend either to try to fix the situation, get defensive, get angry, or withdraw. Even while his wife is still stating the problem, a man's brain is working on a solution: something to fix, a wrong to right, an error to correct.

Women tend to seek security, reassurance, a sympathetic ear, and validation in response from their husbands. Wives don't always want a solution right off the bat. First they need empathy and understanding. Once a wife feels emotionally connected to her patiently listening husband, she may be ready for suggestions on what to do.

Once again Monique awaited Jim's arrival from work with dread. For the third time this year she had crunched their late-model SUV. She knew the consequences well: a traffic fine (it was her fault—again), another insurance deductible to pay, a hike in their already sky-high rates. And this time her traffic citation came with an embarrassing bonus: a requirement to attend what the police officer at the scene referred to as "driving school for dummies." Jim's recounting of all these facts only made Monique feel more inept.

Husbands, if you were Jim, how would you respond? You know the practical implications of damaging a vehicle. You have likely dented a car or two in your time. But that probably isn't what you want to say to Monique. If you're like many men, you want to rehearse the details and lovingly but firmly make sure it doesn't happen again.

But right now Monique isn't looking for a lecture. She needs a response that makes her feel as if you understand her reaction to the accident. Try these: "Are you okay?" or "Was the other driver hurt?" or "Were you okay driving home?" or "Did the officer make you feel stupid?" or "Did the other driver yell at you?"

When your spouse has laid bare his or her soul, a wise response has three elements. Just remember the acrostic A-S-K:

Ask—"What do you need most from me right now?" or "How can I help you?"

Suggest—Offer to assist by saying, "Would it help if I . . . ?"

Kneel—Assume an inner posture of servanthood. Reassure your spouse that you will do whatever he or she needs you to do.

Maybe your spouse already knows exactly what he or she needs in a situation. But how much better to ask proactively, "What can I do to help you?" These are the caring words of serving love.

As we have shared with you about communication skills, maybe you can't imagine expressing your deepest needs to your spouse. Or you may wonder if you're ready to hear what your spouse needs from you. How can couples delve so deeply? What makes deep sharing possible? Barb has an important insight on this topic.

HOW CAN WE DELVE SO DEEPLY?

Earlier in the chapter, Gary explained from our national survey that both men and women identified unconditional love and acceptance as their number one need from their marriage partner. Unconditional acceptance simply means loving and receiving your spouse no matter what. It's a commitment that says, "I will always stay with you. I will always love you. I will always affirm you and support you." Robertson McQuilkin is one of our heroes, a shining example of someone who shows unconditional love.

Now let's be real: Admitting our needs to our spouses isn't very flattering. It's rather humbling. I would prefer to have it all together, to need nothing from Gary or anyone. I want to be an omnicompetent wife, the total Proverbs 31 woman. But God in his wisdom didn't wire me that way. Instead, he designed Gary to love and accept me unconditionally despite my obvious (and not so obvious) needs, weaknesses, and failures. And God designed me to accept my dear but needy and imperfect husband the same way.

This is the beauty of unconditional love and acceptance. I am able to be honest about my needs with Gary because I know he won't pounce on me—put me down with either condemnation or an immediate solution. He will love me, affirm me, and support me because we are committed to each other unconditionally.

Communication of needs flows freely in an atmosphere of complete acceptance. Therefore, it is imperative that husbands and wives continually grow in meeting this critical top need in each other. We need to extend open arms to our spouses, assuring them, "You can tell me anything. You are safe with me."

Let me share something special with you wives. Your husband may be like many men in our culture today, a culture that is far more concerned about image than authenticity. Men are more reticent to admit their weaknesses and pain. Remember: They grew up with the sad and inaccurate mantra, "Big boys don't cry." Even the smallest hurt in your husband's past may have prompted him to cover up with a mask. Like Phantom in the popular production *Phantom of the Opera,* he may still wear a portion of that mask to cover old inner wounds that have never fully healed. He may be trying to cover a fear common to many men—the fear of failing you.

One way your unconditional love and acceptance can minister to your husband is by helping him take off his mask. Wives, God has generously gifted you with the ability to be gentle and loving. Demonstrate these qualities by being transparent about your own weaknesses to show your husband that he no longer needs to hide behind an image of strength or perfection. If your husband acts as if nothing bad ever happened to him, he is hiding behind a mask of false bravado. Your own transparency and your acceptance will help free him to trust you with his pain and needs also.

Husbands, let me share a final word with you. Most guys are quick to rush in with answers to a wife's problems. It might be easy for you to love her in practical ways: unstopping a plugged toilet, mowing the lawn, always being the one to top off the gas tank in the family van. But the real servant not only serves where it is *easy* but where it is *needed*. If you desire to have a servant heart, give yourself humbly to your wife. Ask her what she needs. Listen to her. Study your wife with the intense purpose of a servant who is eager to please.

Husbands and wives, you are launching into the exciting adventure of discovering and meeting your spouse's needs. You are taking another key step in the direction of divorce-proofing your marriage.

A SPECIAL NOTE ABOUT THE JOURNEY

The ministry of discovering and meeting your spouse's needs breeds mutual honor and understanding in your marriage. But there is more to the vital element of serving love than we can put into these two chapters. We recommend that you read *The Five Love Needs of Men and Women* and use *The Five Love Needs of Men and Women Workbook* (see appendix A) to expand your understanding and application of this topic. These resources, explored with a small group of married couples, will further equip you to put serving love into action in your relationship.

Part Four

PERSEVERING
LOVE

Persevering love stays strong in tough times

and helps spouses feel

bonded—best friends for life

eight

LOVE THAT ENDURES
TOUGH TIMES

$\mathscr{B}$arb and I became friends with Dan and Jeannie through
church. Dan is a hardworking, kindhearted Christian guy who
was known around town for cheerfully moving snow for many
of his neighbors. He and Jeannie are also actively involved volun-
teers in many community service projects. And the couple is
doing a great job of raising the kids.

Dan is a bridge builder by trade. One day he jumped from
a half-completed bridge deck to a platform a few feet below—
a deft hop he and his coworkers made a dozen times a day. This
time, however, the platform broke beneath his feet, and Dan fell
thirty-two feet to the ground below. Even though he survived
the fall, the impact severed his spinal cord.

Dan's accident happened a few days before Good Friday,
plunging them into the greatest time of trial and need in the
history of their marriage. After Easter Sunday service at our
church, Barb and I stopped by the hospital to see this dear
couple. We were blown away by what we found. All they could
talk about was their gratitude to God for sparing Dan's life. No

complaining, no blaming God, only gratitude. We had gone to minister to them, and instead they ministered to us! It was one of our most memorable Easters ever.

A short time later, when it was clear that Dan's paralysis from the waist down was permanent, I asked one of his sons if I could do anything to help. With a smile—and not a hint of resentment, bitterness, or self-pity—Matt said, "Don't worry about that, Gary. Dad's got me covered."

Since then, the loving partnership Dan and Jeannie built in the years before Dan's accident has only grown stronger through the adjustments to Dan's new life as a paraplegic. He and Jeannie have fallen more deeply in love. It's a love they have passed down to their children. At their daughter's wedding, Dan proudly escorted his daughter down the aisle in his wheelchair. And when the happy couple said "I do," Dan spun his chair in celebration!

THE POWER TO HANG IN THERE

How would you respond if your world came crashing down like Dan and Jeannie's did? Would a similar tragedy strain your marriage to the breaking point?

Dan and Jeannie discovered a love that thrived in good times and continues to flourish in the worst of times. And they're not the only miracle couple we know. Barb and I have watched in awe as numerous marriages thrived and grew stronger under life's most difficult trials. We are amazed at the faithfulness of couples we know who have stayed connected despite a wide array of problems, such as

- ◆ chronic illness
- ◆ financial ruin

- ◆ a runaway child
- ◆ physical handicaps
- ◆ job loss and extended unemployment
- ◆ the death of a child
- ◆ a spouse who doubts God
- ◆ conflict with extended family
- ◆ sexual addiction
- ◆ depression
- ◆ infertility
- ◆ blended families
- ◆ countless other tragedies

While unfortunate circumstances, poor choices, and even the devil himself could have driven these couples apart, they stayed together and followed God's plan for their marriages. Sadly, we also know countless other couples whose marriages have blown apart under the same pressures.

Like most couples, you face pressures from life's many inconvenient, tragic, or evil circumstances. Sometimes a variety of pressures pile up on you all at once. Sometimes tragedy hits with the force of a wrecking ball, then goes away. Other times the same nagging pressure can hover like a dark cloud for months or even years. It's not a matter of *if* your marriage will face pressure; it's just a question of *when*.

No couple is immune from the kind of pressure that has the potential to threaten a marriage. After the terrorist attacks of September 11, 2001, Laura Bush described the event as "the biggest crisis" of her marriage. Laura and her husband, President George Bush, were in different parts of the country when the planes hit the Pentagon and the World Trade Center towers. Like most of us, neither of them knew what would happen in the subsequent hours, but they knew their lives were in danger. Laura comments on that day: "When he landed in Washington, I went back to the White House. . . . We just hugged." The president later told friends that "he feared he might lose her that day."[1]

What held the First Couple's marriage together during the weeks and months following the crisis? Two things: their friendship and their faith. The Bushes have a close relationship. "She's his confidante, and he's hers," observes a close friend. They find time for each other every day. Their friends agree that "George and Laura are best friends."[2] An adviser to the president said of the couple, "It's been a strong marriage from the very beginning, and that is principally because they both share the same common purpose in life, which is to serve other people. . . . [They] have unwavering love for one another that's grounded in a deep and abiding faith."[3] The Bushes agree. Laura reflects, "Our faith is very important to our marriage. . . . It's gotten so much stronger and deeper."[4]

How can you make sure your marriage, like the Bushes' and like Dan and Jeannie's, will weather the storm? What will prevent your relationship from crumbling under the weight of pain, problems, and tragedy?

If you want to divorce-proof your marriage against the storms and struggles of life, if you want a deeper bond and a richer friendship, you need what Barb and I call *persevering love*. It's the kind of love that triumphs over trials and grows stronger when you are most vulnerable. Persevering love doesn't just hang on through calamity by its fingernails; it hangs in there and thrives. It's the kind of love described by Paul in 1 Corinthians 13:7: "Love never gives up, never loses faith, is always hopeful, and endures through every circumstance." Persevering love bonds husbands and wives into lifelong friends.

What does this kind of love look like? We want to share with you what we have observed in couples like Dan and Jeannie, couples whose marriages are fortified by persevering love. In this chapter we will present six qualities of persevering love. And in the next chapter we will coach you on specific ways you can cultivate persevering love in your relationship.

PERSEVERING LOVE REQUIRES TOTAL COMMITMENT

Paul and Nina were the darlings of their church's high school youth group. Both of their families were influential in the church, so the couple's engagement was big news there. Paul and Nina married after college and returned to their hometown and their old home church to begin their new life together.

Who could have anticipated that the first major attack on Paul and Nina's marriage would come from within the body of Christ? After an embezzlement scandal involving their senior pastor was discovered, Paul and Nina found themselves torn in opposite directions. Paul's family lined up with those in the church wanting to restore Pastor Evans. But Nina's family sided with those who would settle for nothing short of dismissal and prosecution. Each family exerted pressure on the young couple to conform to their respective viewpoints.

Eventually Nina's family left with dozens of other people to form a new church. Paul's family stayed. The couple's extended families weren't speaking to each other. Both sets of parents implied that disagreeing with the family position was tantamount to disobeying Christ. Furthermore, many of Paul and Nina's childhood friends were embroiled in the split and exerting pressure on them.

All eyes were on the young couple. How would they respond to the pressure? Naturally, Paul and Nina each felt a tug of allegiance toward their families. And they personally disagreed on how the scandal should be resolved. These loyalties threatened to pull them apart. Both wondered if their marriage had been a mistake.

But their love endured. They agreed that their commitment to each other superseded their important but subordinate commitment to their parents, families, friends, and church. Paul and Nina kept talking through the tense situation and their disagreement. Instead of pulling away, they took refuge in each other. They affirmed that their relationship was stronger than family pressure. They wisely decided to exit the no-win situation and join a church attended by neither of their families.

From what Barb and I have witnessed and experienced, the starting point for persevering love is an all-out commitment to each other. It's the tough stance that says, "Our marriage is bigger than any issue. No matter who or what is arrayed against us, we will stand together. Neither of us will ever go through a trial alone."

Persevering love doesn't say, "I'll stick with you because I have to—because I promised to" but, "I will hang in there with you because I care for you more than anything in the world."

Have you committed yourself 100 percent to endure together whatever life may throw at you? How are you demonstrating that commitment in the face of life's problems and pressures?

PERSEVERING LOVE REQUIRES UNCONDITIONAL ACCEPTANCE

Right after Travis and Mary celebrated their fifth anniversary, Mary visited her doctor about an incessantly bloody nose. The physician removed a small benign growth from inside her nose, and there was no further treatment.

One morning a year later, after Mary's routine physical exam, the doctor telephoned. He wanted her to come in immediately—that afternoon—for a biopsy. She called Travis at work in a panic and blurted out the news. His response was immediate: "I'll be home within the hour and take you to the doctor.

I don't want you to go alone. I will be right there with you, whatever happens."

The morning after the biopsy, Mary underwent surgery to remove a cancerous growth from her nasal cavity. Despite a painful course of radiation, the cancer returned a year later. Four years and six surgeries later, Mary's determined optimism was fading. Each successive surgery removed additional tissue and bone, until the right side of her face was severely disfigured. Even her eye was removed. While the procedures ultimately bought her another seven years of life, Mary considered herself grotesque.

In order to conceal Mary's disfigurement, a team of artists and doctors created a lifelike mask for her. Although the mask fooled those who saw her in public, she couldn't wear it around the clock. Except for hospital workers, Travis was the only person who saw Mary without her prosthetic in place. And until the day she died, Travis told Mary that she was the most beautiful woman in the world. He had lived up to his promise: "I will be there with you, whatever happens." Their love endured and became strong against the ravages of terminal cancer.

The unconditional acceptance of persevering love says, "No matter how good or bad you look, no matter how much money you earn or lose, no matter how smart or feebleminded you are, I will still love you." That's the stuff of our wedding vows—for better or for worse, for richer or for poorer, in sickness and in health. Persevering love chooses to continue loving even when life dumps on us a world of reasons to fall out of love.

PERSEVERING LOVE REQUIRES DEEP TRUST

Ross and Judi responded eagerly to their church's mission to support an orphanage in Southeast Asia. They gave generously to

help provide shelter and education for several hundred former
street kids. But the couple was moved to do more. Within eighteen months Ross and Judi had adopted three siblings from the
orphanage, two girls and a boy. The kids looked nothing like their
new parents, and they spoke a language the couple could not
understand. Yet Ross and Judi embraced the kids as their own.

All three children struggled to adjust to their new surround-
ings, but by middle school it was obvious that Megan's problems
were the most severe. No matter what Ross and Judi did, Megan
kept acting out, disobeying, and rebelling. She was virtually
uncontrollable. Then one night, their eighth-grade daughter ran
away from home.

Megan's sudden disappearance released a flood of unspoken
questions and accusations that had been lurking in Ross's and
Judi's minds. They were desperately worried for their daughter,
but they were furious at each other: "Why did we want these
children?", "Did we make the right decision?", "Who is this
person I'm married to—the one who can't fix this situation?",
"Why weren't you a better mother to Megan?", "Why weren't
you a better dad?" The conflict raged through that first night.

By four o'clock in the morning, Ross and Judi had vented their
darkest doubts about themselves, their parenting, and their marriage. Then, as they gazed at one another through tear-rimmed
eyes, they realized that they had no one better to trust than each
other and God. They had too much good history together to turn
on each other now. They had made it this far; they could make it
the rest of the way if they continued to trust in each other.

Ultimately Megan returned home, and with the help of long-
term biblical counseling, she was able to address the deep pain and
hurts of her life. She wasn't the only one who went deep. Ross
and Judi learned that this harrowing experience took them to
places they didn't know existed. Yet the pain led them to a deeper
trust in God and each other, enriching their lives.

Persevering love is the product of deep trust between husband and wife. Trust says, "I will depend on you to guard and protect my heart and my life, to fight beside me always." You may need to trust a lot of people to pull you through a crisis. But more than anyone else on earth, husbands and wives should rely on each other.

King Solomon wrote, "If one person falls, the other can reach out and help. But people who are alone when they fall are in real trouble" (Ecclesiastes 4:10). Another rendering of the same verse describes the crisis even more strongly: "Pity the man who falls and has no one to help him up!" (NIV). The wise king continued, "A person standing alone can be attacked and defeated, but two can stand back-to-back and conquer. Three are even better, for a triple-braided cord is not easily broken" (Ecclesiastes 4:12). While these verses do not refer specifically to the marriage relationship, they do reveal that a trust-based relationship, especially one that is "triple-braided"—such as husband, wife, and God— is tough to beat. Allow pressures to bond you together in mutual trust and build your friendship instead of pull you apart.

Trials require a depth of trust that doesn't grow overnight. This is why the trust of persevering love grows richer over time, as you each prove yourselves trustworthy to the other. It may be true that trust begins to build during courtship, and your commitment to trust may be inherent in your wedding vows. But *complete* trust is established over time and under the pressure of daily life.

PERSEVERING LOVE REQUIRES ENDURANCE

As a boy, Jake was ridiculed constantly by his peers for being small, weak, and homely. As a defense, he developed a biting, sarcastic wit. He never thought he would be attractive to a woman, so he was amazed years later when he and Lori fell in love and married after dating only a few months.

Most of the time Jake kept his sharp tongue under control around Lori. But sometimes when she raised an issue, he launched into a barrage of cutting words. Five years and four children later, both Jake and Lori wondered if their choice to marry was a mistake.

Without any input from Lori, some of Jake's male friends from church sat him down and confronted him about his sharp language with Lori. They didn't know the whole story, but they had seen enough to intervene. Jake resisted their efforts. So these men called in the pastor who, in turn, called in the church's board of elders. Jake felt like a little boy again, surrounded by an army of peers who mocked and humiliated him. His anger deafened him to what these Christian friends and leaders were saying. Within three weeks, Jake felt so alienated that he vowed never again to set foot in church.

Lori is still upset by what she calls "SWAT team tactics" used by the men at church. But she knows their efforts were well-intentioned and that they were not the cause of Jake's problems. She even acknowledges that, in some ways, her marriage is better now. The confrontation by the guys didn't change Jake, but it did change her. When Lori saw how Jake overreacted to the threat he perceived in those men, she finally understood what Jake had endured as a child.

For the past three years Lori has treated Jake with a compassion he has never experienced elsewhere. Lori keeps on loving the husband who is confronting the pain in his heart and beginning to sort out his relationship with God. In tender moments he is opening up to her at levels he never thought he could. She has become a model of quiet endurance. She's hanging in with Jake, even though he still loses his cool with her. She is determined to do her utmost to bring him back to God and the church, and she knows the only thing that will bring him back into the fold is firm, steadfast love.

Every kind of trial—emotional burdens, financial difficulties, spiritual questions, physical pain, relational stresses—presents a new opportunity for a husband and wife to persevere. Commitment helps you stay connected to each other through trials; perseverance is the determination to outlast the problems, to help each other get to the other side. Lori is doing most of the persevering in her marriage right now. But think of the intimacy and friendship that can develop in your relationship when *both* of you are committed to persevering through every trial.

PERSEVERING LOVE REQUIRES ABIDING FAITH

Barb and I know a few couples who have gone through fiery trials without counting on God's strength. How difficult that is! But we also know many couples who have discovered that trusting in God, relying on his strength, and walking in his ways were more than sufficient to take them through the flames.

Karen's greatest fear was that her husband's refusal to take care of himself would leave her without a husband and their children without a father. She had good reason to be afraid. Both Brian's father and grandfather had died in their fifties from heart attacks. At forty-eight, Brian's cholesterol was dangerously high, and his power lunches were loaded with high-fat foods.

Brian knew that Karen's warnings (he sometimes called them nagging) were motivated by her love and concern for him. But he was unwilling to change. After ignoring chest pains and Karen's pleas to see a doctor for weeks, Brian suffered a massive heart attack one morning while climbing the steps to work. He didn't die, but he faced a long recovery. And his health would never be the same.

In an instant, Karen's life changed. She worked day and night caring for Brian, being a mom to their kids, and trying to bring order and stability to a household in crisis. With Brian unable to return to his high-powered job, their lifestyle changed dramatically. Karen was forced to take a job outside the home.

Karen knew she faced a choice. She could resent Brian for his stubbornness and careless behavior, or she could forgive him and shower him with the love he didn't deserve. She knew that as long as she withheld forgiving love from Brian, her own anger and resentment would imprison her. So she made the commitment to follow God's plan and allow Christ's love to flow through her.

As Brian was enfolded in Karen's self-sacrificial, Christlike love for him, he realized the depth of pain he had caused his wife and children. He confessed his stubbornness and sought their forgiveness. He renewed his commitment to Christ. Things that once seemed so important to him—country club membership, exotic vacations, large stock portfolio—were replaced by such simple pleasures as a walk around the block. Brian and Karen discovered the joy of spending time together in prayer. And they began to enjoy a level of intimate understanding and connection that they had never experienced during the "good times."

For marital love to really endure life's pressures, it needs to be grounded in a sincere, abiding faith in the God who designed marriage. Like Brian, any of us can stubbornly pursue a lifestyle that our culture deems important and live independently of God. Sometimes a severe trial moves us to let God have his way with us and to see what truly matters in life. We often don't really appreciate the important role faith plays in our marriage until a crisis forces us to throw ourselves on God.

Faith is such a vital facet of the marriage relationship and such a source of strength for divorce-proofing marriage that we will spend all of chapter 13 discussing how you can develop greater spiritual intimacy with your spouse.

PERSEVERING LOVE REQUIRES DILIGENT PREPARATION

Anyone who lives near a hurricane zone knows that the time for action is long before the storm hits. Once the wind is wailing and the surf is boiling and the rain is coming at you sideways, it's time to head for the storm cellar and hunker down. It's too late to board up the windows, buy drinking water and batteries, and add flood coverage to your homeowner's policy.

Extensive hurricane preparation makes a lot of sense, but some people may be lulled into inactivity because killer storms don't strike every day. In fact, years may elapse between serious threats. Yet the time to prepare for a hurricane is during the calm between the storms.

When it comes to marriage, all of us live in a hurricane zone. And since the pressures, crises, and tragedies of life seldom blow in with advance warning, it is during the calm stretches of life that we must get ready for them. Persevering love is founded on the devotion and friendship a husband and wife build before the storm strikes.

Janis peered through the living room sheers watching Pete drive up from his last day at work. She smiled. Pete walked into the house carrying a few files and a couple of balloons. He said the retirement party was "no big deal," low-key just like he wanted it to be. The real retirement party—a surprise to Pete—would be later that evening. Janis had invited Pete's boss, a dozen of her husband's close associates, and their spouses.

Pete had toyed with the idea of retirement six years earlier. He even took a three-month leave from work to see how he liked ditching his job to do whatever he wanted to do. During that time, Pete felt as if he was constantly underfoot in Janis's domain, and they were both clearly irritated with the new arrangement. They had not expected the retirement experiment to become a crisis, but it had.

After a month Pete was back at work. "We kept bumping into each other," he told the guys. But while Pete and Janis were happy to return to a few more years of "normal" life, they both realized that they weren't ready to face each other for twenty-four hours a day. The friendship they had enjoyed as a young couple had waned. If they were to survive Pete's real retirement, they had some work to do on their relationship.

You and your spouse may not be facing the "crisis" of retirement, but one thing is for sure: If you are not presently in a difficult trial, there is one on your horizon—a financial crunch, an injury or illness in the family, a conflict with children, a disagreement between you and your spouse, etc. We're not being fatalistic, just realistic. Hurricane season in family relationships lasts year around. You just don't know when or how soon the next one will hit.

If you and your spouse find yourselves in one of those lulls between storms, rejoice! And while you are rejoicing, take the opportunity to prepare for stormy weather ahead. Now is the time to shore up your marriage. Work on a Bible study together. Take a second honeymoon—or third, or fourth. Read some good books on marriage enrichment and discuss them together. Attend a Christian marriage conference (we recommend a "Weekend to Remember" seminar, sponsored by FamilyLife). Seek out a biblically based Christian counselor, and ask him or her for pointers on how to deepen your friendship. The more you invest in your marriage *between* the storms, the better prepared you will be to *endure* the storms together—and even come through them stronger.

After Pete's failed attempt at retirement, he and Janis admitted to each other their disappointment that retirement didn't feel right. But they determined to do something about the distance that had crept into their marriage. They sought out couples who had retired and who looked happier than ever. And they took the next few years to rediscover each other and enter into each other's areas of interest.

When Pete finally came home for good, they had a head start on many retiring couples. Their only regret was that they had missed out on each other's friendship for so long.

For all the planning Pete and Janis did, Pete's retirement didn't turn out as they expected. Six months after Pete retired, their daughter-in-law committed suicide, leaving their son to raise three small children alone. As Pete and Janis wept and prayed about the tragedy, they realized that they were in a unique position to help their son and grandchildren. They stepped in and took care of the two youngest kids during the day until they reached school age. And for many more years Pete or Janis, or both, were at their son's house to greet their grandkids when they arrived home from school.

Pete and Janis were ready when the storm hit. Having fortified their friendship, they were prepared to help their son and grandchildren survive the devastation of suicide. They had no idea how their bonding over the previous years would benefit their son and his family. But for the first time in their lives, they faced a trial truly *together*.

Are you nurturing your relationship today so you can face whatever tomorrow brings? Are you building a relationship that will be ready for the tests you can't anticipate? In the next chapter, we will see how these six qualities of persevering love—commitment, acceptance, trust, endurance, faith, and preparedness—can see you through when the next storm hits.

nine

WEATHERING
THE STORMS

$\mathcal{I}$f your marriage is anything like Gary's and mine, you live in a
pressure-cooker world. You have more than your share of daily
stress. On top of career demands, you have a spouse to love,
kids to tend, and perhaps aging parents to care for in their golden
years. Each of these relationships is a privilege, but each one also
clamors for priority status in your complex and busy life.

Like every married couple, Gary and I have had our share
of ups and downs: the joy of bringing new lives into the world,
the dark uncertainty of illnesses and surgeries, the fulfillment
of ministry to others, the pain of being ignored by each other.
But through it all we have been committed to facing these ups
and downs together as a team—partners and best friends in the
whirlwind of life. With the help of God we have found our way
through perilous life passages and withstood many trials. And
in each case we came through with greater determination and
devotion and a deeper love for one another because we took the
precarious journey together.

Then the big one hit, a marital storm with the potential to do us in. It rocked our world with the impact of a category-five hurricane. If ever our relationship needed persevering love, this was it.

BLINDSIDED BY GRIEF

It happened in 1997, a year after Gary's father died. Gary was very close to his father, so he struggled with a tremendous sense of grief and loss. The grieving process takes time, but Gary didn't have any time to grieve. A few days after the funeral, he was back to work speaking, counseling, and writing. Caught up in the responsibilities, pressures, and demands of the ministry, Gary did not allow himself to thoroughly process his grief. And he began to pay the price.

As Gary tried to press on with life, it was soon clear that he was in a depression. This was not just a temporary funk but an extended clinical depression. He couldn't concentrate. Some nights he was unable to sleep. Other times he would sleep fourteen to sixteen hours straight. His appetite left him, and he lost twenty-five pounds. He felt sad, helpless, and hopeless most of the time. Life wasn't fun for him anymore.

Gary and I are a committed team both in marriage and ministry. We live together *and* work together. So I was not a bystander in this trial; I was a full-time active participant in Gary's grief and depression. Although I did not suffer clinical depression, his pain was my pain as well. We both felt overworked and emotionally drained.

Some days Gary and I would go to work together as usual. But some mornings he would wake up so weighed down that he just wanted to stay home. On those days I canceled everything on my calendar just to sit and hold Gary as he processed his grief. Neither of us could fully comprehend what was happening. In

our darkest hours, living a day at a time seemed too much.
We were reduced to living five minutes at a time!

Now, I'm a woman who likes a semblance of order in daily
life. But Gary's debilitating depression threw our family schedule
completely out of whack. I felt frightened and absolutely helpless. Needing a sense of control, I increased my public responsibilities in our ministry to compensate for Gary's absence. But
in my private moments, I wept over Gary's anguish and inner
turmoil. He was retreating more into himself, sometimes coming home from work and going straight to bed without dinner.
And I was not handling it well.

Our family had been extremely close, full of love, warmth,
and laughter. But Gary was not himself anymore, and his depression was a dark cloud over our daily life. We still had our share
of lighthearted moments, but most days were difficult for us all.
Gary was sometimes abrupt with our girls, or he would tune
them out completely. I tried to assure Sarah and Missy that their
dad would be all right, but I was afraid that he would *not* be all
right. In my darkest moments I felt like I was sinking down into
Gary's private hell alongside of him.

If you had asked me two years before Gary's depression if
a storm like this could happen to us, I would have answered,
"Absolutely not!" Gary had been a lighthouse of strength for me
over the years. But that strong beam was fading. I didn't know
if this storm would ever end.

As difficult as this trial was for me, Gary was the one bearing
the brunt of it. He now will tell you more of the story.

I must admit that 1997 was the longest, most difficult, most
painful year of my life. Some days I simply isolated myself from
others and shut down. I would sneak out the back door of my
office and drive down the highway looking for a place to be
alone, to cry. I didn't think I could provide for my family. I

didn't think God could use me. I didn't think I could ever climb out of this deep hole.

During these times I would often walk for hours, hoping the exercise would bring relief. It helped some, but the deep feelings of failure and insecurity were almost more than I could bear.

One day I planted myself on a park bench with my Bible and a bottle of water. I cried out to God, "I am not leaving until you reveal yourself and your promises to me in your Word." I read and read. The hours passed. In the fifth hour I came across Exodus 14:13-14: "Moses answered the people, 'Do not be afraid. Stand firm and you will see the deliverance the Lord will bring you today. . . . The Lord will fight for you; you need only to be still'" (NIV).

That was the beginning of the turnaround for me. God had spoken. My deliverance was his responsibility. He was going to war for me against the depression that had crippled me. I sensed the burden begin to lift.

I drove home to Barb, my best friend, and told her what had just happened. "I know there's hope, Barb," I said. "I'm going to come through this."

As we talked that day, Barb reminded me of some basic truths that are foundational in our marriage. "Gary, I don't expect you just to get over this. I expect you to walk through it with me by your side. I also want you to remember that God will fight for you, just as he revealed to you on that bench. You need to trust him and be still. Let him carry you in your spirit, and let me carry you as your soul mate."

She reminded me that I could trust her. "I am sticking to you like glue, and nothing can separate me from you. We are one. The wedding vows we exchanged are the real thing. My promise to you is true. For better or worse means that even at the worst of times, we are a team."

How I praise God that his promises are true. He *did* fight for

me. By his grace and strength, I recovered from depression.
I even gained back the twenty-five pounds I lost. I also praise
God that Barb's promises were true. She stuck by me like glue.
I couldn't have made it without her persevering love.

BUILDING A LOVE THAT ENDURES

Maybe you have yet to be hit by a storm as severe as ours. Or
maybe you are in the middle of something even worse. No
matter what you have faced in the past, you can be sure there
will be trials in the future. Barb and I want to coach you on a
way not only to survive those trials together but also to grow
even stronger in the process.

What we need is a love that provides strength to withstand
life's pains. We believe persevering love is the answer. Persevering love stays strong when the storms howl in your marriage.
Persevering love bonds you even closer together, strengthening
your friendship. How can you make sure that you and your
spouse have what it takes to get through these storms? Here are
five vital keys to building a fortress of love that will endure in
your marriage. Barb will get us started with the first two keys.

Connect and Stay Connected
Your ability to endure together in the hard times is directly
proportional to the depth of your partnership in good times.
Two hearts must link up to grow strong together. If you want to
stay glued together in difficulties, you have to apply the cement
of partnership now.

Gary and I start our day by connecting even before we crawl
out of bed. Gary is the morning person in our house, so he's
usually awake first. I'm still half-asleep when I hear him whisper,
"I love you, Barb. . . . I need you, Barb." But what gets me every

time is when he says, "Baby, baby, baby!" Every time I hear it I laugh, bringing joy to my soul.

Before you go your separate ways each day, give each other a heartfelt, "I love you." Stay connected by calling each other during the day. Find ways to be readily available to each other even as you travel or tote the kids around. Taking time to connect and stay connected builds security and intimacy in a relationship. It's part of what makes a great marriage, a divorce-proof marriage. And it's essential when trials hit.

Jon was in the middle of a prolonged, stressful period with his company. His division was being phased out, and although he still had a job, he was assigned the task of turning out the lights in his area. This meant handing out pink slips by the dozen and enduring months of ugly, confrontational meetings on and off the job site. Jon was seldom in the same location for more than a few hours.

Heather expressed concern for her husband's emotional well-being, saying it bothered her that he was almost impossible to reach during the day. In order to stay better connected, Jon carried his cell phone consistently so that he and Heather could be in contact with the touch of a finger. Jon and Heather both found that it eased their edgy nerves to know the other was only the push of a button away.

Some colleagues heard about it and joked that Jon's wife had him on a pretty short leash. But instead of unplugging his phone, Jon asked a pointed question: "Why don't you feel a need to be connected during this stressful time?"

These days, people might tell you that even a healthy, God-ordained level of dependence on your spouse is a form of sick codependence. Yet in our disconnected world, you need to do everything you can to strengthen emotional and spiritual ties with your spouse. Whether times are easy or hard, your spouse will deeply appreciate your efforts to stay in touch. Do what it takes to feel connected and present for each other even when you're apart.

Make Your Relationship a Safe Place

Jay and Kari know what it's like to suffer the winds of monstrous storms—literally. They live in tornado country. When Jay was in high school, the roof of his parents' house was blown off. The son of Kari's close friend was killed in a tornado. And together this couple has felt the sting of thousands of dollars of storm damage to their own home and property. So when the weather sirens wail in their community, Jay, Kari, and their two small children run for cover.

But their dash for safety is anything but helter-skelter. Jay and Kari have everything neatly set up ahead of time. A box stored in the safest corner of their basement contains not only emergency lighting and a weather radio but a lot more—crackers, candy, juice boxes, some sunshiny storybooks, and a stash of blankets and pillows. By day they make their bolt to the basement an impromptu party. And at night it takes them less than a minute to carry their sleeping kids to the basement and tuck them into makeshift beds. Whether a storm strikes by day or by night, they have created a safe place.

Is your relationship a safe place where both of you can run from the troubles and terrors of life? Your spouse needs to know *now* that your loving arms will always be a shelter in the midst of a trial or tragedy. He or she will sense that assurance only if you practice empathy and comfort now.

Chuck's mother was angry when her children suggested it was time for her to sell the family home and move to a senior citizens' apartment complex. She protested, and the kids—all in their fifties themselves—backed off. When a stroke forced Mrs. Olson directly into a nursing home a year later, she spewed bitterness.

Chuck was utterly devoted to his mother and took the lead in sorting through her things, preparing her home for sale, and overseeing her finances. Yet he was deeply wounded by his mother's constant unkind remarks. He was a terrible son, she said, for moving her out of her own place. In reality, the stroke—not Chuck or his siblings—had forced her move.

Melinda, Chuck's wife, could only watch from the sidelines as he took on all the details of caring for his aging mother. Melinda continued to hold down the fort at home, shuttling their three kids to school, lessons, and other commitments. But Melinda wisely made time to let Chuck express his hurt and frustration and to reassure him that he wasn't mistreating his mother. Melinda gave Chuck—the devoted son who would never complain about his mother—a place where he could feel safe.

Some people feel too threatened to confide in anyone, sensing that no one really cares what they think or feel. Many see this kind of bonding in marriage as potential bondage. Some are so worried about losing personal freedom that they never attain the depth of fulfillment that comes from true closeness.

In reality, your marriage can be a fortress of protection where each of you is safe to show your wounds. Safety happens when your spouse is emotionally present—totally with you—and you are present for him or her. Your relationship becomes a safe place when you lower your defenses and share yourself fully with your spouse, knowing that you are accepted and loved for who you are, that you don't have to pretend to be anything else. If you can provide this safe haven for one another, you are well prepared for any trial.

Another key for weathering the storms of life through persevering love is communication. Gary will share some important insights on this vital skill.

Keep Communicating

Barb and I know from experience that it's tough to communicate during tough times. Even the smallest of trials can drive a wedge between a husband and wife. And if small conflicts can divide you, think how much more some of the devastating blows of life can push you apart. Here are three reasons why trials are a threat to communication.

Trials isolate us in our own thoughts. Trials have a way of forcing even the most communicative people inward. Rosa, for example, had always worn her thoughts and feelings on the outside. Her husband, Andy, said he never had to wonder what was going on in Rosa's head because it was always simultaneously coming out her mouth! Yet when Rosa lost two sisters to breast cancer, she retreated within herself.

Then cancer became a personal issue. When Rosa's doctor recommended that she undergo a radical preemptive mastectomy, she knew she faced a decision only she could make. Her world closed in on her like the long winter in Iowa, where the sun may not be visible for months. Even though the decision was ultimately Rosa's to make, vital information for making this decision came from her husband. He told her that he wanted her around forever and that he would love and treasure her whatever she looked like. Andy asked some key questions to help her start communicating again. We will discuss those questions in a moment.

Trials invite denial or the belief that you can handle it all alone. Denial is the handy psychological term for our tendency not to admit a problem exists. It's a refusal to deal with the facts. Asserting that you can handle a problem alone may be a healthy sign of independence, but it may also be an unhealthy attempt to avoid looking bad or asking for help. It can set us to humming the old Simon and Garfunkel tune "I am a rock, I am an island." Both denial and stubborn independence push your spouse to the periphery, saying, "I don't need to talk about it."

When you uncover deep pain, you also will often find issues of privacy and emotional safety. In fact, it's the fear of not having a safe place to sort through our problems that prompts us to keep those hurts under wraps for so long. That's why developing safe patterns of friendship is so vital *before* a trial hits.

Trials leave us feeling that no one understands. When Michael and Karley learned that their fourteen-year-old son, Evan, had a rare and deadly disease, they felt that no one in the world knew what they were going through. They struggled with this lonely feeling through the next few weeks until their doctor put them in touch with a support group of parents whose children had the same illness and who connected by phone and e-mail.

Michael and Karley received help and comfort from people who knew exactly what they were going through because they had gone through it—or were still going through it—themselves. This couple tapped into what Paul describes in 2 Corinthians 1:3-4: "All praise to the God and Father of our Lord Jesus Christ. He is the source of every mercy and the God who comforts us. He comforts us in all our troubles so that we can comfort others. When others are troubled, we will be able to give them the same comfort God has given us."

Don't believe the subtle lie that "no one understands." Your spouse understands what you're struggling through, though perhaps not fully. Reverse the roles for a moment. If your spouse was going through a crisis and thinking no one could understand his or her pain, you would hate being locked out. You would be hurt if your help and comfort were unwelcome. Why? Because as someone who has also faced hurt in life, you have genuine comfort to offer even in an unusual trial.

If you ever feel tempted to lock your spouse out of your agony, resist that urge. Dare to open up.

When you face times of trial and pain, asking each other three critical questions can help you to keep communication open.

1. *"What's the problem?"* At first glance, the answer is obvious: It's the trial itself—cancer, bankruptcy, rebellious child, layoff, etc. But here's our point. First, the problem isn't us. We're on the same side. The problem is something outside of us, and we are battling it together. Second, the problem is something we can name and tackle together.

Here's how Andy finally got Rosa talking again. When Andy asked her to define the core of her struggle, she said, "You won't like the way I look after breast surgery. You won't love me as much." But Andy quickly disagreed, assuring his wife that his love for her would never change. To him the only issue was her health and survival. Andy's clarification shifted the focus to the main issue—getting rid of her cancer. Assured of Andy's love and acceptance, Rosa was free to elect the surgery.

2. *"What do we need from each other?"* After you have defined the problem, ask yourselves what kind of help you need to solve it. Identify areas where you have the strength and know-how to support each other. Do you need the other to step in with a decision? Do you need some space? How about comfort and encouragement? Perhaps you need your spouse to brainstorm with you or to seek God's truth with you in his Word and through prayer.

3. *"What kind of outside help do we need?"* Resolving a trial or crisis is often beyond your ability and resources. In the case of marriage-threatening trials, in fact, this is *always* the case. God wants to put other people in your life to lift you up. Your task at this stage can be as concrete as making a list of the people you need and what they can do for you.

The greatest resource to meet your needs, of course, is God.

He is the ultimate answer for your every need. God also gave you your spouse to comfort and support you. Christians have the resources of God's church, the body of Christ. And God surrounds you with other people—family, friends, neighbors, physicians, counselors—to help you through trouble. Even if you don't have the skills to meet your spouse's needs, you have a wealth of resources at your disposal. Take advantage of them.

Therese had always led an ordered life. She had everything under control, from precisely monitoring her weight to guarding her emotions to running her house and family with tidy precision. Ron often feared disrupting her orderliness, even when he felt he was being treated like one of the kids.

One night, after Therese had hosted a birthday party for their twelve-year-old daughter, Megan, and a dozen other girls, Ron watched as his very in-control wife curled up on the couch and began to weep. Within minutes she was crying as he had never seen her cry before. Ron had no idea what was happening, but he knew enough to sit down next to her and wrap her in his arms.

After an hour of uncontrolled sobbing, Therese gathered herself and said, "Ron, I don't know how to tell you this. When I was growing up, I was sexually abused by a teenage boy in our neighborhood. I don't know why this is coming out today. I suppose it's because the abuse started when I was Megan's age. Seeing all those innocent little girls . . ." Another wave of tears choked off her words. She eventually cried herself to sleep in Ron's arms.

In the morning Ron called work and said he wouldn't be in. He took Therese for a walk in their favorite park. As they sat together on a park bench overlooking a lake, Therese told him a little bit more of her story in carefully measured words. "Ron, I can't tell you what he did to me. I don't want to sicken you. I feel dirty. I feel guilty for what he did to me. I didn't know how to stop him. I'm watching our own girls grow up, and I can't keep this inside anymore."

Ron had no idea how to counsel his wife through her pain. But he knew it was a crisis they could face together. He knew how to hold his hurting wife. And he knew how to find help.

Obtaining a referral from his pastor, Ron persuaded Therese to see a Christian counselor who had worked with dozens of women dealing with sexual abuse issues from their past. For weeks Ron faithfully sat in the waiting room while his wife met with the therapist. One day Therese invited him into the session. She was ready to bring Ron into the healing process, a process that might never have begun without Ron's help and encouragement.

Husbands and wives, you will face trials that are too big for you to handle, problems you can't begin to address in your own strength and wisdom. As a spouse, your role is simple: Be the best help you can be. But also commit yourself to finding help beyond what you can offer.

A fourth key to building a love that endures involves seeing God's perspective of our trials. Barb will discuss this important key.

Rest in the Truth That God Has a Purpose for Trials

If it were up to Gary and me, we would choose to navigate through life with as few problems as possible. God doesn't see things our way, however. He has allowed trials in our lives to teach us persevering love, to help Gary and me bond together as best friends for life. We can't say the trials have been fun, but we do appreciate what God is building in us in the process.

The trial of Gary's depression was excruciating for both of us. But our experience in that trial has provided us with a foundation to weather other storms God may allow us to face. We have experienced the truth of Romans 5:3-4: "We can rejoice, too, when we run into problems and trials, for we know that they are good for us—they help us learn to endure. And endurance develops strength of character in us, and character strengthens our confident expectation of salvation."

If your confidence is only in your own ability as a couple to make it through life's hardest moments, you are woefully unprepared. But when you acknowledge that God is sovereign over all of life, that nothing can touch you except what he allows, that his purpose in trials is to build your endurance and character, then you are ready to weather any storm. These are truths you can rest in now and forever.

Early one morning during Gary's crisis, I wept uncontrollably through my prayer time. Memories of our happy, love-filled home washed over me. I desperately wanted to go back in time to the way things had always been. "Oh God, I want my home back!" I sobbed. In my private agony, I pleaded, "Please, God, strengthen my husband!"

In that moment, God's unfathomable love embraced me. I sensed that he was my close companion in the midst of the battle. I transferred my needs to the one who promised to carry all of my burdens. Matthew 11:28-29 reminds us so clearly: "Come to me, all of you who are weary and carry heavy burdens, and I will give you rest. Take my yoke upon you. Let me teach you, because I am humble and gentle, and you will find rest for your souls."

As God began to heal Gary of depression, I sensed greater passion and deepened love for God. I began to enjoy closer fellowship with Jesus, an intimacy that I may have missed had the hurricane of Gary's depression not driven me to utter dependence on God.

My perspective on trials has changed since then. I'm not as fearful to face them now because I know they actually produce something good in my life. People continually ask Gary and me where we get our joy. If you didn't know us well, you might think we didn't have any burdens. Well, now you know. Like you, we do have burdens, trials, storms. But we have much joy as well! It's because, just like you, we have a heavenly Father who provides shelter through the storms, a haven so safe and strong that no power on earth can conquer it!

Great marriages are often forged through difficult trials. Whatever you may be facing in your marriage right now, let the words of James 1:2-4 be both instruction and comfort: "Dear brothers and sisters, whenever trouble comes your way, let it be an opportunity for joy. For when your faith is tested, your endurance has a chance to grow. So let it grow, for when your endurance is fully developed, you will be strong in character and ready for anything."

Someone may be saying, "What? Consider our child's illness, my spouse's unemployment, and the termites in our basement as an opportunity for joy? Are you kidding?" No, we're not kidding. It's not always easy, but God desires that we take joy in our trials—not because they are joyful, but because he is using those experiences to strengthen our faith and make us mature.

Gary has one more key for building a love that endures.

Decide to Tackle Trouble Together— Wherever It Takes You

Tyrone was a young, successful foreign service officer. Serena was an artist. They were different in a lot of ways, but they had in common a deep love for God and a keen wit. They instantly became best friends. When they married one bright summer day, Serena had no clue that she would be back in the same church less than a year later—for Tyrone's funeral.

Soon after the wedding, sudden vision difficulties sent Tyrone first to an optometrist and then to an ophthalmologist. Further tests revealed he had an aggressive, inoperable brain tumor.

As radiation and chemotherapy treatment began, Tyrone regretted that he had "dragged Serena into this," as he put it.

Serena reassured him that she hadn't been dragged into anything. She was with him because she loved him. And she would stay with him for the same reason, no matter what happened.

One day, when the situation looked grim, Serena held Tyrone's hand through another round of radiation treatments and chemotherapy cocktails. Suddenly she grinned at him, and he looked at her as if she had gone mad. "I love you," she said. "You throw quite a party. I wouldn't miss this for the world."

It soon became clear that Tyrone wasn't going to get better. They quietly acknowledged that they would never realize many of their dreams for their life together. But they also realized that they had each other for as long as God allowed it, and that was what they really wanted.

One bright winter afternoon, shortly before Tyrone began to lose his mental faculties, he asked Serena if she wished she had married someone else. "Never once," she whispered. "I promised I would be with you. And I will be . . . 'till death do us part.'" Even after Tyrone slipped into a coma, Serena kept her promise. At his bedside she did the only thing she could do: stay beside him until their trial was over.

Barb and I have found that our love for each other is glorious in the good times—the vacations on the beach, the memory-making experiences with the kids, the times of deep intimacy together with Jesus Christ. It's easy to love in the good times. But when our marriage comes under intense testing, we still have in our possession what really matters. We relish a love that won't quit. We know a friendship that only gets stronger as life gets tougher. We find acceptance in our neediness. We have a hand to hold in our pain. In short, no matter where our trials take us, we have each other.

In your times of crisis and unbearable stress, you may secretly wonder if your spouse will draw closer to you and stand with you, no matter what, or turn away and let you battle the storm alone. You may also wonder if you have the strength to hang in there with your spouse or if you will be tempted to walk away. Now is the time to decide and agree together: Together we will tackle anything that comes our way, and we will stay together in it no matter where it goes.

When you commit to this level of persevering love, you are deciding to stick around through the suffering, to walk through pain, and to stay devoted through difficult times—until you are parted by death. You are offering your spouse the assurance that he or she will never be alone when trials come. Persevering love gains you the privilege of walking through every storm with your best friend.

It is a sobering reality that some trials, like that of Tyrone and Serena, end in the death of a spouse. Even then there is joy and triumph. Our spouses who go on to glory gain the presence of Jesus Christ and the end of all trial and pain. Those of us left behind have one of life's most treasured possessions: memories of a love that endured to the end.

A SPECIAL NOTE ABOUT THE JOURNEY

Persevering love is something we all need to keep our marital relationship intimate and rooted regardless of what happens in life. There are steps you can take now to be assured your love will endure. There are ways to make sure that your relationship is a safe place, that communication lines are open, and that you view the storms in your life from God's perspective.

This is why we plan to write a book about persevering love. It's in the works. This book will help a small group of couples cultivate the assurance and confidence that, no matter what trials you face, you will survive them and come through them stronger and more deeply in love than ever before.

Part Five

GUARDING LOVE

Guarding love protects from threats

and helps spouses feel

safe and secure

ten

THE CASTLE OF YOUR HEART

*I*f you lined up five million women," Michelle began her letter to Barb and me, "I'd be the last one you would suspect to have an affair. I was a *pure* woman. My eyes never looked at another man."

Michelle's sad story is one of vulnerability and carelessness. Read it for yourself:

> *I helped lead a Bible study for women facing marital struggles. I saw these women through pain in their marriages and even separations. But I was different. I was faithful and true.*
>
> *When we finally purchased a computer, I found that the Internet contained so many interesting places. I could look up vacation spots, read newspapers. These were all good things, nothing evil. I never realized that I was only a click away from destruction.*
>
> *One day I signed up for a chat room. I chose a clean one, not a porn room. I wanted to just go in and see what was going on. Almost immediately a man began talking to me. He paid attention to me and had an insightful response to every word I wrote.*

I continued to meet this man in the chat room, even though I knew it was wrong. The relationship seemed innocent. We just talked about family and life. Soon we progressed to phone calls. I loved communicating with him. He cared so much.

After some time, we decided to meet. We were in love, or so we thought. After telling my husband I was meeting some girlfriends, I took off and hooked up with this man for what I thought would be a romantic weekend getaway. It wasn't at all what I expected, and suddenly everything came crashing down. I had betrayed my husband and my family.

My careless involvement with the Internet nearly destroyed my marriage. I became addicted, and it eventually led to an affair. I have regretted the day when, with one click on the mouse, I entered a downward spiral of sin and deception. I failed to build a fence of protection around my marriage. I didn't guard my heart.

THE STATE OF THE HEART

Notice Michelle's closing line. She admitted that she had tumbled into an affair with an on-line stranger because she didn't guard her heart. With that poignant insight she nailed both her condition and its cause. Whenever a marriage self-destructs, the *heart* is the heart of the matter.

Your heart, simply put, is the core of who you are. It's everything. It's the source of all life. In our culture, we have neglected this truth while declaring that the mind is the center of our being. Any Hebrew scholar in Bible times would have countered, "No way. Life flows from the heart. Everything we do and everything we are—our very destiny—bubbles up from that deep inner spring." Used in a literal, concrete sense, the Hebrew word for *heart* means the internal, blood-pumping organ buried in our chest. In metaphorical use, however, *heart* became the richest biblical term for the whole of our inner or immaterial nature, encompassing emotion, conscience, thought, and will.

The heart is where your life meets your world. It's the gateway to your emotions and relationships. It's where you feel deep joy and experience deep pain. And where your heart leads, your eyes, mouth, and feet naturally follow.

In Proverbs 4:23, wise King Solomon offers a vivid picture of the importance of your heart to the state of your whole being. He calls the heart "the wellspring of life" (NIV). What is a wellspring? It is the fountainhead or source of a spring, stream, or river. More broadly, a wellspring refers to a seemingly endless supply of something. When Solomon identified the heart as the wellspring of life, he meant that our very selves bubble up continuously from this central, inner source.

Think about an artesian well for a moment. If the source of the well—the wellspring—is good, you will get good, life-giving drinking water. But if there is something wrong at the source, if the wellspring is contaminated by poison or parasites, the bad water that flows from that source may have the power to kill.

No wonder Solomon admonished in the first part of Proverbs 4:23, "Above all else, guard your heart" (NIV). When you read "above all else" in Scripture, you know the message must be important. Guarding our hearts is *very* important. If we fail to keep our hearts free from contaminants—fleshly thoughts, desires, and choices—our entire lives will be negatively affected. Your heart is supposed to be a wellspring of life. Left unprotected, it can become a source of destruction and death, as Michelle found out.

The instruction to "guard your heart" means to purposely place a protective shield around the center of your life. The word *guard* suggests exercising great care over or posting a watch. When you guard your heart, you are guarding all that is truly valuable in life. And the love that identifies and stands against real-life dangers to a marriage is *guarding love*. When guarding love is put in place and vigilantly maintained in your relationship, it will protect your hearts from both internal and external threats. When guarding love is in operation, you and your spouse will enjoy a heightened sense of safety and security in your relationship. And without guarding love, your marriage can never be divorce-proof.

SAFE WITHIN THE CASTLE WALLS

Once upon a time, defending your family from danger and death required something concrete and visible. If you wanted the ultimate in protection for your family, you built a castle. You may hold the romantic notion of a castle as a "tower of love," where the beautiful princess met the dashing prince. But in reality, castles were fortresses designed to keep the bad guys out and the good guys safe.

Castles first appeared in northwest Europe in the ninth century. Many of them were built so well that they still exist more than a thousand years later. One authority catalogs the remains of at least fifteen hundred castles in England alone.

Ever wonder who lived in castles? Besides the lord and his family, the inhabitants of a castle included knights, squires, men-at-arms, a porter who kept the outer door, and watchmen. There was also a ministerial and domestic staff, a steward who administered the estate, and any number of servants. The larger the landholdings, of course, the larger the staff. But one thing was always true: The castle was built to protect them all.

If you study about castles, you will discover a history of warfare. These family strongholds were typically built on high ground, positioned to command the view of the lord's landholdings and a major thoroughfare. Medieval military science basically boiled down to the attack and defense of castles. Castles were constructed to defend the inhabitants from thieves and plunderers. The stronger the castle, the more the attackers schemed to break through its defenses.

There were two ways to attack a castle. In a *frontal assault,* the attackers marched up in plain sight and started hammering away with catapults, battering rams, flaming arrows, and hordes of invaders scrambling up long ladders. The head-on approach was an attempt to break into the castle by brute force.

A second approach could be called a *sneak attack.* A few attackers would try to slip into the castle undetected—by night over the wall, through an underground passageway, or other means. Once inside, the infiltrators could disarm the guards and throw open the castle gates for the army concealed outside. And the castle would fall from within.

There is a clear parallel between the castles of old and the defense of our marriages and families. Let's face it: Marriages are objects of attack in this country. Our godless culture is attacking marriage and the family on every side. There is the frontal assault of the media: movies, TV programs, music lyrics, and Internet Web sites that mock sexual purity, abstinence, marital fidelity, and family values. And there is the sneak attack, Satan's subtle attempts to twist our minds and our hearts away from God's plan for marriage and family.

We must be well prepared to stand against this onslaught and protect those dearest to us. If we are going to fight the battle, we must understand both the nature of the assault and the weapons of defense at our disposal.

You may say, "I'm really not that vulnerable to attack. After all, I'm a Sunday school teacher and choir member at our church. I don't rent R-rated videos or visit pornographic Web sites. You must be talking to husbands who spend a lot of time away from home on business or to wives who are always bemoaning the lack of fulfillment in their marriages."

Holding such a casual attitude is like leaving the castle gate wide open at night. Don't underestimate the enemy of your soul. We are all at risk, all vulnerable to attack. Ask Michelle. We must heed Solomon's advice to build a secure castle around our hearts. To lose our hearts is to lose everything.

THE FATE OF UNGUARDED HEARTS

Michelle isn't the only Christian whose unguarded heart became contaminated and whose marriage suffered the consequences. Compromised hearts come in all shapes and sizes:

◆ Acting on her lifelong dream, Sheila tells Ray she is quitting her day job to join a band. She overspends on high-end sound equipment, putting the couple deeply in debt. Then she leaves Ray for the guy who manages the band. Sheila's heart has been stolen by the fantasy of fame and then by another man.

◆ Jim seeks out tough assignments, extra hours, and long trips at work as his way of leaving his mark on the world. Feeling abandoned by her husband, Angela strikes back by furnishing their house well beyond their means and hosting lavish parties. Her latest find? A throw rug for the back entry "that can get dirty when the kids track in mud." The cost? A mere three hundred dollars. Jim and Angela's hearts have been contaminated by the drive to look good.

◆ David can remember as a boy finding stacks of pornographic magazines in his dad's workshop. As an adult, he feels that his own sexual needs aren't being met by Kathy. So like his father, David turns to pornography. He tells himself that viewing hardcore porn on the Internet is better than being unfaithful to his wife. David's heart has been poisoned by sexual temptation.

◆ When April first dated Joe, she loved how he pulled her onto the back of his motorcycle for rides that terrified her parents. Now married, April is constantly irritated by Joe's rough style. She mocks everything about him—his "biker" behavior, his clothes, and the beat-up truck he drives to a dead-end job. April's heart is possessed by a critical attitude.

◆ Jerry frequently claims that he doesn't have time for his wife or kids. Yet every fall he disappears for at least four weeks during hunting season. Where is he? Crouched in a stand of trees with his bow, poised to skewer a deer. Jerry's heart has been taken over by a hobby.

◆ Jill won't let her children play with any of the neighbor kids, whom she fears may say or do something that will corrupt her kids' morals. When her husband watches TV, opens a magazine, or reads a newspaper, she goes on and on about her disapproval. She is making everyone's life miserable. Jill's heart has capitulated to fear.

The Bible reminds us that "the human heart is most deceitful and desperately wicked. Who really knows how bad it is?" (Jeremiah 17:9). We all have an inclination to minimize the vulnerability, weakness, and sinfulness of our own hearts. And Barb and I don't claim to be exempt! Until we were confronted by our daughter's family picture (see chapter 1), we did not realize that our marriage was under siege. We had convinced ourselves that our marriage was utterly secure. It was not. The enemy was on the offensive. In many ways, our hearts had been left unguarded.

This is why we are compelled to constantly guard our own hearts—and to urge you to do the same.

ARE YOU PREPARED FOR THE BATTLE?

Guarding love will serve your marriage the way ancient castles served their inhabitants. Guarding love will help you fend off attacks on your marriage from without and within. Guarding love will keep your focus where it belongs—fixed on your first love. Without guarding love, you risk disconnecting from each other and connecting to other people, things, or activities that will pull you away from your spouse, even toward emotional or legal divorce.

When you guard your heart, you are protecting everything that is most important to you in life. You are guarding the love you have always dreamed of. What more do you want than a spouse who loves God, who loves you more than anything on this earth and is wholeheartedly committed to you, and whose heart is pure and true? Isn't this your dream for your marriage? Wouldn't you do anything to protect it? Of course you would. That's why you need the fortress of guarding love around your hearts and your relationship.

Satan's agenda is to draw you and your spouse away from each other. He is subtly at work to accomplish his goal at this very moment! While failing to guard your heart may not lead you into a full-blown marital affair, it always leads to trouble. If you intend to foil the enemy's agenda, you need a plan to nurture guarding love. If you want a divorce-proof marriage, you must take charge of your own heart and help guard the heart of your partner.

It is important to know that the threats to a man's heart are somewhat different from the threats to a woman's heart. And Satan knows where we are most vulnerable, so our defenses must be fortified in those areas. In this chapter we will identify these specific areas of potential weakness, and in the next chapter we will discuss how to counter these threats to men and women.

MEN UNDER ATTACK

Let's look first at the points where men are most vulnerable to attack, starting with external threats, Satan's frontal assault through our culture. Then we will look at areas where women are most vulnerable.

Career pressures. God created all of us to be involved in meaningful work. Most men, and many women, work outside the home. But when a man allows the world's formula for success to capture his heart, he is playing with dynamite! How many men do you know who have lost their wife and children because their job was more important to them? The pressure from supervisors or peers to make a man's work his life can be a serious threat to his marriage relationship.

Worldly distractions. In a man's most inspired moments, he may set godly goals for growth in Christ, family enrichment, and job success—usually in that order of priority. But the daily grind and hourly interruptions sometimes blur or bury those goals. Distractions may come in the form of pleasure (recreation, entertainment, etc.), power or position (influence at work, at church, in the community, etc.), or paychecks. While all of these elements are fine in their place, if they distract a man from the primary values of faith and family, his heart is left dangerously unguarded.

Relationship pressures. Some days a man feels that everybody wants a piece of him, and most of the time he wants to comply in a loving, helpful, "Christian" way. The boss wants him to work a little later or come in for evening meetings. The neighbors want him to help them roof their house or move furniture. The Sunday school superintendent is in desperate need of more teachers. The missions committee needs a chairman. And the guys keep bugging him to spend more Saturdays with them out on the lake. If a husband allows these relationship pressures to dominate his life, if he is trying to please everybody who needs something from him, his marriage and family will suffer.

Sexual temptation. Here's an obvious one—and it's a deadly peril. Barb and I can't even count the marriages we know about that have been shattered by sexual sin. For every ten guys on your softball team or in your Sunday school class, four or five have fallen in some way—an emotional affair, a physical affair, addiction to pornography, some sexual sin. These flaming arrows fly at men from every direction in our culture. A husband cannot let his guard down for a moment.

In addition to threats launched at us from outside, we can also fall prey to internal threats.

The search for significance. What man doesn't want to make his mark on the world? Properly directed, a husband works to use the gifts God has given him to become part of God's great plan for the world. His greatest significance is bringing glory to God. But some men can become so sold out to "I am what I do" that they lose all sense of balance. They claw their way up the corporate ladder and develop their careers while sacrificing their families. Success can take over a man's heart when it becomes his primary purpose in life.

Passivity. As Barb and I speak across the country, the number one lament we hear from wives concerns the passivity of their husbands. Passivity is when men back off and do little or nothing to nurture the relationship. A passive man has the attitude, "Hey, I work hard to make a living for the family. My wife should take care of the responsibilities at home—including the health of our marriage." Passivity is when a man stops running hard and fast after God's best for his family.

Control. Let's face it: Most men like to be in charge. But God never intended for a husband to control his family. Rather he is called to love and serve his family as Christ loves and serves the church. Control is going all-out to get things your way, and it can come from fear, insecurity, aggression, or low self-esteem. Whatever the source, a controlling husband and father can be poison to a family relationship.

Competition. Most men love to compete. Competition in balance is called a sport. Competition out of balance is a war. If a man's priorities are not firmly in place, the drive to compete can unravel what matters most to him: his family.

A woman's heart is just as vulnerable to attack as a man's heart. Yet these attacks are often different. No one knows better than a woman some of the ways Satan tends to capture a woman's heart, so Barb will lead us through this section.

WOMEN UNDER ATTACK

Ann met Rusty at work. Like Rusty, Ann was a Christian. Both were married. She was attracted to his big heart, which in her mind was surely an outgrowth of his Christian faith. Ann noticed how Rusty truly cared about the people he worked with. He seemed like such a neat Christian. One day Rusty found Ann crying. He put his arm around her, consoled her, and prayed for her. He had no idea that her husband wasn't doing a good job of meeting her emotional needs. At that moment, Rusty touched Ann's vulnerable heart.

After that incident, Ann felt spiritually and emotionally connected to Rusty. She began thinking about Rusty a lot. She dressed to impress him and sought him out at work. Until Ann started reaching out to him, Rusty thought that he could not be tempted by another woman. He and Ann were just friends, after all, and he was just ministering to her.

Can you see how inadvertently Ann and Rusty developed an emotional bond? It was a bond that ravaged both their marriages.

Even as Christians they were not exempt from a heart-poisoning relationship.

Let's look at some of the dangers women need to guard against. Here are some of the more obvious, external temptations:

Relationships with other men. As Ann discovered, wives must protect themselves when interacting with men other than their husbands. While a woman may be attracted by a man's physical attributes, she is many times more likely to be lured by an emotional connection. Wives must not allow themselves to be emotionally dependent on other men—or vice versa.

Preoccupation with children. When a wife continually puts the children before her husband, the marriage becomes unbalanced. True, she can't ignore the runny noses or the homework that's due tomorrow morning. But a wife must do whatever it takes to manage her children's needs in a way that doesn't ignore her husband's needs.

Failing to meet personal needs. Women often spend their time meeting the needs of everyone around them and then fail to refill their own tanks. That leaves wives vulnerable to many threats that can disconnect them from their husbands, including bitterness and anger. If these threats are not addressed, they lead women to be vulnerable to the attention of other men. Take care of yourself. Get the rest you need. Spend time with female friends who encourage and energize you. Refresh yourself daily by spending time in prayer and in God's Word.

Wives, you might not get drawn into an emotional or physical affair. But your heart may be drawn away by something seemingly as innocent as some of these internal threats:

Worry. It's natural to be concerned for the people you care about. But all-consuming worry pulls you away from trust in God. Worry is a distrust of God's resources and an attempt to live by your own devices.

Critical attitude. Most women hold an ideal for their marriage and family life. When a wife feels that her husband doesn't support these needs and wishes, she may develop a critical attitude, especially toward him and her children. A critical spirit is a real love killer.

Comparison. Some women tend to compare themselves to others on everything from the intelligence of their children to the address and square footage of their homes. This unhealthy habit can lead to dissatisfaction with themselves and their relationships—especially the person they may hold responsible for any shortcomings: their husband.

Control. It is the nature of many women to take charge, to coordinate their families, and to make things happen. But God's plan for marriage involves family leadership from the husband. Women who assert unreasonable control may cause great discomfort to their husbands. It is a sure way to push him even farther away than he may already be.

TREASURES WORTH GUARDING

Gary and I want to strongly admonish you to continually pursue guarding love for your relationship. We need to be vigilant in guarding the love of our lives. Any of the external and internal threats we have mentioned can pollute an unguarded heart and poison your marriage. No matter how positive your legacy as a couple may be at this point, the enemy will continue to pound at your gate, attempting to steal your dream and nullify your example to others. He knows that *in one single unguarded moment* you can lose your testimony, your platform for counsel, and your positive influence as role models of a loving marriage. What a frightening thought! It's like spilling a bottle of black ink across the carefully written pages of a beautiful life story.

You may find it hard to believe that your heart could ever drift from devotion to your husband or wife or become poisoned by other loves. Relational ruin happens to other people, not you. Don't be lulled into a false sense of security. You are wise to heed the caution of 1 Corinthians 10:12: "If you think you are standing strong, be careful, for you, too, may fall into the same sin." Or as Proverbs 16:18 pointedly teaches: "Pride goes before destruction, and haughtiness before a fall." Your success at developing guarding love depends on recognizing that your hearts and your marriage *are* vulnerable to devastating attack.

It is likely that you have already experienced the pain resulting from severe attacks on your heart. Perhaps you have even tasted the humiliation of a major defeat in your marriage. Is there still hope for plundered hearts that were left unguarded?

We want to assure you that there is always hope. Take courage from the good news at the end of Michelle's Internet affair. Eventually she was confronted with her behavior and confessed her sin. Although she had not intended to hurt anyone, she hurt a lot of people. Even her children knew what she had done. Yet in spite of all the lies and hurt, God has given this husband and wife the courage and strength to rebuild their marriage. "We are taking back our home and telling Satan to get out," she writes. "We have a lot of work to do, but I know it will be worth it." Michelle and her husband have discovered the great worth of guarding love.

In the next chapter, you will learn how you can put guarding love into action. We will share with you how to protect your heart and the heart of your spouse. The result will be a greater sense of safety and security in your relationship than you have ever known.

eleven

BUILDING WALLS
OF PROTECTION

$\mathcal{S}$ix years ago, Conner landed the position of junior vice president in a Fortune 100 company. With a dozen years of experience in the industry, an MBA from a prestigious business school, and a no-holds-barred work ethic, Conner knew he had the tools to do his job and do it well.

After a few steps up the corporate ladder, his momentum stalled. He went two years without a promotion, and by his mid-thirties Conner feared that he had topped out with the company. Whichever way he pushed to expand his responsibilities, he was met with resistance. His personal, cynical motto became "I work for idiots." He knew that his judgmental attitude was neither charitable nor Christian, but he felt it captured the reality of his situation.

When he was passed over for the job of president of his division, Conner was more than a little rattled. Frustrated by his inability to advance, he went to visit a career coach, who signed him up for a group seminar on finding meaning in work. The first exercise was to think through a list of a hundred items such as honesty, balance, generosity, and security, with the goal of determining the half dozen or so qualities that mattered most to him in life. Conner rapidly narrowed his list down to five: personal growth, achievement, competence, challenge, and advancement.

For several moments, Conner sat and pondered the five words he had chosen. Then, suddenly, he bolted from the room. One of the seminar trainers found him sitting alone in a stairwell, staring down at the floor, tears staining his shirt. Conner explained what had happened. When he examined his priorities, he realized that he had excluded family relationships from his list. That stark insight slashed through his heart like a knife. He might as well have pushed his wife, Sasha, and two small sons out the front door of his heart, slammed the door, and thrown the dead bolt.

When Conner returned to the seminar room, he redid his list to reflect the values he *wanted* to have—with his family coming ahead of his work goals. With the fresh certainty of what really mattered to him, he wrote that his new mission in life was to put his family first and to guard against anything that would rob his family of its rightful place in his priorities.

"That was a turning point in my life and in our marriage," Conner says. "As I sat in that stairwell I thought about everything I had to lose if I didn't do something different with my life. I knew Sasha was slipping away from me because I had left her behind in my business pursuits. I decided that day to stop clawing my way to the top and to be content with my position. I have mastered my current job, which is really an advantage at this stage of my life. I can do my job and still have energy left for Sasha and the boys. We're on our way to healing the wounds I caused. A promotion right now would put them back at the bottom of my list. And I don't ever want to hurt them again. I think I am finally realizing that significance is more important than success. I *can* win in the marketplace, but I *have* to win at home."

GUARDING YOUR OWN HEART

Barb and I are encouraged by Conner's decision to take a stand against the enemies of his heart and his family. We have witnessed scores of couples who have made the same decision to build a protective castle around their relationship. If they can do it, so can you. In fact, you *must* commit yourselves to guarding love if you want to divorce-proof your marriage and live the dream for your life together.

Guarding your heart isn't a one-person job. It won't do to send a husband scurrying out of the castle to defeat the ravaging hordes single-handedly. It isn't a wife's job just to stay behind in the castle and worry about her husband. Your relationship is a partnership in every way, including the defense of your marriage.

We will look first at how you as husband and wife can post guards over your own hearts. Then we will share how you can help guard each other's heart. Your marriage and your legacy depend on winning this crucial battle.

Be Committed to the Task

The Bible has some strong words about the task of guarding our hearts. In addition to the admonition in Proverbs 4:23, "Guard your heart," the Bible tells us how seriously God wants us to take our job. Jesus repeatedly coached his disciples to be on guard against hypocrisy (see Matthew 16:6-12), greed (see Luke 12:15), persecution from others (see Matthew 10:17), false teaching (see Mark 13:22), and, above all, spiritual negligence and lack of preparation for the Lord's return (see Mark 13:32-37).

More cautions echo throughout the Scriptures.[1] *"Be careful* that you don't fall"* (1 Corinthians 10:12). *"Be careful* to do what is right"* (Romans 12:17). *"Be very careful,* then, how you live"* (Ephesians 5:15). *"Be careful* that none of you be found to have fallen short"* (Hebrews 4:1). *"Be careful* to do what the Lord your

God has commanded you" (Deuteronomy 5:32). *"Give careful thought* to your ways" (Haggai 1:5).

Barb and I say the same thing to you. Be careful!

Don't let down your guard. The threats to your marriage are real. The dangers are even more dire for those who don't realize they are under attack.

If you think you are wavering in your commitment to the task of guarding your heart, take a moment to catalog everything you stand to lose if you fail to protect your innermost heart. Like Conner, you will find that nothing is as valuable as the priceless treasure of your family's love.

Ask the Lord to Protect Your Heart

Roger and Sharon are not millionaires, and they don't have jobs in a Fortune 100 company. But they feel amply protected in life. They have a decent bank account, paid-up life insurance, a service contract on the furnace, and an extended warranty on their vehicles.

These are good things. But there is only one totally trustworthy source of protection for a marriage: God himself. David said it well in Psalm 61:1-4, when he cried out to the Lord:

> *O God, listen to my cry!*
> *Hear my prayer!*
> *From the ends of the earth,*
> *I will cry to you for help,*
> *for my heart is overwhelmed.*
> *Lead me to the towering rock of safety,*
> *for you are my safe refuge,*
> *a fortress where my enemies cannot reach me.*
> *Let me live forever in your sanctuary,*
> *safe beneath the shelter of your wings!*

When you realize that the internal and external threats to your hearts are real, you can pray as David prayed. Maybe you have never "prayed Scripture" with your spouse. But you can use Psalm 61 as your script.

Tell God, "I will cry to you alone for help. You are my safe refuge, a fortress where my enemies cannot reach me."

Plead with God, "Hear my cry. Listen to my prayer. Lead me to the towering rock of safety. Let me live forever close to you. Shelter me beneath your wings."

Jesus invited us to trust God to safeguard our hearts when he taught his disciples to pray, "And don't let us yield to temptation, but deliver us from the evil one" (Matthew 6:13).

Spending time daily in God's Word and in prayer is vital to keeping our connection to Christ. And by protecting our relationship with Christ first, we can avoid falling into traps. Daily obedience to Christ is the best defense we have against the enemy of our hearts and our marriages.

Establish Openness with God

I for one don't like going to the cardiologist. I don't enjoy having electrodes taped to my chest and running on a treadmill until my lungs burn and my stomach churns. And that's only part of why I don't like going to the heart doctor. My ego doesn't like the possibility that there might be something wrong with my ticker. But in reality, learning what may be wrong with me—and as soon as possible—is the more direct route to getting well. So an occasional heart checkup is a good thing.

Even more important is a spiritual checkup, a *real* heart checkup. We need to be open and honest with God about what is going on at the wellspring of our lives. Few of us, men or women, are eager for our weaknesses to be exposed. But allowing God to probe us helps detect any areas of the heart that may be weak and in need of spiritual repair.

God, the Great Physician, wants to see us more than once a year, however. He can keep our hearts strong by seeing us daily. Psalm 139:23-24 shows us how we can come to God and let him do a heart exam. It's another passage of Scripture you and your spouse can pray together in order to guard your hearts:

> Search me, O God, and know my heart;
>   test me and know my thoughts.
> Point out anything in me that offends you,
>   and lead me along the path of everlasting life.

As you expose your heart to God on a daily basis, he will show you what you need to do to keep the wellspring of life healthy and flourishing. He will help you guard your heart.

Our deepest fear in facing any doctor is that he or she might uncover a problem for which there is no cure. However, there is no inner heart problem that cannot be completely healed. Through the death of Christ, God has provided a way to cleanse us from our sins. Here is his prescription for getting rid of sin once and for all: "If we say we have no sin, we are only fooling ourselves and refusing to accept the truth. But if we confess our sins to him, he is faithful and just to forgive us and to cleanse us from every wrong" (1 John 1:8-9).

Do you have an open relationship with God that allows him to examine your heart and point out where it needs to be guarded? When you allow God to search your life daily for wrongdoing and confess and turn from that wrong as soon as God brings it to your attention, you establish a habit that offers powerful protection to your heart.

Keep Short Accounts with Each Other

In the chapters about forgiving love, Barb and I shared that it is crucial to close the loop and resolve all the hurts and anger we cause each other in marriage. When we hang on to hurt and withhold forgiveness, it makes us bitter people, and the hearts of bitter people are exceedingly vulnerable to attack.

Several years ago I spoke at a conference with a couple named Jim and Renee Keller. During his talk, Jim said something about forgiveness that knocked my socks off. He described the pattern of communication he and Renee have used since the first day of their marriage. We think it is an excellent way to guard your hearts by keeping short accounts.

Before they were married, Jim explained, he realized that both he and Renee were a little headstrong. So he knew they needed a plan for dealing with the inevitable conflicts they would face. So he promised Renee that whenever they had a conflict, he would initiate the resolution of the problem and the process of forgiveness, no matter who was at fault.

I sat in the back row of the auditorium waiting for the punch line. But he had already delivered it. Jim had committed to initiate conflict resolution and forgiveness—even when Renee was the offender. I was in awe.

Later that afternoon I took Renee aside and said, "Okay, Renee, this is just between the two of us. You have been married well over a dozen years. How many times has he violated that promise?"

"Never, Gary," she replied with a smile and a twinkle in her eye. "He has initiated forgiveness every time."

Again I was awestruck. Renee admitted that there are times when Jim is 100 percent right and she is 100 percent wrong. Yet he still takes the first step toward forgiveness and reconciliation.

Jim is determined to douse any coals of resentment before they burst into flame. He is a peacemaker. He is also reflecting incredible servantlike male leadership. Keeping short accounts with Renee is more important to him than his pride and ego.

Just think how such an approach would keep the air clear in your
marriage, especially if both you and your spouse adopted Jim's
attitude.

Stay Accountable

I have a close relationship with five men who ask me the tough
questions. I have met with the same small group of men (Jerry,
Mike, and Tim) since 1979. These three guys, along with my
buddy Steve Farrar and my son-in-law (Scott), have carte
blanche to ask me anything they want about my life. My accountability partners can pelt me with honest questions about guarding
my heart in every area of life, including marriage. The questions
can be brutal: "What has been dominating your thoughts this
week?" or "Have you put yourself in a compromising position
with another woman this past week?" or "Have you been in the
Word?" or "What issues are you and your wife dealing with this
week?" or "Are you in your kids' lives?" or "Are you shooting
straight with me, or are you blowing smoke?"

I don't get together with my small group or connect with
Steve or Scott to snitch on Barb's flaws. I focus on my faults and
struggle points, not hers. These guys are trusted advisors. They
encourage me to follow God's best. In addition to accountability
we experience deep friendship and healthy male intimacy. We
spur each other on toward growth in Jesus and in turn sharpen
each other's ability to serve.

Why do I do this? Because I'm convinced of the truth of
Proverbs 27:17: "As iron sharpens iron, a friend sharpens a
friend." We need each other! Think about it, men. When we
were boys, we had buddies to play with. We built forts and tree
houses, played baseball, or—if you're a little younger than I
am—video games. Oh sure, sometimes we got into arguments
and fights, but those guys were our pals and were in our lives
day in, day out.

But then something happened in adolescence. We discovered girls. We stopped hanging out with the guys. We headed off for college or work, and we met some new friends. But by the time we settled down and got married, a lot of us had lost our best male friends. Not having close male friends leaves a gaping hole in a man's heart. We all need other men who will help us guard our hearts.

Accountability is a pressing need for women as well. Barb will share the feminine perspective of staying accountable.

When Gary talks about men's accountability groups, all I can picture is a hardcore meeting of the president's cabinet. Various officials offer status reports on the state of the nation. Men get down to business and deal with issues and events. Yet women need accountability as much as men do, first to our husbands and then to a few Christian female friends. But our accountability sessions may look quite different.

My accountability meetings involve people as varied as my daughters to women from church to other solid Christian female friends. Our times of open sharing, Bible study, and prayer encourage me. Sometimes my sisters in Christ challenge my attitudes and behavior. But more often we need support.

Women, be honest. How many of your girlfriends support you in your marriage—unfailingly prod you toward faithfulness and friendship in body, soul, and spirit with your husband? And how many of your friends get together just to have a gripe session? You need women to step close to you and risk saying something that may be hard to hear, to point out a mistake so you may grow deeper in Christ, and to help you guard your heart. But you need a group that doesn't spend its first fifty-nine minutes taking "prayer requests" (sometimes another term for gossip) before devoting its final minute to prayer. Find women who share your devotion and love for God.

In addition to guarding your own heart, you can do several positive things to guard the heart of your spouse. First, I will share some helpful ways that wives can help their husbands guard their hearts, then Gary will do the same for men.

SEVEN KEYS TO GUARDING YOUR HUSBAND'S HEART

A man's heart is a precious and private thing. A man is less likely than a woman to bare his soul or communicate every thought. His heart is often locked up and protected, a great treasure stored in a secure vault. This inner wealth represents the core of a man's whole being, the hub of all his activity, his identity as a man.

As his wife, you hold the key to your husband's heart. You are the one person who knows his deepest needs, the quiet longings of his soul, his search and struggle for significance, his God-given strengths, and even his frailties, the weaknesses he can hide from others but not from you.

Make no mistake: You have significant influence in his life. I believe a great deal of a man's personal success and right choices can be traced back to the woman who whispers affirmation and encouragement in his ear at night.

A woman was walking down the street with her husband, who was the mayor of a small town. As they passed a construction site, she stopped to say hello to a worker, who happened to be one of her old high school boyfriends. As they walked on, her husband commented, "Aren't you glad you're married to a mayor and not a construction worker?" His wife replied, "If I had married him, *he* would be the mayor."

Yes, women, you hold the power to help or to hurt your husband. The pastor who officiated at our wedding ceremony said a bad woman can break her man and a good woman can make him better. Here are ways you can demonstrate guarding love and make your husband a better man.

1. *Honor him and his world.* Most men would admit that deep inside every man is a boy and his dreams. Wives, close your eyes for a moment, and envision your husband as an energetic, clear-thinking, bright-eyed ten-year-old shooting baskets—totally in love with life! His future at that point was all promise. He had great dreams and plans, perhaps to be a basketball star, a global adventurer, or president of the United States.

Now think about your husband as he is today. Has he quit dreaming? If so, when did it happen, and why?

Men need their wives to dream with them, to envision the possibilities and walk courageously into change. Often a woman can be so preoccupied with the security of her husband's current job that she can't even consider the great things that may await him in a different company or a new career field. A man longs for the freedom to fully be who he is, assured that his wife will stand beside him through it all.

2. *Avoid sabotage.* I trust you would never intentionally mean to do harm to your husband, but you can inadvertently sabotage him without realizing you are doing so. How? By misusing power.

Do you have any idea how influential you are in your husband's life? It's your voice that whispers into his ear at night. Your beliefs, behaviors, and decisions have as great an impact on him as most other forces. He listens to you and trusts in your advice and counsel. This incredible influence carries with it great responsibility. Make sure you do not mismanage your power in his life and end up wounding him.

"How could I be wounding him?" you may be asking. Many of us women like to be in charge, and sometimes we like it too much. I love being efficient! I'm good with organizing our

household, family schedules, time with our grandbaby, appoint-
ments, my daily workload. It takes a concerted effort and
control to maintain order and stay on task. But I create a problem when I begin thinking that my control extends to others,
especially to Gary.

At times I've been guilty of questioning or doubting my
husband, and in the process I have undermined his God-given
leadership and personhood. To avoid sabotaging our marriage,
I have learned to guard our relationship by surrendering my
need to be in charge.

3. *Love him unconditionally.* A wise older woman once explained
the difference between love and infatuation in this way: "Infatuation is when you think he's as sexy as Tom Cruise, as smart as
Albert Einstein, as witty as David Letterman, and as athletic as
Kurt Warner. Love is when you realize he's as sexy as Albert
Einstein, as athletic as David Letterman, as witty as Kurt Warner,
and nothing like Tom Cruise . . . but you'll take him anyway!"

Every one of us longs to be loved with no strings attached.
Do you love your husband for who he is—right now, with all his
imperfections? Or do you watch his every move with a critical
eye? Do you place your expectations for him so high that disaster
is inevitable?

You can measure your own love for your husband by comparing it to the standard described in 1 Corinthians 13. Are you
patient and kind? Or are you envious and proud? Do you keep
records of your husband's wrongs, then drag them out when they
might be advantageous for you? Do you continue bringing things
up that should have been dealt with and forgotten long ago?

Guarding love is deeply and passionately proud of the man
you married. If you do not love your husband for all he is, you
are leaving him vulnerable and your marriage unguarded.

4. *Understand your differences.* Yes, men and women are different. One of the most reckless things a woman can do is insist that

her husband want what she wants, feel as she feels, behave as she behaves, think as she thinks. Likewise, I don't know a woman who would want her husband to insist that she want, feel, behave, and think the way he does. A husband is 100 percent male; a wife is 100 percent female. Your husband isn't your girlfriend any more than you are his buddy. Respect the gender differences by encouraging him to be all the man God created him to be!

You can learn about your husband's uniqueness only as you study him. Listen carefully to him. Communicate by opening up and sharing with him. And when you talk to him, tell him honestly what you think and feel. But always be tender. The more you understand and respect your husband's male characteristics, the more you can intimately meet his need for you—and help guard his heart in the process.

5. *Honor his friendships.* Can you remember some of the guys your husband hung around with when you first met—the ones who resented you for stealing their buddy away? Well, some of those guys have grown up. Your husband needs like-minded Christian men to reinforce his character qualities. He needs to be around guys who want to follow Jesus Christ regardless of the cost. Give him space to connect with other men who will sharpen him as iron sharpens iron (see Proverbs 27:17).

6. *Clarify your family roles.* When God created Eve, he made her in his image, with qualities not found in Adam. He gave the woman an incredible title of honor and strength, calling her "helper" (see Genesis 2:18, NIV). The Hebrew word translated "helper" can also be translated as one who brings unique strengths and qualities to the other; these qualities, found only in the woman, complete the union between man and woman.

Elsewhere in the Old Testament, this word is used in reference to God himself. Psalm 54:41 tells us that God is our "helper." It is a title of honor and great worth.

By understanding the meaning of your role as helper, you can be encouraged to use your distinctive strengths to build up your husband and contribute to his life. Your very uniqueness can offer your husband qualities that fully complete him—as no one else can!

You can complete your husband and guard his heart by working with him, not against him. How? If your husband is struggling in an area, pray for him. Talk to him if he is open to that. Listen to what he is saying and *not* saying. And then get out of the way, and let God work in his heart. God will open his spiritual eyes as you obey the scriptural command to win him by a "gentle and quiet spirit" (1 Peter 3:4). You are a major part of the equation to help your husband understand his role in the family. But you can't do it alone or by nagging. You have to let God do it in his good timing.

7. *Commit yourself to him and to God.* A wife may feel that she made a commitment once and for all to her husband on her wedding day. And in a way, she did. But recommitment needs to happen each day.

Similarly, your lifetime commitment to God should be renewed daily as you seek to follow Christ moment by moment. Without a doubt, the most lasting gift you can give your husband is your rock-solid faith in Jesus Christ. I want to live my life with God as my first love. When I experience God's unconditional love, he fills me to overflowing. And after me, who benefits the most from my walk with God? Gary, of course. He benefits from the overflow of my dependence on Christ.

Don't make the mistake of putting your husband on a throne that only God should occupy. God alone is God, and your ultimate source of strength is found in him. But after God, your next allegiance is to your husband. These are your two primary, daily commitments.

Gary will now share tips for how men can express guarding love to their wives.

SEVEN KEYS TO GUARDING YOUR WIFE'S HEART

Men, if your goal is to maintain a heart-to-heart connection with your wife, here are seven ways you can guard her heart:

1. Listen! I remember a weekend a few years ago when our daughter Missy was a high school senior. It was homecoming weekend, and she was on homecoming court. This was a big deal for my three women—Barb, Missy, and Sarah. To put it mildly, the emotional tide in our home was at flood stage. Insecurity and anxiety over the event pushed Barb to tears. Missy and her big sister experienced their fill of emotional swings too. It was a classic woman thing.

What did I do? I reminded myself, *Okay, Gary, Barb says that both short-term and long-term marital success depends on a husband's ability to meet his wife's emotional needs.* I knew that with a word, a look, or an attitude I could either tune in to or turn off these women who are so important to me. My wife and daughters needed my soft side during this time, not my logical, hard side. So I listened. I exercised compassion in the midst of their emotional stirrings.

The way my best female friends in the world reacted to the homecoming thing was an issue of "heavenly wiring," not a character flaw on their part. That's the way God made them. When that wiring trips a breaker and the emotions bubble over, a man is tempted to fix it, to tell his wife what to do. At that point, however, she doesn't want to know what to do. She just needs you to be with her through the range of feelings she is experiencing. Save the advice until she has had a chance to express her heart—and then think hard about saving it until she asks!

Guys, have you ever just held your wife when she was struggling with something? I tried it recently when Barb was stressed. I just looked at her and said, "May I just hold you?" She melted in my arms. I couldn't believe it. After several minutes and a few tissues, she looked at me and said, "Thanks, Gary, for supporting me." I was stunned. It worked!

Trust me, men: A supported wife is a guarded wife.

2. *Offer practical help.* If you have children, you know how your wife notices the kids' needs, which you sometimes overlook. Often she is the one present when they have needs, and she does what it takes to keep the children safe and content.

God gave children two parents for a reason. It's tough for a mom to go one-on-one with an energetic child, much less get double- or triple-teamed by other kids in need. You can protect your wife's heart from a heap of bitterness and resentment if you pitch in and help with the kids. Dying to selfishness is lived out by serving your wife in the day-to-day things. Don't save your practical help only for special occasions; make it an everyday occurrence. There is wisdom in the familiar kitchen motto informing us that the secret passageway to a woman's heart runs right through the daily chores: "I like hugs, and I like kisses, but what I need right now is help with the dishes."

3. *Make time just for her.* Husbands, have you picked up on what draws a woman to a man who is not her husband? It usually doesn't have anything to do with brains, bucks, or brawn. It's what won her in the first place: a man's time and undivided attention.

If you don't meet your wife's need for friendship and emotional intimacy, you will leave her vulnerable. She may withdraw from you, or she may not feel free to respond to you sexually. Worst-case scenario, she may begin to look elsewhere to have her needs met.

When you sense your wife withdrawing, it's probably not because she has decided you were right and she should "stop nagging." She has given up on connecting with you. Something is very wrong. From a woman's perspective, it means you are not a harbor of safety to her but a threat. If you do not address this pattern of withdrawal, you may end up as two strangers coexisting under the same roof, sharing meals and the same bed but walled off from each other emotionally.

4. *Give her time for herself.* Many women who work so hard to meet the needs of their husbands and children fail to meet their own needs. A wise, guarding husband will make sure his wife has time and opportunity to rejuvenate herself through spiritual growth, physical exercise, or emotional interchange with female friends.

This is not as simple as your baby-sitting and watching a ball game on TV for a couple hours while she's out. Your wife will be recharged when she knows her duties at home are being done—not just delayed—while she's gone. For example, yesterday, while Barb and I were working on this book, I would take intermittent breaks to throw a load of clothes into the washer, fold some laundry, and empty the dishwasher. These small acts of service took just a few minutes, but they allowed Barb extra time for her writing and filled her love tank.

If your wife just needs a temporary respite, step up and take over some of the chores. But if she feels constantly behind, you probably need to rethink completely the division of labor at your house. It may cost you some time and effort, but it also may get her thinking and feeling more positively about you.

5. *Love her unconditionally.* I hope you regard your wife as the most wonderful woman in the world. I hope you are her greatest encourager. But you are also the person who sees her faults most clearly—not because you are critical of her but because you know her better than any other person does. What should you do with what you know about her weaknesses?

A woman's acceptance of herself hinges on so many things. Seeing herself through your eyes is perhaps the biggest of them. You are her mirror. She sees herself most clearly in how you respond to her. You guard her heart by loving her despite her flaws. You protect her by loving her even if she doesn't change. When she looks at you and sees unconditional love and acceptance shining back at her, she will more readily accept herself. Let her know through your words of affirmation, your supportive prayers, and your positive body language that she is your one and only.

6. *Demonstrate spiritual leadership.* The apostle Peter wrote, "In the same way, you husbands must give honor to your wives. Treat her with understanding as you live together. She may be weaker than you are, but she is your equal partner in God's gift of new life. If you don't treat her as you should, your prayers will not be heard" (1 Peter 3:7). The point about your wife being "weaker" does not mean she is morally or mentally inferior to you. Rather, it most likely refers to relative physical strength between the sexes.

God has called you to devote yourself to honoring, understanding, and accepting your wife as your equal partner in life. He is asking a lot of you! But you have chosen to accept this mission. And know that your wife longs to experience the fulfillment that comes from knowing that you love God and are willing to serve him by being an effective husband and father. So as you strengthen *your* relationship with God, you will help your wife strengthen *her* relationship with God and with you.

When I see a guy struggling with his wife's response to his leadership, I help him focus on his relationship with Jesus. Bottom line: When he gets his relationship with God in sync, his wife's positive response will invariably skyrocket.

Barb and I both read *The One Year Bible* (Tyndale House) each year. I read it each morning, before I even look at the sports page. This discipline took some time to develop, but I know that it not only enriches my life spiritually but also gives Barb incredible security to see me leading by studying the Bible consistently.

When I tell her what I am learning in the Word, it leads her to trust me because of the work Christ is doing in my life.

7. *Pray for and with her.* A husband who prays with his wife will find her more trusting of him. She will be motivated to be one in mind and spirit with him. If you want a biblical family, then you must initiate prayer with your wife. God has promised to bless that kind of spiritual investment.

Before Scott married our daughter Sarah, I took him aside and said, "Scott, you have the opportunity to base your marriage on prayer and spiritual intimacy with Sarah. Start your marriage relationship by loving Sarah as Christ loved the church. Every morning when you wake up or at night right before you go to sleep, take Sarah's hands and pray out loud together. I'm not legalistic. If you miss a day occasionally, it's no big deal. But how about being one of the few guys in America who commits to pray daily with his wife?"

Every so often I check with Scott to see how he is doing. I am thankful to say that he is on target in this vital area.

As much as Barb and I pray together now, we didn't always have a good track record. I didn't start as strongly as I wished in our marriage, but I am hitting the mark now. I'm not perfect, but I am enthusiastic about my role as the servant leader of our home. Your record may not be perfect either. But praying with your wife consistently will draw the two of you together in spiritual intimacy. Nothing will make her feel more safe, secure, and protected than your prayers *for* her and *with* her.

A SPECIAL NOTE ABOUT THE JOURNEY

We have shared with you what we have learned about the areas where men and women are most vulnerable to attack. We have also shared how you can help guard your heart and the heart of your spouse. We encourage you to take the next step and form your own group for loving support and accountability, if you are not already participating in one. Study our new books *Guard Your Heart* and *Guard Your Heart Workbook* (see appendix A). By systematically working through the biblically based content and following through on proven marital exercises, you will find that the various facets of guarding love will provide the safety and security your marriage needs in order to be divorce-proof.

Part Six

CELEBRATING
LOVE

Celebrating love rejoices in the marriage relationship

and helps spouses feel

cherished and captivated

twelve

REKINDLE THE JOY OF BEING MARRIED

𝕸en, do you remember how you felt when you brought home the first love of your life? You couldn't wait to show her off to your family and friends. You fawned over her. You expected a wink of approval from those whose opinions you trusted most. She was the apple of your eye.

We're not talking about bringing your *girlfriend* home to meet your mom and dad. We're talking about your love affair with your first *car.*

Chances are your first set of wheels cost you plenty. Whatever it looked like, you were thrilled to drive it home. Whether it was brand new or just new to you, you carefully parked it away from other cars to avoid those ugly parking-lot dings. You kept it spotless inside and out. You may have spent your Saturday afternoons waxing and buffing it to a blinding sheen.

Eventually, however, your first car's beauty began to dim. You couldn't prevent the dings from accumulating or the carpet from wearing thin or the vinyl from cracking or the paint from fading. And if you had the bad luck of crunching your car in an accident, your love affair may have ended even sooner. You couldn't wait to trade in your old clunker for a pretty, new model.

Your marriage is a lifelong commitment, not something you can trade in when it has lost some of its just-married luster. Yet Barb and I know of countless men and women who "swap out" a spouse for something newer, nicer, prettier, or more exciting— either through divorce or by attaching themselves to an object or activity that seems more appealing.

Why do they do it? Because one or both spouses lose sight of the infinite value of the love they already have. They need a love that remains fresh and vibrant as the years roll by.

ARE THE MILES SHOWING ON YOUR MARRIAGE?

On your wedding day you were flooded with joy over your spouse, and you gladly proclaimed your undying commitment to each other in front of family and friends. It was a moment when all the emotion of King Solomon's love poem came fully alive: "I am my lover's, and my lover is mine" (Song of Songs 6:3).

But maintaining the I'm-rejoicing-over-you attitude isn't automatic once your relationship has logged some miles and picked up a few dents and dings. It's even worse if you carry around lots of unresolved disappointments. What if your wife looks more like her aunt than the woman you married? What if your husband wears the same size pants he wore in high school—with forty added pounds hanging over his belt? What if the sparkling extrovert you married has turned into a couch potato? Where did the magic go? Is there any way to get it back?

As married couples grow older, they lose some of their showroom luster. Some of us have been around the block of life a few times and are showing a whole lot of wear and tear. Many couples grow apart over the years, and their marriages are marked by everything from ho-hum to hatred. Feelings of boredom, disdain, or being taken for granted can drive a couple all the way from disappointment to emotional divorce.

If this is the case, what is there to be excited about as the years go by? What do you have to celebrate? Can you really expect your marriage to get better with age? Or do you just have to make the best of it with the same old model?

Marriage holds no joy for those who feel stuck with the same old model. But it holds infinite happiness for couples who learn to celebrate their one-of-a-kind love. Barb and I call this facet of love *celebrating love.*

LOVE WORTH CELEBRATING

Celebrating love revels in the emotional, physical, and spiritual connections that bond you to your spouse. It's a love that protects you and your spouse from drifting apart and enables you to fall in love and feel discovered all over again. Celebrating love rejoices daily in the marriage you have and helps you feel cherished and captivated by each other.

Celebration is an inescapable element of God's love. Maybe you have never thought about God's enthusiastic love for us. The Bible tells us that "the Lord . . . is a mighty savior. He will rejoice over you with great gladness. With his love, he will calm all your fears. He will exult over you by singing a happy song" (Zephaniah 3:17). God is so excited about his relationship with us that he celebrates his love by bursting into song! And Solomon's biblical love poem, Song of Songs, is a romantic celebration of marital love and sex. No doubt about it: God celebrates us!

Let us share one example of what celebrating love looks like in today's world. Barb and I received this e-mail from a friend.

While waiting to pick up a friend at the Portland, Oregon, airport, I had one of those life-changing experiences that you hear other people talk about—the kind that sneaks up on you unexpectedly. This one occurred merely two feet from me.

Straining to locate my friend coming off the jetway, I noticed a man coming toward me. He stopped right next to me to greet his family. First, he motioned to his younger son (about six years old) as he laid down his bags. They gave each other a long, loving hug. As they separated enough to look into each other's face, I heard the father say, "It's so good to see you, Son, I missed you so much!" His son smiled somewhat shyly, averted his eyes, and replied softly, "Me too, Dad!"

Then the man stood up, gazed into the eyes of his older son (about nine), and while cupping his son's face in his hands, he said, "You're already quite the young man. I love you very much, Zach!" They too hugged a most loving, tender hug.

While this was happening, a toddler (about two years old) was squirming in her mom's arms, never once taking her eyes off her dad. The man said, "Hi, baby girl!" as he gently took the child from her mother. He kissed her face all over and then held her close to his chest while rocking her from side to side. The little girl instantly relaxed and simply laid her head on his shoulder, motionless in pure contentment.

After several moments he handed his daughter to his older son and declared, "I've saved the best for last," and proceeded to give his wife the longest, most passionate kiss I've ever seen. He gazed into her eyes for several seconds and then silently mouthed, "I love you so much!" They gazed into each other's eyes, beaming big smiles at one another, while holding both hands. *For an instant they reminded me of newlyweds, but I knew by the age of their kids that they couldn't possibly be.*

I puzzled about it for a moment then realized how totally engrossed I was in the wonderful display of love not more than an arm's length away from me. I suddenly felt uncomfortable, as if I were invading something sacred. I was amazed to hear my own voice nervously ask, "Wow! How long have you two been married?"

"Been together fourteen years total, married twelve of those," he replied without breaking the gaze from his wife's face.

"Well, then, how long have you been away?" I asked. The man finally turned and looked at me, still beaming his joyous smile. "Two whole days!"

"Two days?" I said, stunned. By the intensity of the greeting, I had assumed he had been gone for at least several weeks, if not months.

Wanting to end my intrusion, I said, "I hope my marriage is still that passionate after twelve years!"

The man suddenly stopped smiling. He looked me straight in the eye with a force that burned right into my soul. Then he told me something that left me a different person. He simply said, "Don't hope, friend. Decide!"

He flashed his wonderful smile again, shook my hand, and said, "God bless!" With that, he and his family turned and strolled away together.

I was still watching that exceptional man and his family walk out of sight when my friend came up to me and asked, "What are you looking at?"

Without hesitating, and with a curious sense of certainty, I replied, "My future!"

That's the power of celebrating love. It's not just a dream. It's a facet of love that we all have experienced and can recapture in our marriages. It produces great joy—and it will divorce-proof your marriage! If you stumbled onto the airport scene our friend did, we suspect you would stare with just as much amazement. Who wouldn't give an arm and a leg to be in a relationship like that? Who would ever think of walking away from that kind of love?

RECAPTURING THE JOY

Without celebrating love, your relationship will stagnate—or worse. But when you cultivate celebrating love in your marriage, you will reconnect with the heartfelt love you discovered when you first fell head over heels for each other—and better. Celebrating love allows you to grow deeper in love year after year, rediscovering what you almost forgot about each other, appreciating again what may have lost its shine, and displaying affection and appreciation for all that you find in each other.

If we asked you to give three reasons for celebrating your love, what would you say? Or would you come up empty? You may feel you have nothing to celebrate. You may think that the days of passion, joy, and excitement in your marriage ended when the babies began arriving and you took out a second mortgage. "The party's over," you glumly report.

The Bible offers strong guidance on how we can recapture the celebrating aspect of love, which may have grown cold through the years. We see the solution in the book of Revelation, where Jesus scolded the believers in Ephesus for forsaking their deep love for him and for one another: "But I have this complaint against you. You don't love me or each other as you did at first!" (Revelation 2:4).

Then the Lord immediately tells them two things they must do to correct the problem: "Look how far you have fallen from your first love! Turn back to me again and work as you did at first" (2:5). Jesus doesn't tell them to wait for the old, warm feelings of love to well up again. He commands them to act by *recalling* their former love for him and *returning* to their former habits of devotion to God.

This passage coaches us to all-out commitment to the Lord. But the same principle applies to your relationship with your spouse. If you think back to the early days of your relationship, even to the days before you got married, what do you recall? How great was your love at that point? How did you demonstrate that love to one another? What kinds of loving attitudes and habits did you practice? If you have lost the sparkle and intensity of your love for each other, how can you return to those expressions? How can you return to the excitement you once sensed for each other?

FIVE KEYS TO CELEBRATING LOVE

The words spoken by the man at the airport—"Don't hope, decide!"—have stuck with Barb and me from the moment we first read that e-mail. In marriage, every day is cause for celebration, and enjoying each other is a choice just like any other divorce-proofing facet of love. Let's look at five keys to developing celebrating love in your marriage.

1. Put Each Other at the Top of the List

Fred was a workaholic. Fifteen-hour days as a consultant in the tech industry consumed him, and he thrived on conquest, whether beating people in games of one-upmanship or closing a deal and nailing the competition. He was proud of the lifestyle he had provided for his wife, Peg. After all, he had achieved the American dream of having it all: a large home with a three-car garage, pricey cars, a plump stock portfolio, and a four-season cabin complete with a shed full of snowmobiles and a boat so sleek it looked like a spaceship. Peg felt as if she had everything—except her husband.

A severe downturn in the tech sector left Fred scrambling for work. The months of joblessness stretched on and wiped out most of Fred and Peg's assets, leaving them struggling to pay their bills. When bankruptcy was unavoidable, Fred hit bottom.

Peg had a different outlook. She was confident they could start afresh, just as they had when they were young. And she was secretly glad to be rid of many of the things they had lost. She gently told Fred that she didn't need all the things he had worked so hard to accumulate. What she really wanted and needed was him.

The first key to celebrating love is to move each other to the top of your to-do lists, just below your love for Jesus. You must make spending time together a priority, just as you did when you were first dating. Barb and I are amazed at how many people buy into the idea that "quality time" with our spouses and children is sufficient. Quality time is a myth. I am ashamed of how many in my field of counseling have perpetuated that myth.

You need hundreds of hours of *quantity* time before you can enjoy real *quality* time. You need frequent periods of time away from the kids and other responsibilities. Find enjoyable activities to do together—everything from hobbies to foreplay to conversation—activities that will rekindle intimacy of the heart and spirit. Give your spouse priority access to your time instead of just the leftovers. Here are several ideas to help you elevate celebrating love in your schedule.

Put family second, right after your relationship with God. Plan the together times you need, and write them on your calendar—in ink. That means not only date nights and getaway weekends but also smaller time slots each day, like dinner together, time with the children, and time to talk, play a game, or watch a favorite TV program together after the kids are in bed.

Be cautious when making commitments outside your family. Ask yourself: Do I really have the time, energy, and resources to make this happen without compromising my commitment to "family second"?

Cultivate enriching relationships. All of us deal with people who sap our strength. These are the people who always seem to be in crisis, people who mostly take from us and are unable to give of themselves. In addition to these "ministry opportunities," you need friendships with people who energize you instead of drain you.

Make communication a priority in your relationships. Take advantage of time in the car and around the dinner table to promote meaningful conversation. Don't clutter your life with the noise of constantly droning TV, radio, or music.

Let your body language demonstrate that your spouse is your priority. When you talk together, put down the newspaper and turn off the TV. Make eye contact. Give undivided attention. Ask God to give you the ability to focus directly on your spouse. When you walk together, hold hands. When you are together with other people, touch each other or make eye contact across the room in ways that say to each other and to people around you, "This person is the love of my life."

Instead of evaluating your daily success by how many tasks you check off your to-do list, ask whether they are the *right* tasks, those that properly balance God time, personal time, and family time. Your attention to the Bible, prayer, and fellowship with God will give you access to the only power source that will ultimately satisfy, allowing you to properly honor your family.

2. Confess to Each Other

We're back to this important point of closing the loop through forgiveness.

When Fred's work as a consultant dried up, he and Peg had to deal with issues that were even bigger than their financial problems. Peg was hurting from years of not being at the top of Fred's priority list and from their lack of emotional connection. She didn't know where to take all these issues, so she stuffed them inside, buried her pain alive, if you will.

After declaring bankruptcy, Fred finally found work at one of the few surviving tech companies in his area. He began to contemplate what Peg had said about getting along just fine without "all that stuff." He asked her how she felt about their old life and how he had wounded her. In short, he became teachable. As he began to understand all the hurt he had caused Peg, he confessed how wrong he had been and asked for her forgiveness. For the first time in their marriage, Fred began to factor Peg's thoughts and feelings into his career decisions.

Unresolved offenses block all kinds of intimacy—emotional, physical, and spiritual. Barb and I know this from our own experience and from talking to countless couples whose love has grown cold. Trying to get close while those hurts remain is like trying to hurdle a hundred-foot wall. It won't happen.

When you sense a wall between you and your spouse, something is very wrong. Husbands, why not take the lead to address the pain, close the loop, and restore intimacy? Become responsible for the tone of the relationship and get your marriage back on course, especially if you are guilty of contributing to the pain.

Barb is going to discuss another key to celebrating love, the importance of getting to know one another deeply.

3. Get to Know Each Other Again

Most men tell Gary and me that they were far more successful at connecting with their wives before marriage or before children. And many women report to us that as family responsibilities and challenges mount, they lose track of their husband's most heartfelt needs. Recapturing the joy of celebrating love in your relationship requires that you get to know your spouse all over again.

How? Demonstrate your love by showing that you are deeply interested in your spouse. It takes effort to rediscover your wife's strengths, personal interests, and uniqueness. It requires focus to rediscover things about your husband that you have overlooked for years. Yet detecting these deep, hidden qualities will bring new excitement into your marriage. Here are some tips for getting started.

Study your spouse. Watch closely to discover what makes your spouse's eyes brighten. Men, make it your goal to know your wife better than she knows herself. Women, do the same. You will learn what he or she is thinking about, what his or her focus is, what is important in his or her life, and what he or she gives time and energy to. The more you study your spouse, the better prepared you will be to serve him or her.

Really listen to each other. Give your spouse your complete attention, even if you don't have a clue what he or she is talking about. Ask questions. Notice what your spouse gets excited about in conversation and what causes him or her to slow down and reflect. Pay attention to your spouse's choice of words when talking about a subject close to his or her heart.

Work alongside each other. You may have devised a tidy division of labor to keep your household humming along smoothly: He always fuels the car, she does everything in the kitchen; he handles outside chores, she does homework with the kids. It may be efficient and orderly, but it isn't much fun doing your chores and tasks alone. And in a busy household, it can mean constant separation. Try flip-flopping some of the roles and responsibilities, or better yet, team up with your spouse to do them together.

Try some of your old favorites again. What are some of the things you and your spouse did when you first met and married? You know the things I mean: hobbies, sports, shopping, cheap dates, even parking beside the lake. Your spouse's interests don't have to be your favorite things to do, but you can take turns participating in each other's favorites. Honoring your spouse means sacrificing some of your own agenda to please each other.

Get away together. Go on a picnic. Go for a walk. Send the kids to their grandma's or a friend's house for the weekend, and take off for your favorite bed-and-breakfast. Or spend the weekend at home. Take a minivacation each year without the kids. And during a normal, busy week at home, spend a part of every day or evening with each other, just the two of you. Your getaways don't have to cost a lot of money, but the effort to be together will pay significant dividends in your marriage.

Be captivated by the love of your life. Barb and I recently spoke to hundreds of students at our daughter Missy's college campus. We delighted in seeing these young men and women thirsty for biblical truth about godly relationships. As I was coaching the guys, I taught them what Solomon wrote in Proverbs 5: "Why be captivated, my son, with an immoral woman, or embrace the breasts of an adulterous woman?" (v. 20). In this Scripture passage Solomon confronts us by describing the futility in seeking pleasure from someone other than the love of our life: a wife—or for that matter, a husband. To really bring this teaching alive, read verses 18-19 and capture the king's instruction: "Let your wife be a fountain of blessing for you. Rejoice in the wife of your youth. She is a loving doe, a graceful deer. Let her breasts satisfy you always. May you always be *captivated* by her love" (emphasis added).

You should have seen the eyes of these eager young men bulge as I described being *captivated* by the wife of my youth. Being captivated by Barb isn't being trapped or stuck. To the contrary, being captivated means celebrating the reality that I am enthralled with Barb. It is being caught up and bound to each other. It is the experience of not seeing another woman in the room because I have eyes only for the one I am sharing life with. Captivating love celebrates God's design for marriage. And it doesn't get any better than that!

4. Rethink Your Thinking

Gary and I know a lot of people like Dale, who always sees the dark side of everything. Whether the subject is work, church, or his wife, he notices flaws and failures everywhere. By constantly focusing on the negative, Dale misses the brighter side of life, especially in his attitudes toward his wife, Katie. His mind endlessly cycles a negative commentary about her, like a looped tape recording. If Dale doesn't break this gloomy pattern, he and Katie are doomed to a marriage devoid of celebration.

What tapes are you playing about your spouse? Can you change the way you think about your spouse? Absolutely. We believe it is possible to learn to fall in love again, and we have two simple coaching tips to get you started:

1. Be willing to fall in love with your spouse again. Being in love begins in your mind with the choice to surrender to feelings of love. Celebration is a learned response to the way your partner looks and feels, to the things your partner says and does, and to the emotional experiences you share. Only when you have made this basic choice can you train yourself to look for the good in your spouse and be glad for it.

2. Control your thoughts. The New Testament encourages us to control our thoughts, to take them captive and make them obedient to Christ (see 2 Corinthians 10:5, NIV). We can do that in our marriages. When a negative thought about your spouse comes along, arrest it, lock it behind bars, and throw away the key! When you see a positive trait in your spouse, embrace it, think about it, comment on it, and enjoy it. Change the focus of your thinking to the qualities that caused you to fall in love with your spouse in the first place.

When you are with your spouse next, look closely at him or her. Look at his or her hands. Do you remember when just holding hands made you tingle? Look in his or her eyes. What makes those eyes sparkle? Think about your spouse's passions and dreams. What makes him or her excited to be alive?

Then tell your spouse what you see. Give words to your love. Express your love aloud, and do it often.

Ask God to refresh your love for your spouse. Even if you currently complain to yourself about your spouse a hundred times a day, even if you genuinely feel your marriage has gone bad, even if many days you don't feel in love anymore, you can change. God can still help you develop a celebrating love.

5. Rekindle Romance and Physical Intimacy

Romance and sex may be the first thing you associate with celebrating love. Sex isn't all there is to celebrating love; there is more to feeling cherished and captivated than what happens in your most private and intimate moments together. However, Gary and I are as glad as anyone that celebrating love includes this special kind of husband-wife closeness!

But let's look for a moment at the full extent of captivating love. Men, I have found that as a husband demonstrates being captivated by his wife, she flourishes and revels in his love. Captivating love is reflected when a man is mesmerized by his wife. He connects to her and is entranced by her. His eyes light up when he is in her presence and reflect warmth and tenderness when he speaks of her in her absence. He is charmed by her, and others just know that there is something special about this love that reflects celebration. Captivating love leads to the expression of sexual intimacy in the marriage relationship.

As we discuss the component of sexual intimacy in celebrating love, let's start with a foundational truth: God created men and women to be different. "So God created people in his own image; God patterned them after himself; male and female he created them" (Genesis 1:27). In addition to the obvious differences in physical anatomy, have you noticed how this difference works out in everyday life? For example, while a woman is thinking about a dirty kitchen floor or sleep or errands or bathing the kids, her husband may be thinking about sex. And when he is in the garage rebuilding a carburetor or refinishing a piece of furniture with a ball game blaring on the radio, his wife may be thinking about a quiet conversation over a cup of tea.

Back in chapter 7 we said that most men spell intimacy S-E-X and most women spell it T-A-L-K. This basic difference can lead to enormous confusion and outright conflict. But here's the good news: The difference was God's idea, his design. He created a wife with all the incredible, unique gifts and needs she brings to her relationship with her husband— including her need for talk. And he created a husband with all of his wonderful, unique gifts and needs—including his need for sexual intimacy.

So how do a husband and wife bridge these differences so that both enjoy the sexual intimacy of celebrating love to the maximum? It happens when we understand and lovingly accommodate the unique intimacy needs of our spouses. First, I will coach you husbands on how to meet your wife's intimacy needs. Then Gary will coach you wives on meeting your husband's unique needs.

UNDERSTANDING YOUR WIFE'S INTIMACY NEEDS

Shared emotional arousal between husband and wife is a catalyst in the development of a passionate physical love. What husbands must realize is how their seemingly nonsexual activities help to satisfy a wife's hunger for physical intimacy. At the heart of these nonsexual actions is the emotional bond of being friends. "The determining factor in whether wives feel satisfied with the sex, romance, and passion in the marriage is, by 70 percent, the quality of the couple's friendship," says marriage expert John Gottman, and "for men, the determining factor is, by 70 percent, the quality of the couple's friendship. So men and women come from the same planet after all."[1] A key quality in married friendship, for men and women alike, is staying interested in your partner and keeping your partner interested in you. No gimmick—flowers, candy, or a candlelight dinner—works unless your partner is genuinely interested in you and his or her face lights up when you enter the room. Especially for wives, the pathway to sexual intimacy is *emotional* intimacy.

Husbands, don't underestimate the power of the small signs of affection that communicate to your wife all day long that she is loved. This is vital to your wife's sexual fulfillment. Susan gives a personal example:

> For years I have tried to encourage my husband to show affection outside the bedroom. He just can't seem to say anything nice or touch me without wanting sex in the next five minutes.
>
> One day we got together with another couple, Matt and Leann. Matt was a high school friend—not a boyfriend, but he could have been. The four of us spread out a picnic. I watched Matt throughout the afternoon as he

held Leann's hand. He said kind things about how much
he appreciated her. He carried everything from the vans
and helped serve lunch to the children. He even kissed
Leann good-bye when she and I took the kids for a trip to
the rest rooms.

Watching Matt love his wife hit me hard. He's someone I've thought about a lot over the years, wondering
if I missed something by not dating him when we were
younger. Seeing his minute-by-minute connection with
Leann sure didn't help me feel content with my husband.
I really had to give my attitude to the Lord and ask him to
help me be patient with my husband. He's a great guy in
so many other ways.

A wife starved for emotional intimacy and nonsexual affection
may withdraw from you physically. She may seem distracted and
distant, spending more than the usual time at work or in other
activities. She could be "too busy" or "too tired" for sex and avoid
spending time with you. And you might notice that your children
are a higher priority for her than you are. These are all warning
signs that a wife's need for friendship and nonsexual affection is
not being met. She does not feel that you cherish her. She does not
feel captivated. Celebrating love is not part of her experience.

Every husband reading this book is married to a walking, talking marriage manual. You will be amazed at what you can learn
about her needs if you just watch her and ask her. A woman tends
to be naturally gifted with the ability to show her husband the
keys that will emotionally strengthen their marriage. Husbands,
your wife is your greatest guide to discerning how to be tender,
tuned in, and teachable. But you won't learn anything if you
don't pay attention to her.

Wives, Gary has a few important paragraphs to help you
cherish and captivate your husband.

UNDERSTANDING YOUR HUSBAND'S INTIMACY NEEDS

Men talk to Barb and me all the time about their frustrations regarding sexual intimacy in their marriages. Few women understand the depth of anguish a husband feels when his need for sexual intimacy is not fully met.

"I felt that I was meeting Olivia's emotional needs," Owen says. "She even said I was. I was doing everything I knew to do, and she told me how much she appreciated how we talked and how I treated her. But when it came to my desire for sex, it was completely up to what kind of mood she was in. Some days she was preoccupied, as if I was last on her list, not worth her attention. Other days she just didn't feel like it. When I told her I wanted to get close to her, I felt as if I was begging. It was humiliating."

With his one legitimate, God-appointed outlet for sexual intimacy cut off, Owen retaliated by shutting down the emotional connection Olivia so enjoyed. His tactic backfired when his wife pushed him away and started a relationship with a man at work.

Sexual frustrations can lead to more serious marital problems. A husband whose wife ignores his drive for sexual intimacy feels rejected as a person and as a man. He often shuts down or pulls away, perhaps turning to pornography or affairs to meet his needs. We do not condone or excuse these activities no matter who is at fault. A man or woman who steps away from God's moral guidelines is personally responsible for the painful consequences. However, such actions can be averted if a wife is attuned to the depth of her husband's need for physical intimacy.

Wives, you can view your husband's strong need for sexual intimacy as a negative thing—a problem to manage—or you can delight in the fact that your man has such a deep hunger for you. If sexual intimacy is a struggle for you, begin by taking the issue of your sexual relationship to God: Ask him, "What is blocking me from enjoying the sexual aspect of our marriage? Is there hurt between my husband and me? Is there unresolved conflict or lack of forgiveness? Am I bringing past pain from other relationships into our marriage bed?"

Until you resolve your own issues, it will be nearly impossible for you to enjoy a healthy, active sexual relationship with your husband. Women with unresolved emotional pain have difficulty taking the risk and opening their hearts and bodies to their husbands.

If you want to maximize your sexual relationship with your husband, follow these coaching tips:

Don't stay angry. Anger robs you of intimacy, and unresolved tension brings a frosty chill to your bedroom. Confess your offenses, forgive his offenses, and be done with it!

Exchange tips with your husband. Outside the bedroom, in the calm light of day, ask your husband how he would like you to give him pleasure the next time you are together sexually. Ask him to make a list of things you can do to please him. Then create your own list of three to five ways he can give you sexual pleasure. Exchange your lists, and take turns treating each other to the new ideas.

Confront the darkness. More and more women confide to us that their husbands bring pornography into the bedroom for erotic stimulation—sexually explicit magazines, videos, etc. If it's happening in your relationship, put a stop to it. Keep your marriage bed pure.

Pray about your sex life. God isn't intimidated or embarrassed by your sex life. He invented it! Invite the originator of sex into this arena of your marriage, and let him guide you in cherishing and captivating your husband.

LITTLE THINGS MEAN A LOT

You can do much to rekindle celebrating love in your marriage by paying attention to the little things. Small acts of love can ignite a bonfire of passion in your spouse's heart. Barb and I have listed a number of ideas below. You may recognize some of them from the early days of your courtship and marriage. Select a few to put into practice. As you do, feelings of being cherished and captivated will follow.

IDEAS FOR CELEBRATING YOUR HUSBAND

- ◆ Send him off and welcome him home with a smile and a kiss.
- ◆ Let him know you're glad he's home just because you love him, not because the sink is clogged or you need to get away from the kids.
- ◆ If you arrive home after your husband does, find him before you do anything else and tell him how glad you are to be home.
- ◆ Let him know you care. Buy a mushy card, and send it to his office, hide it in his briefcase, or slip it into the book he's reading at bedtime.
- ◆ Write down a list of reasons why you love him, then share the list with him over a romantic dinner.
- ◆ Leave him a surprise note with an encouraging Bible verse.
- ◆ Buy attractive new nightwear for yourself—and hide his!
- ◆ Give him massages.
- ◆ Pray for him before he leaves for work.
- ◆ Join him in his favorite activity even if you aren't crazy

about it. Try doing with him some of the things he enjoys doing with his buddies.

◆ Say, "I'm sorry" when you are wrong, and forgive him when he is wrong.

◆ Initiate sexual intimacy.

◆ Listen to his opinions on spiritual issues. Ask him what type of activities would fuel his spiritual growth. Don't impose your ideas on him.

◆ Leave him a voice-mail message saying you love him and are praying for him.

◆ Eat breakfast with him, and enter his world at the start of the day.

◆ Accept your body, and enjoy experimenting with him sexually.

IDEAS FOR CELEBRATING YOUR WIFE

◆ Be accessible to her—always! Tell her where you will be and how long you will be gone.

◆ Let your coworkers know you can always be interrupted when she calls.

◆ Repeat your wedding vows often. Tell her that if you had it to do all over again, you would choose her again—and again, and again . . .

◆ Continually promise and reassure her that your love for her and faithfulness to her is "till death do us part."

◆ Invite her to tell you how she desires to be loved, then seek to love her in that way.

◆ Give her a head-to-toe massage.

◆ Compliment her, especially for the little things.

◆ Send flowers or chocolates or whatever little gifts she likes.

- ◆ Attend a marriage conference together. Take the initiative to locate one, make all the arrangements, including a baby-sitter if that is necessary. Join us at one of our conferences. Check our Web site (www.afclive.com) to see if we are going to be in your community this year!
- ◆ Lavish her with nonsexual touch.
- ◆ Call her during the day just to say hello.
- ◆ Put your arm around her or hold her hand in public.
- ◆ Say "I love you" before she does. Begin and end each day with encouraging words.
- ◆ Write notes to her regularly telling her how proud you are of her.
- ◆ Hold her hands, and pray for her.
- ◆ Send her cards or love letters.
- ◆ Bring her breakfast in bed.

Celebrating love doesn't need to be extravagant or showy. It can be expressed by a hand-in-hand walk, a single rose, a carefully placed note, and the creative thoughtfulness that comes from the heart. You can start with affirmation and compliments, because a lack of appreciation for your spouse will kill anything else you try.

One more component of celebrating love is so important that it requires its own chapter. Let's consider what spiritual intimacy can do to help you and your spouse feel cherished and captivated.

thirteen

BUILDING SPIRITUAL INTIMACY

𝒯he following letter is from a woman we will call Nicole. She wrote in after listening to our radio program, *America's Family Coaches . . . LIVE!* Barb and I hear sad stories like this from our listeners and conference attendees quite often. They remind us of the critical nature of spiritual intimacy in divorce-proofing a marriage.

> *Dear Gary and Barb,*
>
> *My husband and I listen to your radio program daily, and we have attended your marriage conference and read your books. I'm glad my husband has been involved in your material. But there is also a problem with him. It's like there are two men in my life. The public side of Trent goes to church and does all the acceptable Christian things. But at home, where it really counts, Trent lives a private life that doesn't match his profession. I know I sound critical, and perhaps I am. It's because the man I thought I was marrying is not the man I live with. Let me explain.*

Trent grew up in a Christian home. He went to Sunday school as a boy and was taught Christian principles. When we dated, he appeared to have a relationship with Jesus. But soon after our marriage, he gradually fell away from what little faith he had. I saw it in his business dealings, as he moved into gray areas financially and violated biblical principles. I saw it in his personal habits. He would stay up late at night watching TV, and if he heard me coming into the room, he would quickly switch the channel.

The Internet became an obsession with Trent. I went on-line once to check out a plane fare and found that he had logged a string of visits to a porn site that made me gag.

But it wasn't only the money and sexual things that bothered me. It was the heart things. Trent would attend men's conferences, buy the books, and appear to be seeking spiritual things, but he wouldn't share anything with me. Sometimes I would see him talking to his small-group buddies in the church hallway, laughing and enjoying rich fellowship. But I was crying on the inside because he never shared this kind of joy with me.

I heard you say to one radio listener that a hurting wife should express her heart to her husband. I did that to Trent. I heard you encourage another listener to pray. I have prayed, over and over again. And then I heard you tell one caller to get out of the way and let God work. That's the only thing I haven't done. I am afraid that if I do move out of the way, Trent will never move closer to me or to God.

I long for Trent to pray with me. I long for him to say, "Nicole, look what I just read in the Word." I long for him to initiate spiritual discussions with me. I see other women growing spiritually with their husbands, but on the inside I feel as if I am dying. I want to love Trent unconditionally. I want to encourage him, and most of the time I do. But more than anything, I long for the "marriage of three" you two talk about

*on the radio—a marriage of Jesus, Trent, and me. I don't
want more stuff, I want more of my husband—his thoughts
and feelings. Most of all I want more of his spiritual heart.*

*I won't leave Trent. I am committed to him. I also know
that I am part of the problem. I expect things too quickly, get
short with him, and get critical at times. Please pray for us:
Trent and Nicole. Pray that I won't get discouraged and that
somehow we will experience a breakthrough without facing a
big crisis. I've heard you say so often that pain is the precursor
to growth. I am fearful of what could happen, what God could
allow, to lead us to that growth. But I am willing to surrender
if God would take his rightful place in our home.*

Thanks for being there. I am praying for you two.

Nicole

These kinds of letters break our hearts. Sadly, this isn't
the only Christian home in which a spouse has subtly or deliber-
ately allowed the spiritual underpinnings of the marriage to
crumble. We find so many couples living in a daze, wondering
what piece of the marriage puzzle is missing. Often it is spiritual
intimacy.

As the result of our listening to couples, we have identified
several telltale signs that suggest a marriage may be languishing
in spiritual impotence. Look over the list, and see if any of them
describes your marriage.

You may experience conflict in many areas. The spiritual dimension provides the foundation for how the game of life is to be
played. It's tough to play well in marriage if you and your spouse
don't equally value God and Scripture. You wouldn't want to
play a game of baseball if people didn't agree on the rules. It's
true of marriage as well.

You may feel incomplete. You may be on top of your game in
every other area of your relationship, but if you don't connect

spiritually, you will always feel like something is missing—because the most important element *is* missing! Without a spiritual connection you miss out on the closeness and joy God intends. The deepest part of your spouse will go unexplored, leaving the greatest joys of your marriage untapped.

You may lack a firm foundation for your marriage commitment. The Bible declares marriage to be a sacred, unbreakable union. But without that biblical foundation in your life, it is easy to see marriage as an arrangement of convenience rather than commitment. And when it is no longer convenient, you want out.

You may lack boundaries for guarding your marriage. The Bible provides absolute standards for right and wrong. God's people enjoy confidence that the boundaries they live by were erected by a kind and loving God. But without the spiritual dimension, your marriage lacks God's protection and provision.

Many of these signs are evident in Trent and Nicole's marriage. But there is great hope for this couple and others who are struggling in the area of spiritual intimacy. Developing and enriching spiritual intimacy in marriage is a vital element of the celebrating love that helps husbands and wives feel cherished and captivated.

A MARRIAGE OF THREE

It is relatively easy to understand the *emotional intimacy* that bonds a husband and wife heart-to-heart and the *physical intimacy* that brings them together body-to-body. But every couple also needs soul-to-soul closeness. If you want to enjoy the deepest level of connection and celebration, you need to develop and grow *spiritual intimacy* in your relationship.

Bonding spiritually can be an enormously puzzling area of getting along as husband and wife. Even when you want it, you may struggle to achieve it. Even if you both set a goal to bond spiritually, you may have difficulty deciding how to get there. And if only one of you wants to pursue spiritual depth in your relationship, you may never get there at all.

So what is spiritual intimacy? There is nothing weird or mystical about it. Spiritual intimacy occurs when you as husband and wife surrender your lives and relationship to the Lord. You bond and grow together spiritually when you live out your marriage relationship according to God's ways and aim to please him in all things.

Spiritual intimacy is an ingredient available only to those who have a personal relationship with God through Jesus Christ and who live their lives seeking to please him. When you are joined with another Christian in marriage, you have the wonderful privilege of seeking spiritual intimacy in your marriage. When a husband and wife are growing in their vertical relationships—individually with God—the horizontal relationship between them tends to come together as well.

Barb and I believe that spiritual intimacy in a marriage is a "God thing." It's a marriage of three—an intimate relationship between God, a husband, and a wife. Profound intimacy happens when two hearts, two bodies, two souls connect with the God who created them and designed marriage. It can be pictured as you, your spouse, and God positioned at three corners of a triangle. As you and your spouse draw closer to God, you naturally draw closer to each other.

Most of our world doesn't understand spiritual intimacy in marriage. Sadly, many Christian couples haven't grasped this profound truth either. But when a husband and wife truly begin to understand the significance of a marriage of three, their relationship begins to flourish. Ecclesiastes 4:12 offers a great picture of what we mean by this intimacy of three. "A person standing alone can be attacked and defeated, but two can stand back-to-back and conquer. Three are even better, for a triple-braided cord is not easily broken."

Later in this chapter we will look at practical ways you can make spiritual intimacy a reality in your relationship. But first we want to explain exactly what achieving spiritual intimacy can accomplish in your marriage. And we want to speak frankly about the harm that can come to marriages missing this all-important foundation.

THE BENEFITS OF SPIRITUAL INTIMACY

You may not realize the power of spiritual intimacy in creating celebrating love in your relationship. Barb and I often describe it this way. Emotional and physical intimacy ignite the rocket in your marriage, but spiritual intimacy fires the afterburners and gets you into orbit. Emotional and physical attraction is what drew you together, but the spiritual connection is what keeps you together. Spiritual intimacy is indispensable to achieving the marriage of your dreams and fully divorce-proofing your marriage.

Spiritual intimacy will be the source of your greatest joy as husband and wife. It is also the source of the strength you need to divorce-proof your marriage. In fact, we can't limit the role of spiritual intimacy to celebrating love. It is the foundation for all six key kinds of love we present in this book. Your vital relationship with God through Christ empowers

- ◆ the grace in forgiving love
- ◆ the humility in serving love
- ◆ the patience in persevering love
- ◆ the wisdom in guarding love
- ◆ the joy in celebrating love
- ◆ the power in renewing love

You, your spouse, and God are an unbeatable team. No matter what life throws at you, no matter how the enemy tries to thwart you, no matter what mistakes one or both of you make, a marriage of three can get you through it and go deeper. Spiritual intimacy and closeness in marriage is the greatest connection of all. Here are just a few key benefits of spiritual intimacy:

Spiritual intimacy empowers celebrating love. A spiritual connection won't make your marriage perfect, but it will keep you in touch with the author of marriage who has the answers to your deepest marriage problems. Bonding spiritually enables you to accept each other as people forgiven by God. And as God reminds you of the true nature of your union—that your love isn't between two persons but three—you will experience the depths of uniting body, soul, and spirit. It is impossible to keep such a connection from igniting into feelings of being cherished and captivated.

Spiritual intimacy allows you to connect at the deepest level. God designed husbands and wives to join together emotionally and physically. And these connections are electric! But he also created you to come together at the deepest level of your being—soul and spirit. If you want the deepest possible connection with your spouse, this is it. As you seek God together, your hunger for wholeness will be satisfied.

Spiritual intimacy links you with God's purposes and plans for you. In the Old Testament, God told his people, "'For I know the plans I have for you,' says the Lord. 'They are plans for good and not for disaster, to give you a future and a hope'" (Jeremiah 29:11). This promise is for you today too. God has good plans for your marriage. He guarantees to make your marriage an adventure as you trust him to guide you together through life.

Spiritual intimacy allows you to bless each other with God's love. In the Bible, God often uses the intimacy of the marriage relationship as a metaphor for his love for humankind. As a husband or wife, you can demonstrate what God's love for your spouse looks like. You can be God's voice and arms of love and care. What a privilege! As you meet your spouse's needs, you are God's love "with skin on."

Spiritual intimacy brings your deepest values and desires into agreement. Barb and I believe that the Bible not only communicates how you can know God and connect with your spouse but also lays out principles for what is right and important in life. As you and your spouse grow spiritually intimate and submit to the teachings of Scripture, your biggest goals and beliefs will be in harmony.

Spiritual intimacy opens the door to the deepest levels of communication. One of the fundamentals of intimacy is being honest about who you are—warts and all. As you grow in spiritual intimacy and transparency, your communication will expand from the physical and emotional levels to include the spiritual element of your lives and relationship. Spiritual intimacy permits profound sharing you cannot enjoy at any other level.

Spiritual intimacy empowers your marriage to survive. Every couple encounters circumstances in which they feel overwhelmed. The power of God is bigger than any situation you will ever face, and he can enable you to stand firm in the storm. Barb and I have seen a number of Christian couples collapse under trials and conflicts. But these collapses happened only after one or both partners compromised or abandoned their core spiritual values.

Spiritual intimacy connects you to a supportive body of fellow disciples. A husband is the strength of his wife, and a wife is the strength of her husband. But no marriage survives or thrives by itself. God has given you his people, the church, to stand with you when you struggle and celebrate with you when you triumph. If you are not connected with a local body of believers who support your marriage, make that connection! It is a benefit God doesn't want you to live without.

WHAT SPIRITUAL INTIMACY LOOKS LIKE

Spiritual intimacy is more than going to church together and holding hands during the service, as nice as that may be. Carl and Danielle's story gives us a peek into what spiritual intimacy looks like in a marriage relationship.

"Danielle and I met at the state university," Carl explains. "All I knew was that I couldn't stop staring at the young woman across the room in my sophomore literature class. I had no shortage of physical attraction to her, and I found out later that she had no shortage for me.

"When I approached Danielle about starting a study group, she agreed, provided we met in a place like a restaurant or the library—not the dorms. She also insisted that other people be in the group. I had no idea where all these 'rules' were coming from. But I was willing to jump through some big hoops to get to know her."

"To me," Danielle interrupts, "they weren't just rules. I was a Christian, and these boundaries made sense. I had no idea who this guy was, other than that he was smart—and cute. The 'rules' protected our long-term good."

"The big change," continues Carl, "came when I asked her out on a date. Danielle turned me down flat. By that time, our studies had touched on some spiritual topics, and she and I both knew I wasn't a Christian. She said that if I wanted to get closer to her, a good place to start would be joining her at church."

"You have to imagine how I felt at that point," Danielle says. "Carl was a great guy. But he was clueless about God. I knew one of God's boundaries for me was not dating a non-Christian. I didn't want to let my heart get attached to a guy if he didn't trust in Christ, but I also didn't want him to fake a spiritual awakening just to get a date. He had to realize the truth of the Bible for himself—and for real. And he did."

Carl explains, "Not only did Danielle make me wait until I became a Christian before we dated, she made me wait most of another year to 'make sure it stuck.' She said her older sister married a guy who always nodded when she talked about spiritual issues. He is a really compassionate guy who works with kids in the city. But faith in Christ isn't real for him, and they have struggled ever since. Danielle wasn't going to go there.

"Danielle didn't allow physical attraction to drive our relationship. In fact, she told me to keep my hands to myself— another one of those boundaries. She said she wanted her body to be a gift to her husband. But I got to unwrap the package later, after we got married.

"Meeting Danielle and meeting God revolutionized my life— not so much in *what* I did but *why*. Before I became a Christian, I was a good, moral person, but I didn't have a relationship with God. When I learned that Christ died for me, and that his death made me acceptable to God, I realized that I needed God and I wanted to live for him. The real change in me took some time— almost six months. It didn't happen overnight."

"That was fifteen years ago," Danielle says. "We married knowing that our lives were fully committed to God. Our strong and growing faith has helped us stay close to God individually and support each other's growth. And our spiritual life together has had a huge impact on how we bring up our children and what we teach them about faith and life.

"I think one of the ways we are different from non-Christian couples is that we make decisions God's way. First, we always pray and tell God that we want to follow his will for our lives. Then we look hard at the Bible to see what it says about our situation. We don't argue about what *I* want or *he* wants. Sometimes we can't agree on what *God* wants, but we leave it up to

God to show us through the Bible or through the other ways he can guide us, like prayer and wise Christian counsel."

Carl adds one last point. "When I became a Christian, this was all a mystery to me. But it's not a mystery anymore. It's all about having a close relationship with Christ and with my wife, loving each of them with all my heart."

ROADBLOCKS TO SPIRITUAL INTIMACY

Maybe your response is, "That's a wonderful story, but I can't see it happening in our marriage. I already have a hard time maintaining a spiritual focus in my own life, let alone worrying about developing spiritual intimacy with my spouse. How can I cram more into life?" Or maybe you're saying, "My spouse just isn't interested in spiritual things. What can I do?"

Barb will walk you through three major hurdles to spiritual intimacy and how we can overcome them.

"I don't have time for spiritual things. We have more pressing issues right now." If I walked out to the garage tomorrow morning and found that my car wouldn't start, I would investigate. (Actually, I would ask Gary to investigate!) He would first check to see if the battery had somehow drained overnight. He would double-check that the car had adequate fuel. But the problem might run deeper than the obvious. There is no substitute for keeping your battery charged and putting gas into the tank, but sometimes the engine needs an overhaul. Surface fixes won't do the job.

That's the situation with our lives. Smaller concerns are pressing and urgent, but none is as important as developing spiritual intimacy. Even if your life is in shambles, the most important thing you can do is make room for God.

"I'm afraid God will expect more than we can do." That's a fear many of us experience whenever we contemplate going deeper

with God. It's the fear that God will force you to give up something you like or lead you down a painful path. Yes, giving yourselves to God often involves making hard choices regarding your activities and possessions. But remember that his purpose is to "give life in all its fullness" (John 10:10). And you can trust him to do that as he builds you into a couple who lives close to him.

"My spouse isn't interested in spiritual matters." If your spouse is struggling with this whole area, pray for him or her. Share your own convictions if your spouse will listen, and then let God work in his or her heart. God will gradually open your husband's spiritual eyes as you obey the scriptural command to win him by a "gentle and quiet spirit" (1 Peter 3:4). Or God will work in your wife's heart as you "treat her with understanding" (1 Peter 3:7). You can be God's instrument in reaching your spouse. But you must let God do it in his good time.

The truth is, the only person you can change is you. So let God do his work in you. Open your heart to him, and continue to pursue a faithful, obedient relationship with him, giving him your whole heart, soul, and mind. At the same time, pray faithfully for your spouse. You might even want to ask some of your trusted friends and prayer partners to pray with you that God will work in your spouse's life. Then be patient. Don't give up, ever.

Back in the early days of our marriage, both Gary and I were growing in our faith—with a lot of maturing yet to do. I remember a conflict that had spiritual implications. One summer our house badly needed painting. Gary decided that since he couldn't paint during the week because of work, he would stay home from church for four Sundays and paint one side of the house each week.

I didn't think that was a good idea. I was excited about going to church and didn't want to miss out. And I was afraid that four weeks away from church would have a negative effect on Gary's growth and on our marriage. I could have nagged, complained, or even enabled his behavior by staying home with him. But I decided to surrender the issue to God, keep up my own relationship with God, and let God handle Gary. So I went to church that month while my husband painted the house.

It turned out to be a pivotal time in Gary's growth. After missing church four weeks in a row, he realized more than ever the value of the worship, teaching, and fellowship he missed. When I got out of the way, God, in his time, had his way with Gary.

GETTING STARTED ON YOUR SPIRITUAL JOURNEY TOGETHER

Maybe you are looking at the possibilities more than the roadblocks. "I like what you're talking about," you say, "but I don't know where to start." That's an attitude Gary and I enjoy working with. It's the place we all find ourselves at some point.

How do we go deeper with God? How do we make a spiritual connection with our spouses? Let us coach you on some tips for getting started on your spiritual journey.

As an accountant in a rapidly expanding business, Denise is exhausted most of the time. She carries a laptop full of work home each night and continues to answer e-mail and phone calls late into the evening from clients across the country. Her job was once enjoyable and challenging. Now she feels like quitting. But she can't, because Denise and her husband, Ken, need the double income.

Ken knows that Denise's needs right now run deeper than what he can meet himself. He knows she is making the best of a difficult situation at work, but she has been ignoring her own spiritual needs. When Ken suggests that she join a Monday evening Bible study for working moms, Denise scoffs. Then Ken explains that he will clear his own schedule on Monday evenings so he can take care of the kids. Denise deeply appreciates his sacrifice and accepts his offer. Within a few days she has notified key clients that she won't be available on Monday evenings. With her husband's loving assistance, Denise finally gets some much-needed soul nourishment.

You and your spouse need to be growing spiritually. And while you are not ultimately responsible for your husband's or wife's growth, you can help or hinder that growth in significant ways. Encourage each other into settings where you can grow in your relationship with Christ: Bible studies, prayer groups, accountability groups, conferences. And then do what you can— such as providing child care—to allow your spouse to take advantage of these opportunities.

Here are a number of specific ways to encourage spiritual intimacy and celebrating love in your home:

Encourage personal time in prayer and Bible study. One time Gary opened the door to our walk-in closet and found me there in the dark, on my knees. I was a bit surprised but not any more than he was! That's when Gary discovered that I truly do have a "prayer closet" and how precious that time is to my spiritual growth. If I neglect prayer or focus on my worries instead of praying about them, my heart can quickly become hard. So one way I commune with God is by going into a secluded place to pray. Now that Gary knows how vital this private prayer time is for me, he does everything he can to make sure nothing interferes with it.

So what do you pray for when you get alone with God? Wives, pray for your husband; pray daily that God would give him wisdom, strength, knowledge, and power to overcome temptation. Pray for areas where he needs help and guidance. Pray for areas where you disagree, and ask God to reveal his plan to both of you.

Husbands, pray for God's help. Ask God to reveal ways you can create more meaning and value in your wife's life. Earnestly seek God's insight and leadership as you learn new ways to express your love to her. Tell her you are praying for her, and encourage her by sharing what you are learning.

Each of you should study the Bible daily for yourself. But you can double your insight by sharing what you learn with your spouse. You may both want to use something like *The One Year Bible* (Tyndale House), which divides the Bible into 365 daily readings. When you're each reading the same passage each day, you can talk about what you learned from it. Or you can read the same devotional book or study guide in your individual devotional time, sharing insights with each other at another time. Gary and I recommend using *Night Light: A Devotional for Couples,* written by Dr. James and Shirley Dobson.

Encourage participation in fellowship and worship. Beth and Steve had always been committed to regular Sunday church attendance. They loved to meet with their Christian friends, to worship, and to hear the teaching. When Steve's schedule changed, he was forced to work some weekends. Even though Beth preferred going to church on Sunday, she understood Steve's need for flexibility in getting to church. She held her husband accountable for his need for active involvement in church. Some weeks they were able to worship together on Sunday mornings. Other weeks they attended the Thursday night service. And when Steve's schedule kept him from all services, Beth gently encouraged Steve to attend an early morning men's study on Wednesdays.

Weekly involvement with a body of believers is what Christian community is all about. You and your spouse need to have regular contact with people whom you can know and who can know you. Hebrews 10:25 says: "Let us not neglect our meeting together, as some people do, but encourage and warn each other." Make sure you and your spouse stay involved, even if it requires some creative scheduling.

Encourage expression of spiritual gifts. Thad found great fulfillment in being part of a ministry that installed and maintained a tiny-tot playground at church. His wife, Lisa, wasn't so mechanically inclined, but she enjoyed teaching Sunday school for the toddler's class. Thad was no teacher, but he and Lisa had a ball leading singing and games together for the little ones. They were committed to using their gifts individually when needed and together whenever possible.

The gifts of the Spirit are the special abilities God gives all believers to do his work in the world (see 1 Corinthians 12 and 14; Romans 12:4-8; and Ephesians 4:11-16). God has chosen to involve us in the building of his kingdom. "We are God's masterpiece. He has created us anew in Christ Jesus, so that we can do the good things he planned for us long ago" (Ephesians 2:10). Each of us should use our unique gifts for the kingdom of God, and we should encourage our spouses to do the same.

It's great fun to discover a shared ministry. You may not be drawn to the same interest, but if you find a place where you and your spouse can minister as a team, you will experience wonderful spiritual harmony.

TIPS FOR GROWING SPIRITUALLY TOGETHER

Spiritual growth is the job of both husband and wife as individuals. But spiritual intimacy happens when you experience God together and share what you have learned. Here are some ideas Gary and I recommend for growing spiritually as a couple:

1. *Read the Bible.* Schedule daily times to read God's Word. Make an appointment with God, and keep it.

2. *Share the Word.* Talk together about what God is teaching you.

3. *Pray aloud together.* You can't get any more intimate than praying together as a couple. If you haven't prayed with your spouse before, start slowly—but start today.

4. *Hold hands and pray.* Joining your hands as well as your hearts and voices as you pray is a great way to draw close.

5. *Study together.* Do a Bible study or devotional book together, or work through a study independently and then discuss it together.

6. *Make Sundays relaxed.* Plan ahead so that going to church is not a hectic event. Replace the race to church with relaxation and heart preparation. If you have children, share the responsibility for getting them ready and in their classes before you sit down for worship.

7. *Be accountable to each other.* Your spiritual relationship will grow deep if you allow yourselves to share and receive correction from each other.

8. *Encourage accountability to others.* Help each other find an accountability group—men for him, women for her—that will serve as a sounding board and spiritual support. Choose groups that will ultimately strengthen your commitment to each other, not weaken it.

9. *Spend time with other couples.* Choose wisely. Link up with couples who are intent on developing strong marriages and have boundaries.

10. *Find mentors.* Ask a mature Christian couple with a healthy marriage to mentor you as a couple.

11. *Speak up.* When you see your spouse take steps of spiritual growth, compliment him or her about it. Cheer your spouse on to more of the same.

12. *Seek God's will for your life.* Start by telling God that you want to do life his way. Read Scripture, and heed the

advice of more mature Christians in discovering what it means to live out God's will.

13. *Teach your children to follow God.* One of the greatest responsibilities of your shared commitment to Christ is passing on your faith to your children. Strategize together about how to make faith vital for each of them, and act on your plans.

14. *Count your blessings.* Set aside time to thank God for everything he has done for you.

Whatever ways you find to build spiritual intimacy, don't ever stop doing them. One of the greatest gifts you can give your lifelong partner is a lifelong commitment to spiritual growth.

But don't put off getting started. As Gary will share, ignoring or delaying your spiritual journey together does not work in favor of celebrating love.

START NOW

Many Christian couples Barb and I talk to wish they had a deeper spiritual life together. They know how important it is, but somehow they just never get around to making it happen. Their intentions are good, but their excuses take precedence. Just think how powerfully God could work in your marriage if you would allow him to get started.

You can learn from the experience of Alex and Karla, who recently visited my office for counseling. Alex had broken his wife's heart—again. He had distanced himself from her and the kids, worked too many hours, and disconnected from her and the Lord. He had caved in to temptations. Karla had responded with bitterness that was demoralizing Alex and exacerbating the problem. Trust had broken down. Neither of them was seeking the Lord, and their relationship was in danger.

Karla pleaded, "Gary, I don't know how to get through to him. I want our marriage to be rich in Christ. I miss the quiet times with Alex, the prayer times we used to experience. They are distant memories now. Help!"

I saw the couple five times and tried to break through some of the pain. Nothing seemed to click. When they arrived for their sixth appointment, I could tell right away that something had really changed. Alex was more responsive. Karla was more gentle. I looked at them and said, "What happened? You two look like completely different people!" They shared their story.

"Gary," Alex began, "last week at work I was so angry with Karla that I decided to write a letter to you. It was five pages long. I pointed out everything she had done to hurt me recently. I was just plain hot. I ragged on her sloppy housekeeping. I blasted her coolness in the bedroom. I hammered on her flagrant money mismanagement. I went on and on.

"I felt a little better after getting all that off my chest, so I decided to write a letter to Karla. I had the pen in hand, ready to pour out all the poison I had written in my letter to you. Then a lightning bolt hit me. I just thought, *What am I doing? I want so much for my wife to connect to me. I want so much to experience God the way I used to. I want so much for our two kids to grow up in a healthy Christian home, and here I am just messing it up.* It's as if my desire to be connected to Karla is somehow blocked by my not connecting to God first. I hadn't prayed. I hadn't read the Bible. I was just playing church on Sundays. I realized in that moment that as I confessed my hard-heartedness toward God and truly sensed his forgiveness, I could then deal with my hard heart toward Karla. Just like I have heard you say, Gary, a marriage really is a marriage of three."

As I listened to Alex pour out his heart, Karla was captivated by his words. She was looking at him as if he had just conquered Mount Everest. In a way, he had.

"Instead of lambasting her," Alex continued, "I started to pour out my hurt in that letter. I confessed to her that I wasn't the man I knew she needed me to be. I asked her to forgive me. I prayed for another chance from God and from her. I prayed for another opportunity to connect to my wife and kids. I prayed that Karla would really listen to me.

"When I got home, I read Karla the letter. Gary, it was unbelievable. She started to cry and open her heart to me. We just sat on our sofa holding each other. Our two-year-old son came up to us and patted us both on the backs. It was as if I had my family back. And I don't ever want to lose my wife again."

What happened to this family? Alex and Karla reconnected, but not before Alex reconnected with God, experiencing his grace and mercy. As the Lord convicted his heart and as Alex restored his vertical relationship with God, the horizontal relationship with his wife opened up again. As Karla saw the work God was doing in her husband's life, it bolstered her trust in God to restore their relationship. She still had to rebuild her trust in Alex. But her trust in God allowed her to take the first steps to reconnect with her husband.

Alex and Karla still have some distance to travel in rebuilding their marriage, but they are on the right path. Their two hard hearts, broken before Christ, are healing through his power. The celebration is returning to their relationship. They are feeling cherished and captivated once again.

Karla is experiencing being Alex's "one and only." They are reveling in their oneness with God and each other. She is experiencing a captivating love that is endearing them to each other. Theirs is becoming a marriage that will not only go the distance but also experience a cherishing and captivating love along the way.

This couple is discovering the joy and fulfillment of spiritual intimacy. The same discovery—or rediscovery—awaits you. And there is no better time than now to start on the journey.

A SPECIAL NOTE ABOUT THE JOURNEY

Maybe you have never built into your relationship the discipline of following God together. Or maybe the coals of your marriage could use some stoking. Whatever the case, we all need to keep our relationship fresh through celebrating love. The key is to create a pattern of consistency and constancy in your love life. We plan to create a celebrating love book that will help you establish and reinforce healthy patterns that will not only bring immediate blessing to your relationship but also divorce-proof your marriage.

Part Seven

RENEWING LOVE

Renewing love refreshes and supports the

marriage bond

and helps spouses feel

confident and rooted

fourteen

A LOVE THAT
IS FRESH DAY
AFTER DAY

*O*ne of the favorite parts of the radio call-in broadcast that Barb and I do is meeting and talking with couples who have been married fifty years or more. In fact, we regularly invite golden-anniversary couples to join us on the program just to drink in their wisdom. We can't help but admire love that has endured a lifetime.

We have searched for clues as to why these marriages have remained strong through the years while others have crumbled. One of the things we ask the couples who have been married for five decades is this: "What do you have to say to those of us who aren't as far along on the journey? What works? How have you done it?" Here are the kinds of things we hear:

"Gary and Barb, we take time daily to listen to each other and learn what the other has experienced that day."

"We love to spend time with each other. We just enjoy being each other's best friend."

"It's a little embarrassing to say on radio, but Barney taught me a long time ago that when I meet his sexual needs, he feels valued. When I listen to him and encourage him, he feels respected. When he prays with me, I feel so safe. When I spend time with him, he makes me feel like a million bucks!"

"Mildred reminds me often that my words of belief in her are the only words—next to God's—she really needs to hear. So I learned to speak up. Yes, we have been married fifty-four years, and I think the marriage is going to take, don't you, Barb and Gary?"

At the other end of the marriage timeline from the golden anniversary couples are people like our daughter and son-in-law. It seems like only yesterday that Barb and I picked up Sarah and Scott at the airport after their honeymoon. We were overjoyed to hear Sarah say from the backseat, "Oh, we're so happily married." They had that just-married sparkle about them. Do you remember it? Do you recall how hard you worked day in, day out to keep love alive and growing?

So where are you now? You may be at the beginning of your marriage or near its end. You may have babies on your hip or teenagers in your hair. Or perhaps you are alone together in an empty nest. Will your marriage flourish to the end, "till death do us part"? Will the two of you still be glowing on your golden anniversary? What is your plan to keep your relationship fresh, vital, and fulfilling for the long haul?

Wherever you are in your marriage journey, you have the opportunity each day to strengthen your relationship with the man or woman with whom you are spending the rest of your life. Your investment in a lifetime marriage is an investment in a divorce-proof marriage.

LOVE THAT GOES THE DISTANCE

Barb and I were twenty-one and twenty-three respectively when we got married. At that young age we had no way to wrap our minds around the meaning of a lifelong relationship. Yes, we had watched our parents' love sustain them for decades. But only after logging twenty-seven-plus years together have we gained enough firsthand experience to understand what a lifetime commitment means.

We have discovered that married love is more like a potted plant than cut flowers. The stunning brilliance of a bouquet of cut flowers lasts for only a few days. Then the blossoms dry up and crumble. A blooming plant lasts much longer. The flowers can blossom again and again. What we all need is a love that allows our relationship to grow continually and blossom repeatedly. We need a dimension of love that refreshes and supports our bond as a married couple, one that helps each partner feel deeply confident and rooted in the relationship.

Barb and I call this facet of love *renewing love.* Renewing love keeps the marriage commitment alive. It continually refreshes the solemn, heartfelt pledge of undying love we made to each other before God, our families, and our friends.

What was that commitment about, really? It may seem like a silly question, but we know plenty of people who assume that their marriage commitment was simply about sexual fidelity or not ever getting divorced. But the marriage commitment is so much more than that. The real heart of renewing love is a commitment to keep growing together. It's an ongoing promise to love to the utmost of your ability— never to leave. It's a commitment sealed by the unbreakable bond God formed between you and your spouse when you made that one-of-a-kind promise. It's a living commitment powered by God.

Renewing love refreshes and supports that unbreakable bond and helps you and your spouse feel confident and rooted.

Look at some of the profound benefits you will enjoy. Renewing love

- provides an environment in which the deepest level of human trust can form;
- supplies the *security* that allows *intimacy* to fully develop;
- protects you and your spouse from the fear of broken promises;
- helps you rediscover the roots of your relationship and stay vitally attached to the love of your life;
- provides *security for the children* raised in your home; and
- undergirds all the other divorce-proofing loves and allows them to flourish.

WAYS TO NURTURE RENEWING LOVE

We all know couples who fully intended to keep the promises they uttered on their wedding day but whose marriages have dried up and died. They neglected the living bond between husband and wife, a bond that must be tended daily and enthusiastically. They didn't refresh and renew their love, so when trouble developed, their marriage could not endure. It came up by the roots.

Barb and I want to share with you five keys to renewing love, specific ways you can refresh and support your marriage commitment.

Decide to Pursue the Dream

We hope you realize that the dream marriage we described at the beginning of this book isn't a mirage. It's a real place on the marriage map—just as real as disappointment, distance, disconnect, discord, and emotional divorce.

But remember: When we talk about the dream marriage, we are not talking about a marriage in which we love each other perfectly and never wound each other. We're not saying that you will be immune to difficult circumstances or that you won't have to work at intimacy and communication. The dream describes the *quality of your relationship* to each other, not the *quality of your circumstances*. As you put into practice the kinds of love that divorce-proof your marriage, you can get back to the dream and have a vibrant marriage even in the midst of stress and struggles. Working hard on your relationship is the normal state of a healthy marriage, even when you're living the dream!

The dream is the kind of marriage we were all hoping for when we committed our lives to each other at the altar. It is a marriage in which husband and wife are diligent to forgive each other; meet each other's needs; conquer difficulties together; guard each other from threats and temptations; enjoy ongoing emotional, physical, and spiritual closeness; and commit to keeping the marriage fresh and alive.

God wants this kind of marriage for you even more than you do. And he has the resources to get you there. But there's a prerequisite: You have to decide that you will pursue the dream. If you want your marriage bond to grow strong, it won't happen by accident. If you want your union to be everything it can be, you can't leave it to chance. We believe that without a basic commitment to pursue the best for your marriage, your efforts to implement the six loves we have talked about in this book will fail. The first step of renewing love is to decide in your heart that you want to pursue the dream. It takes commitment to propel you toward the dream and the qualities that will make your relationship flourish.

Commit to Christ

Barb and I are doing our best to equip churches and couples to divorce-proof their marriages. We urge you and your spouse to settle for nothing less than God's best in your relationship. This is not our idea; divorce-proof marriages are God's idea. These high standards for marriage—the six facets of love we have presented— are rooted in Scripture. So the attitude you must have as you seek renewing love in your marriage is the same attitude of humility and service that Jesus had (see Philippians 2:1-11).

Once you commit to pursue God's dream for your marriage, you need to draw on his power to make it happen. Your commitment to pursue the dream starts with a commitment to Christ. Only by staying connected to Christ will you find the resources for the journey God has for you. Jesus said, "I am the vine; you are the branches. Those who remain in me, and I in them, will produce much fruit. For apart from me you can do nothing" (John 15:5). This is as true for our marriages as for our individual lives of service to God. We need Jesus.

But beware: The enemy will do whatever he can to lure you away from the life-giving sustenance that is yours through your connection to Christ. As one couple discovered, the disconnect is not always the result of flagrant disobedience or rebellion. The enemy can lure you away from your dependency on Christ in very subtle ways.

When Paul and Tasha moved to the West Coast for Paul's new job, they enjoyed visiting a number of large, high-profile churches. Yet every Sunday they felt like two lonely spectators among the throngs. After months of church shopping, they still hadn't found a place where they thought they fit. So the couple decided to take a break from the teaching and fellowship that had nurtured their relationship up to that point. Paul had been in church every Sunday of his life. Missing a few Sundays surely wouldn't hurt. And Tasha thought it would be great to sleep in on Sunday and head to the beach by noon. Because they were away from family and friends, they had no one to check up on them and lay a guilt trip on them for skipping church.

The couple soon realized that their decision was not the best for their marriage. "After a few months of sleeping in," Tasha explains, "we noticed that our spiritual passion was sliding away. We seemed never to have time to pray or to share any spiritual insight with each other. But what really prompted us to take notice was that we started fighting over all sorts of things. We were being selfish in ways we had been giving before.

"Looking back at that time, Paul and I feel as if we missed a turn in our lives and drove off the road. God had led us to our new home, but we neglected to ask him where *he* wanted us to attend church. As soon as Paul and I asked God where we should go, we were able to find a church that suited us. We called it 'the little church under the freeway.' The people there welcomed us. They even remembered us from the first time we visited. We felt surrounded by caring people for the first time since we moved west, and once we got a fresh dose of God's love for us, we had more love for each other. We were surprised at how much a simple step like making a connection with a group of Christians could get our marriage back on track."

God doesn't intend a commitment to him to be a chore. Sticking close to him is simply his primary way of empowering your commitment to each other.

Barb had an experience that introduces another key to building a foundation of renewing love in your marriage. She'll share it with you.

Enter Your Spouse's World

I was having lunch with some of my female friends when one of the women started complaining that her husband played golf far too much.

"Why don't you go with him?" I asked.

"I can't stand to golf!" my friend exclaimed.

"But you love your husband, Stacey. Go out and play with him. Join him. Enter into his world."

At first she brushed me off, but by the end of our lunch she decided to sign up for a beginners' golf class. She didn't tell her husband about the class because she wanted to surprise him.

Several weeks later Stacey showed up on the golf course when her husband was scheduled to play. He was a bit puzzled, but when she announced that she was part of his foursome, he was delighted. Since then they have enjoyed playing many rounds of golf together, and they even have a standing date for an evening game each week during the summer months.

When husbands and wives commit to entering each other's worlds, they are often in for a real eye-opener. Your spouse may live in a world you seldom explore. Getting firsthand experience in his or her interests and activities—ranging from job to hobbies to favorite books and TV programs to family members and friends—can be a rich source of understanding for you. Entering your spouse's world is a great way to renew your bond of love.

Women, you don't have to be good at everything your husband does, and you don't have to be as enthusiastic about his interests as other guys are. But if you want to bond with your husband deeply, you need to validate his interests and join in some of his activities. If he bowls, go along with him sometimes to watch, cheer him on, or roll a few strikes—or gutter balls— on the lane next to his. If he watches *Monday Night Football* religiously, microwave a bowl of popcorn and watch with him. If he putters in the garage, spend some time there watching, asking questions, and handing him tools.

The same holds true for men. Husbands, open your eyes to the experiences that make up your wife's world. Most women lead interesting and busy lives. Have you ever noticed the effort, the planning, and the intricacy that goes into your wife's daily schedule? Whether her days revolve around a job or caring for the kids or juggling both, spend a day or two in her shoes every month or so. What can you do with her or for her so she can enjoy some downtime and make room for recreation each day?

We're not suggesting that you force your way into your husband's golf foursome or that you barge in on your wife's book club. Look for fun things the two of you can do together. Get with your spouse in his or her world. Take him to the pro shop to pick out his birthday present six months early. Go with her to the gift store to discover her favorite fragrances. Don't just hand your spouse a gift certificate. Get in his or her world and get the gift yourself!

You can also explore the more serious facets of your spouse's life. How much do you know about your partner's job, whether inside or outside the home? If it's appropriate, visit his or her work site. Get to know the people your husband or wife interacts with forty or more hours a week. If you can't visit the work site, flip through trade publications to learn more about the job. Attend a business conference or trade show together. If one of you stays home, it's only fair for the other partner to take that job for a day now and then. Learn the scheduling complexities, the social world that the stay-at-home spouse relates to.

You can also enter your spouse's world by asking questions: "What did you do today at work [home]?" "How did things go?" "What victories did you have?" "What were your major struggles?" "How did you handle them?" "What one thing do you wish you could change about today?"

The more time and energy you invest in experiencing your spouse's world, the stronger the bond between you will be.

Keep Cheering Each Other On

Gary is my number one cheerleader, and I am his. There are two things to understand about being a cheerleader. First, support from the sidelines can turn a game around. Knowing that someone has confidence in you when you no longer believe in yourself is an incredibly powerful motivator. Second, cheerleaders always stick around. Unlike the fans, who file out of the stadium early when the game appears to be lost, the cheerleaders stay to the end. And they always show up for the next game, even if the home team got walloped the last time.

It is hard to imagine anything more encouraging than your husband or wife cheering you on while the battles of life rage around you. Sometimes your spouse can even motivate others around you to join in. Broadway and screen actress Celeste Holm once said, "We live by encouragement and die without it. Slowly, sadly, and angrily." Her words are never more true than in a marriage. It saddens Gary and me that authentic encouragement is rare in many homes today. Both men and women need encouragement. When we surveyed men and women on their top needs in marriage, we found that *both* men and women ranked encouragement as their number four need.

Because men and women are different, your encouragement for each other will take different forms. Notice how similar needs are fulfilled differently between husbands and wives.

HUSBANDS NEED	WIVES NEED
1. A card once or twice a year to tell them they are loved	1. Daily doses of "I love you" (cards and flowers work well too!)
2. An evening out every so often	2. One evening every week with just the two of you
3. A golfing (or sailing, or bowling) buddy	3. A female friend in whom she can confide
4. A new challenge every five years to keep life interesting	4. Frequent time-outs from her routine to recharge her battery
5. A slap on the back from the guys on the basketball court	5. Supportive hugs from her female friends

One of the most refreshing and renewing things you can do for your marriage is to offer continual support to your spouse. That's the way you stir up team spirit. When Gary and I run into a problem, it's never me against Gary or Gary against me; it's both of us against the problem. Sure, strife and anger sometimes flare up in our home, just as they do in yours. Yet Gary and I agree that for the sake of our marriage we will humble ourselves and honor each other through every word we say to each other.

Husbands, complaining and arguing can be devastating to a woman. When you speak harsh words to your wife, it's as if you are throwing stones at her. Wives, when you don't support and encourage your husband, it's as if you are jeering at him instead of cheering for him.

You will also be a great source of encouragement and support when your spouse hears you praying aloud for him or her. For example, how would you feel if your spouse held your hands over the breakfast table and prayed, "Dear Lord, help me to be the most loving and supportive wife [husband] I can be today. Help me to love my husband [wife] as you love both of us. Change my heart and correct my faults where I am wrong. And bless my husband [wife] with a joyful, fulfilling day."

How encouraging is it to know that your spouse cares enough to invoke God's best for you? How blessed do you feel knowing that your spouse is asking God to change him or her to be the best possible partner? You can provide that kind of daily encouragement as you pray together for one another.

Since Gary and I work together as well as live together, we deal with potential conflict situations all day long. You can't imagine how many couples have told us that they couldn't work with their spouses. But we wouldn't trade our situation for anything, even though we do have our rough spots.

One day after a round of heated debate and decision making

at the office, one of our newer staff members pulled me aside. She was taken aback by how Gary and I handled the situation on which we didn't agree. "Even when you're in conflict," she said, "you honor each other."

That's what being your spouse's cheerleader is all about. That's what it means to be on the same team, urging each other on toward a common goal. We need to be able to face off on important issues, but we must commit to love, honor, and cherish each other in the process. Help your spouse know that he or she is more important to you than any issue and that your relationship is never at risk, even when you argue. Always be encouraging and supportive. It will renew the bond of love between you.

We have one more tip for renewing love. Gary will share the importance of hanging in there when other couples are bailing out.

Commit to Keeping Your Covenant

Some people have gotten married in unusual ceremonies. If you look under "unusual weddings" on the Web, you'll discover that a couple can get married riding on horseback, sailing aboard a cruise ship, bungee jumping, sky diving, scuba diving, flying in a helicopter, paddling in a canoe, soaking in a hot tub, perching atop a speedway winner's stand, floating in a hot-air balloon, or galloping into a ghost town. A woman who calls herself Reverend Karyl "I'll Marry Anybody" Miller offers "sweet, lighthearted personalized ceremonies" ranging from "way-cool cheapo weddings" to "your-daddy's-rich weddings." You can get "linked at a rink" or "tie the knot on a yacht." She'll even do the ceremony on a roller coaster "as long as you provide an airsickness bag."

Although Barb and I have nothing against creative, personally meaningful ceremonies, we suspect that for the couple who gets married while parachuting, the real significance of marriage might hit the ground without a chute.

Sadly, the undoing of marriages is often treated just as casually as a novelty wedding. We live in the land of prenuptial agreements and no-fault divorce. Having talked with thousands of couples, Barb and I have found that divorce is contagious, kind of like the flu or a cold. When couples come to us and announce that they are getting a divorce, the first question we often ask is, "Who else do you know is getting divorced?" Often it's a close friend or relative of the person. A divorce creates an atmosphere of acceptability for others around that couple to abandon their marriage as well.

At the heart of renewing love is the continually reaffirmed commitment to the permanency of marriage—to love to the utmost of your ability and never to leave. This commitment is much more solemn than most people understand. It's so far beyond a run-of-the-mill commitment that we need a different word for it. It's a *covenant*. That's a term we don't use much anymore. A covenant is a binding, unbreakable agreement between two people.

You can understand the significance of the term when you consider its usage in the Bible. God made a covenant with Abraham when he promised to make his descendants a mighty people. God made a covenant with Moses and the Israelites when he gave them the Ten Commandments. God made a covenant with David when he swore that his throne would last forever. God made a covenant with us when Christ died for our sins and opened our way to God through faith in him.

These biblical covenants are serious, permanent, and irrevocable. Your marriage is also a covenant, and it should be regarded just as solemnly. God's covenant of grace moved Jesus Christ willingly and unflinchingly to the cross. Your marriage covenant should move you to any lengths necessary to love, honor, and cherish your spouse for life.

Living out your covenant of marriage daily is what brings

a sense of confidence and rootedness to your relationship. You don't need to wonder whether or not you will stay together; the decision has already been made. And when you affirm that decision day by day through loving service and commitment, even during the tough times, you will feel confident and rooted in your unbreakable bond.

Hudson Taylor, the great missionary to China, once said that when stress comes down on a relationship, it either drives a wedge between two people, pushing them into isolation, or it comes down at their sides, pushing them closer together. When we are in a covenant relationship, we allow no room for stress to divide us. It can only push us closer together. Such a commitment gives us the ability to say confidently, "We're going to persevere. We're going to make it. We're going to paddle upstream in a culture that doesn't applaud commitment. We have a love that would say 'I do' all over again."

DIVORCE IS NOT AN OPTION

Husband and wife, the very survival of your marriage depends on your recognizing the scope of the covenant you made on your wedding day. Renewing love says with absolute conviction, "Divorce is not an option. We are married for life." Without this firm pledge to God and to each other, your marriage is vulnerable to defeat from every angle. But when you take a stand on your lifetime promise, your marriage can survive anything.

Here is what one of our conference participants wrote to us about the permanence of marriage:

> *My husband and I attended an "I Still Do" conference where you spoke. We have been married for eight years, and we've had our normal ups and downs, like any couple. But our first*

year or so was extremely difficult. Although I was filled with
joy all through our engagement and wedding, from the
moment I stepped out of the church to go on our honeymoon,
I became increasingly disillusioned with married life.

From that very day, a thought was planted in my head that
I allowed to remain—the thought that we would probably
get a divorce someday. Now, my parents never divorced, and
neither did my husband's parents. But my marriage never
seemed "right" to me. We just weren't meant for each other. I
felt we had both made an awful mistake (and I'm sure he felt
that way too). Each of us thought we'd married a monster.

By God's grace, we made it through those first few years.
But thoughts of divorce still had a foothold in me. However,
at the same time God was beginning to teach me something
I'd never realized or understood before: our marriage was not
a mistake. I was married to the right person. I began to change
my attitude to be the wife God wants me to be.

At the conference someone said that marriage is for life. I
realized then that I had never rejected that little thought of
divorce in my mind. But, praise God, I have now made a
conscious choice. My husband is my husband for life. I am
committed to him as long as I live. He is God's perfect gift to me.

We need to forever banish the idea of divorce from our
thinking. Our marriages are only safely divorce-proof when we
commit to never using the "d word"—*divorce*. Before we can ever
know the deep security and confidence God intends for us to
enjoy as a couple, we need to be certain in our heart of hearts
that our relationship is rooted in a love that will never give up.

Renewing your commitment to your spouse is so essential to
divorce-proofing your marriage that we want to explain in the
next chapter how you and your spouse can keep your commitment
in the forefront of your minds and at the center of your marriage.

fifteen

NURTURING
A LIFETIME
MARRIAGE

*W*hen Mike and Cheryl, whose story we shared in the opening chapters of this book, celebrated the twentieth anniversary of their remarriage, the crowd around them knew that this husband and wife had come full circle. When they had been divorced twenty-three years earlier, the young couple saw no chance of reconciliation. The anger and abusive words that had passed between them, and the sense of certainty that these hurtful patterns would never change, drove them apart. The animosity and pain were so great that for seven months after the divorce, they would not even speak to each other except for brief exchanges as they handed off their young son.

But two decades later, Mike and Cheryl stood together before hundreds of people in the rotunda of the Iowa state capitol building. Their special anniversary happened to fall on the Day of Marriage and Family proclaimed by the governor of Iowa. The crowd of people were attentive as Mike and Cheryl shared their story and then signed a covenant marriage agreement—a restatement of their vows that recognized the permanence of the God-designed bond of marriage.

Mike and Cheryl Wells have indeed come full circle. Instead of delivering milk, Mike is now an executive in the family business, the $700 million Wells Blue Bunny Corporation, makers of Wells Blue Bunny Ice Cream. The couple's painful past is gone, replaced by forgiveness, unselfishness, and unwavering commitment. Mike and Cheryl have four children now, and they can't believe how awesome their marriage is. They see each day as a beginning, another step on the journey. And their story of rebuilding a marriage from the charred ruins of their divorce is making a difference in marriages across the country.

When they were divorced, Mike and Cheryl honestly thought they could escape each other. Then they came face-to-face with a life-changing reality. Their marriage—the first one—had knit them together in a sacred bond. "From the day of the divorce, I was the most miserable person in the world," Mike says. "The night the divorce was final, I went out drinking with the guys. Someone came up to me and said, 'Wow! You must feel great. You're finally divorced.' I told him that I had never felt more empty in my entire life. Part of me had been taken away. Part of me was missing."

Mike thought that pulling away from Cheryl would make everything okay. Although the legal papers said they were no longer one, they could not sever the emotional bond that had formed between them. For them, divorce made them feel as if an arm or a leg had been ripped off.

Mike and Cheryl did not understand at the time that when they uttered their first "I do," it was a lifetime promise. God had bonded them to one another on the basis of their commitment, and he wanted them back together. He wasn't going to let them go without a fight, even after the divorce!

This is our message to you: No matter where you are on the

marriage map—even if you are languishing in emotional divorce, even if you have initiated separation and legal divorce—good things are possible because a bond exists between you, and God will not let you ignore it. He created the marriage bond—that solemn covenant—to be unbreakable. Renewing love keeps it that way, helping you and your spouse feel confident and rooted in each other's love.

MARRIAGE IS FOR LIFE

God is serious about the covenant you made on your wedding day. It's clear that he intends marriage to be a lifelong commitment.

Recognizing the pain of shattered relationships, God counsels us in the strongest possible language against divorce. In the last book of the Old Testament, the prophet Malachi wrote:

> You cry out, "Why has the Lord abandoned us?" I'll tell you why! Because the Lord witnessed the vows you and your wife made to each other on your wedding day when you were young. But you have been disloyal to her, though she remained your faithful companion, the wife of your marriage vows. Didn't the Lord make you one with your wife? In body and spirit you are his. And what does he want? Godly children from your union. So guard yourself; remain loyal to the wife of your youth. "For I hate divorce!" says the Lord, the God of Israel. (2:14-16)

In this brief passage, Malachi teaches us a number of core principles for the covenant marriage:

1. God is a witness to the marriage covenant.
2. The marriage covenant is at the top of God's list of concerns for his people.

3. God makes husbands and wives one in body and spirit.
4. God seeks godly offspring.
5. We are to guard ourselves and not break faith with our spouses.
6. God hates divorce.

Do you see why Barb and I are so passionate about divorce-proofing America's marriages? Divorce-proof marriages are God's idea!

God calls us to divorce-proof our marriage not only for our good and his glory but also for the benefit of our children. He desires godly offspring. The benefits of a covenant marriage always spill over and bless our children.

Our daughter Missy was ten years old when a man in our neighborhood left his wife and four boys under the age of twelve. As we passed those boys playing in the street on their bikes, I pulled our car to the curb. I cupped Missy's face in my hands and said, "Missy Rosberg, I'm going to tell you something."

"What, Dad?" she said, wide-eyed.

With my eyes boring into hers, I said forcefully, "I will never, ever, *ever* leave your mother."

Missy smiled. "I know, Dad," she said, "because if you try, I will sew your bodies together so you can't ever pull apart." I think her reply impressed me even more than my proclamation impressed her!

Kids today need to know that marriage is for life. More specifically, your kids need to know that *your* marriage is for life.

We need to divorce-proof our marriages for the sake of the next generation. Don't just tell your kids you are committed for life, *show* them. Demonstrate that your commitment to one another permeates every attitude and action.

In the Malachi passage God didn't just diagnose the problem. He also pointed out the solution; he showed us the way back into the center of his will. "Guard yourself," he said; "remain loyal to the wife of your youth" (v. 15). The New International Version translates "remain loyal" as "do not break faith." This is exactly what we are calling you to do. Be on the alert to anything that could compromise or kill your marriage. Consistently practice forgiving love, serving love, persevering love, guarding love, celebrating love, and renewing love. Never

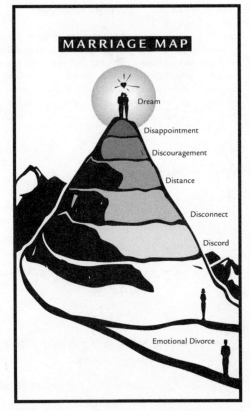

break faith with your husband or wife. That's building a divorce-proof marriage.

THE STATE OF YOUR UNION

Now it's time for a reality check. Barb and I want to ask you a question: How are you doing in the process of building a divorce-proof marriage? Exactly where are you on the marriage map? A major part of the rebuilding process for Mike and Cheryl, for ourselves, and for other couples mentioned in this book was coming to an honest realization of the state of our marriages.

So think carefully about the state of your union.

THE STATE OF OUR MARRIAGE

Review the seven stops on the marriage map as described below, then check one or two that you think most closely describe your marriage today. Realize that your spouse may have a different perspective on the state of your marriage. That being the case, Barb and I recommend that you both complete the exercise independently and then discuss your evaluation together. If it makes you feel too vulnerable to put your responses in the book, make two photocopies of the checklist (see appendix B for a checklist that you can photocopy) and record your responses there.

H   W

DREAM

❑   ❑   We communicate freely and keep no inappropriate secrets.

❑   ❑   We forgive one another and seek forgiveness.

❑   ❑   We seek to discover and meet each other's needs.

❑   ❑   We face and conquer difficult circumstances.

❑   ❑   We guard our marriage against threats and temptations.

❑   ❑   We enjoy ongoing emotional, physical, and spiritual closeness.

❑   ❑   We are committed "till death do us part."

DISAPPOINTMENT

❑   ❑   We have difficulty affirming each other.

❑   ❑   We are surprised by each other's flaws.

❑   ❑   We feel let down by each other's imperfections.

❑   ❑   We cause each other hurt and anger.

❑   ❑   We have conflict over our differences.

❑   ❑   We compare each other to other people.

❑   ❑   We wish we could change things in each other.

H   W

DISCOURAGEMENT

❑ ❑ We often wonder if our marriage is missing something.

❑ ❑ We have reasons to be dissatisfied with our marriage.

❑ ❑ We don't understand each other or meet each other's needs.

❑ ❑ We feel unimportant to each other.

❑ ❑ We are not successful at meeting each other's needs.

❑ ❑ We have difficulty expressing our needs to each other.

❑ ❑ We wonder if we chose the wrong partner.

DISTANCE

❑ ❑ We do not see a letup in our difficulties.

❑ ❑ We do many activities alone, without each other.

❑ ❑ We have given up most expectations for each other.

❑ ❑ We feel little excitement about being married to each other.

❑ ❑ We sometimes feel and act like strangers.

❑ ❑ We keep many of our thoughts and feelings from each other.

❑ ❑ We face a problem that may eventually drive us apart.

H   W

DISCONNECT

❑   ❑   We sometimes feel lonely even when we are together.

❑   ❑   We don't feel an emotional connection to each other.

❑   ❑   We seldom have much to say to each other.

❑   ❑   We often misunderstand and misinterpret each other.

❑   ❑   We direct our attention and activities away from each other.

❑   ❑   We doubt that our marriage can change for the better.

❑   ❑   We are not very interested in each other.

DISCORD

❑   ❑   We think and act negatively toward each other.

❑   ❑   We lash out and hurt each other verbally.

❑   ❑   We wonder what it would be like if we weren't married.

❑   ❑   We wonder what it would be like to be married to someone else.

❑   ❑   We feel that we are at war.

❑   ❑   We lack tenderness and sexual intimacy.

❑   ❑   We cannot hide from others that our marriage is severely strained.

H   W

EMOTIONAL DIVORCE

❏   ❏   We are staying married for some reason other than love.

❏   ❏   We have no hope that our marriage can be better.

❏   ❏   We pretend that our marriage is okay to keep up appearances.

❏   ❏   We only want to protect ourselves from further pain.

❏   ❏   We have separated or have considered separating.

❏   ❏   We are emotionally attached to someone else.

❏   ❏   We have already walked away from our marriage emotionally.

YES, IT CAN HAPPEN TO YOU

Being honest about your starting point—the present condition of your marriage—is the first step to charting a course back to the dream. Yet some couples are startlingly *dis*honest about the true state of their marriage. The sheer number of couples who divorce each year should be sufficient to scare us into honesty. Don't beat yourself up by saying your marriage is worse off than it really is. But also don't be fooled into thinking you are immune to the disappointment, discouragement, distance, disconnect, and discord that can lead to emotional divorce. Renewing love begins by seeing it and telling it as it is.

You may say, "Most of the time I am committed to renewing my marriage, but sometimes I don't feel so committed. What's wrong with a marital 'bad-hair day' once in a while?" Unfortunately, even an occasional lag in commitment can lead to more serious marital trouble. Marriage expert and psychology professor John Gottman notes that a creeping dissatisfaction with marriage can reflect a longer season of marital strain experienced by many couples.

Gottman states that every marriage goes through a cycle of hot and cool phases. The first seven years is often a hot, highly committed phase of marriage during which we really try to learn and practice conflict resolution. At times we butt heads and can even become harsh, but we work through it. In the second seven years, we enter a cool phase where we become distant, suppressing our emotions. The cool phases are potentially deadly. If we fail to address our problems, we can wind up in a marriage with no laughter, no love, and no interest in each other.[1]

Gottman also warns against four indicators of imminent danger in a marriage. His methods accurately predict a 94 percent chance of divorce in marriages in which these four indicators are present:

- *Complaining.* Complaining can be *to* your spouse or *about* your spouse, but your husband or wife gets the message.
- *Defensiveness.* A defensive spouse says, "I'm putting my guard up. You are the enemy, and I don't want you near me."
- *Contempt.* When walls of defensiveness go up, there is anger. And anger can breed contempt. This is the discord we talked about.
- *Withdrawal.* This means emotionally or physically removing yourself from the situation. You've checked out.[2]

Have you ever complained to or about your spouse? Do you see where such an "insignificant" lapse in commitment can lead?

Barb and I are serious about this. If you are not perpetually experiencing renewing love, your marriage is in danger of heading in the wrong direction.

THE ROAD BACK TO THE DREAM

Now here's the good news. Wherever you are on the marriage map today, you can find your way back to the dream by building divorce-proofing elements of love into your marriage one by one. We have shared the stories with you in this book.

- ◆ *Forgiving love* reconciled Mark and Shannon after Mark revealed his addiction to pornography.
- ◆ *Serving love* enabled Robertson McQuilkin to minister to Muriel when she fell victim to Alzheimer's.
- ◆ *Persevering love* preserved Dan and Jeanie after Dan's paralyzing fall in a construction accident.
- ◆ *Guarding love* erected a new wall of protection for Michelle after her affair with a man she met on the Internet.
- ◆ *Celebrating love* brought Carl and Danielle together in spiritual intimacy.
- ◆ *Renewing love* saw Mike and Cheryl renew their commitment to each other and keep it fresh daily.

Where you are in your marriage is important, but where you're headed is even more crucial. So Barb and I want to ask you a few other questions: What will you do to build the various kinds of divorce-proofing love into your marriage? Which kind of love do you most need today to begin divorce-proofing your marriage? Knowing that you can't tackle every problem at once—and that divorce-proofing is a lifelong process anyway—where are you and your spouse going to concentrate your efforts right now?

GETTING BACK TO THE DREAM

Look at the list below, and check the loves that you feel will most effectively bring the growth your marriage needs. Then indicate in the blanks to the right which love you feel deserves the highest priority in your strategy to get back on the road to the dream. Identify your top three priorities. Complete the exercise independently, and then discuss your evaluation together. If it makes you feel too vulnerable to put your responses in the book, make two photocopies of the checklist (see appendix B for a checklist that you can photocopy) and record your responses there.

H   W

❑   ❑   Forgiving love (priority: _____)

❑   ❑   Serving love (priority: _____)

❑   ❑   Persevering love (priority: _____)

❑   ❑   Guarding love (priority: _____)

❑   ❑   Celebrating love (priority: _____)

❑   ❑   Renewing love (priority: _____)

One word of advice: If you want a rock-solid commitment in your marriage, start with renewing love. It will set all the others in motion. You need the divorce-proofing elements of forgiving love, serving love, persevering love, guarding love, and celebrating love to make your marriage last a lifetime. But without a deep commitment to experience—and keep experiencing—these various expressions, you will lack the confidence that your marriage can survive the pressures of twenty-first-century culture.

Love may be a choice, but it is more than a decision of the heart and mind. You must commit your full energy to nurture, feed, and care for your spouse.

You see, God's design is that the person to whom you said "I do" will be the love of your life. Your commitment to that person must be renewed with each passing day so that your love will grow and deepen to a level of intimacy beyond your wildest dreams. This is no fantasy. It is a living reality for those who come to understand the meaning of love and who commit to love this way.

We have referred throughout this book to a collection of workbooks that will help you live out divorce-proofing love in a practical, fulfilling way. The tool designed to solidify your commitment to the process of keeping your love alive and relevant is the workbook entitled *Divorce-Proof Your Marriage Workbook*. This workbook will help you understand just what each of the divorce-proofing loves means to your marriage. It will also help you deepen your commitment to the accountability process of experiencing these loves on a consistent basis. Barb and I encourage you to take advantage of this workbook and invite your friends to join you in the exciting adventure of discovering the love of your life all over again (see appendix A).

GOING IT ALONE

You may be reading this book and applying its lessons alone because your husband or wife is not interested in divorce-proofing your marriage. Barb and I are praying for you because our hearts ache for you. If we could sit you down and listen to your personal story of pain and isolation, we would coach you that your commitment is first and foremost to God. Let him be your partner in the process of divorce-proofing your marriage from your side of the relationship. There is no greater place of blessing than to be sheltered by God's love and care.

We also want to offer you reasons to keep at the process of divorce-proofing your side of the marriage even if your spouse doesn't come along. Do it for the sake of your own faithfulness to God. Do it in the hope that your partner will change. But also do it for the sake of your children and the other people in your life. It may be difficult, but try to think beyond your own pain to those who will benefit from your commitment and example of divorce-proof love. Your children may not look back and say that their parents had an ideal marriage, but they will look back and say that they saw their mom or dad display a commitment to love.

One of the great challenges of going it alone in renewing your marriage is trusting God for the work he will do in the life of your husband or wife. The potential for restoration when you as a spouse exercise humility and obedience is so significant. Don't stop believing what God can and will do through you.

In the meantime, you may experience pain and disappointment. You need to express your feelings and receive encouragement. The best place to take your pain is to a mature, supportive Christian of the same sex: a pastor, pastor's wife, Bible study leader, counselor, mature Christian friend, etc. As you do, continue to hold out hope for what your great God can do for your marriage as you maintain the commitment you made on your wedding day.

CATCH THE VISION

Not too long ago, Barb and I were eating lunch together in Carmel, California, where we were speaking at a marriage conference. As I gazed across the table at my wife and partner in ministry, I said, "Barb, what is God doing in our ministry? I mean, he is doing tremendous things. We host hundreds of radio programs and speak at conferences each year. We have a great partnership with Tyndale House Publishers. I have the privilege of meeting with hundreds of men every week in our Cross-Trainers ministry.

"All of that is great," I said, "but does God have a purpose for us beyond what we are already doing? Could it be that he desires to combine these elements to launch a campaign that will have a profound impact on our nation, a campaign that will touch tens of thousands of churches and hundreds of thousands of homes? Has God been preparing us all this time to be his instruments in divorce-proofing America's marriages and families?"

Barb looked at me quizzically. "Gary, where did that come from?"

"I believe it came from the Lord, Barb," I said. And I was serious.

God doesn't typically reveal himself to me through visions. He does it through his Word and prayer. But that day God's vision was very clear to me. Barb and I were being called to take a stand for the homes of America, to challenge the church and God's people to draw a line in the sand and declare, "As for me and my house, we will serve the Lord." We were being positioned to serve the body of Christ, to give our lives and ministry to help take back what the enemy has stolen: the Christian marriage and family.

Then I began to think: What more worthy endeavor could we undertake than to challenge, edify, and teach the Bible-based principles you have read in this book for building loving homes and divorce-proofing America's marriages? For us, there is no greater call. And we want to help you in your marriage and in your churches to divorce-proof America's families.

The bottom line is this:

If we don't do it together, who will?

If we don't do it *now,* then when?

If it doesn't start here—with our family and yours—then where?

Barb and I believe that a holy fire can ignite across this land. If you take the principles we have shared with you and let them take root and grow in the soil of your marriage, you are well on your way to divorce-proofing your home. But it doesn't stop there. If you—as a couple, a pastor, a small-group leader, an adult Sunday school teacher—share these principles with other couples you care about, you will become a hero to families. Think of the impact as God's divorce-proofing guidelines change couple after couple, family after family.

Let me crystallize the vision and tell you how God has already used this material to change the marriages of one church. In the fall of 2001, we launched this campaign in our local church—Valley Church, in West Des Moines, Iowa— where we field-tested this material. We ministered to about five hundred people for eight consecutive Sunday nights. On the closing night we held a covenant service where 220 couples signed personal covenants as well as a churchwide covenant, pledging themselves to go the distance in their marriages. That evening we saw couples married less than a year and couples married forty or fifty years celebrate a lifelong commitment to marriage. We had four generations of one family witness a husband's and wife's recommitment to their wedding vows. We had little girls dressed up in bridesmaid dresses for their parents.

Weeks later an eighty-some-year-old grandmother approached me and told me that she had been in the sanctuary that night with her son and daughter. Her comment said it all, "Gary, I was at their *first* wedding twenty-some years ago, and I wouldn't have given a plug nickel for their making it. But after seeing how God has transformed them through this series, I *know* they are going to make it."

One couple proclaimed that after sitting in the church parking lot on three Sunday nights following the series, planning their divorce in the midst of despair, God restored them. Then with tears in their eyes they showed us their brand-new wedding bands celebrating their commitment. Today the churchwide marriage covenant hangs in the Welcome Center of our church, proclaiming Valley Church as the first church in this movement to divorce-proof America. Husbands and wives, kids and grandparents, friends in good times and bad can return to that document to be reminded of God's grace and proclamation of a family of believers committed to going the distance in their marriages. We even ended the last evening with a wedding cake, punch, and a celebration with kids, grandkids, and friends!

Yes, we can launch a nationwide campaign and see countless homes transformed. But beware. If we do not teach these principles to our own children, we risk missing the greatest opportunity of all: to pass our legacy of godly homes to the next generation. Barb and I believe that, *for the sake of the next generation,* there is no more worthy cause. This holy fire must purify our own homes first.

So prepare yourselves for action. Put on that armor of God. Take the Word of God into your heart and into your home. Stay on your knees in prayer. Stay clean before each other and the Lord Jesus. Experience his grace and forgiveness when you struggle, and then get back in the race. And spread the good word that God is not finished with America's homes. He is simply looking for couples who are willing to join him in the ministry of divorce-proofing America's marriages for the sake of the next generation.

You can count Barb and me in. We are here to help you and your church or small group. And since you are still reading at this point in the book, we believe you are with us.

We will see you in the battle or on the other side. God bless you!

Appendix A

CAMPAIGN RESOURCES FOR DIVORCE-PROOFING AMERICA'S MARRIAGES

$\mathcal{D}$ear friends,

The resources for the Divorce-Proofing America's Marriages campaign are designed *for you*—to help you divorce-proof your marriage. You and your spouse can certainly read and study these books as a couple. But it's only when you meet with a small group that is committed to divorce-proofing their marriages as well that you'll fully experience the power of these ideas. There's power when believers unite in a common cause. There's power when men and women keep each other accountable. To take on this challenge, you must have a group of friends who are encouraging you every step of the way.

There are several ways you can connect to a small group:

◆ Start your own Divorce-Proofing America's Marriages small group in your church or neighborhood. For workbooks, leader's guides, videos, and other resources for your small group, call 888-ROSBERG (888-767-2374) or visit our Web site **www.divorceproof.com.**

- ◆ Give this information to your pastor or elders at your local church. They may want to host a Divorce-Proofing America's Marriages small group in your church.
- ◆ Call America's Family Coaches at 888-ROSBERG (888-767-2374), or e-mail us at afc@afclive.com and we will connect you with people and churches who are interested in Divorce-Proofing America's Marriages.

Yes, together we can launch a nationwide campaign and see countless homes transformed into covenant homes. But beware. If we do not teach these principles to our own children, we risk missing the greatest opportunity of all: to pass our legacy of godly homes to the next generation. Barb and I believe that, *for the sake of the next generation,* there is no more worthy cause. This holy fire must purify our own homes first.

Gary and Barb Rosberg

DIVORCE-PROOF YOUR MARRIAGE
ISBN 0-8423-4995-2
Audio CD (3 CDs) ISBN 0-8423-6592-3
Audiocassette (2 cassettes) ISBN 0-8423-6894-9

DISCOVER THE LOVE OF YOUR LIFE ALL OVER AGAIN (workbook)
ISBN 0-8423-7342-X

Your house is weatherproofed. But is your marriage divorce-proofed? In this foundational book of the Divorce-Proofing America's Marriages campaign, Gary and Barb show couples how to keep their marriages safe from the threat of divorce. Divorce doesn't happen suddenly. Over months and years couples can slide from the dream to disappointment and eventually to emotional divorce. However, they can stop the slide by learning to love in six unique ways. Small groups will enjoy the *Discover the Love of Your Life All Over Again* workbook, which includes eight sessions. Together couples will practice healing hurt in their marriages, meeting their spouses' needs, strengthening each other through difficult times, guarding their marriage against threats, celebrating their spouses, and renewing their love for each other day after day. A weekly devotion and assignment will help couples practice what they learn in the context of the encouragement of couples who are committed to the same goal of divorce-proofing their marriages. This workbook includes an easy-to-follow leader's guide.

THE 5 LOVE NEEDS OF MEN AND WOMEN
ISBN 0-8423-4239-7
Audiocassette (2 cassettes) ISBN 0-8423-3587-0

SERVING LOVE (workbook)
ISBN 0-8423-7343-8

You, too, can learn how to become your spouse's best friend with *The Five Love Needs of Men and Women* book and workbook. In this book, Gary talks to women about the deepest needs of their husbands, and Barb talks to men about the most intimate needs of their wives. You'll discover the deep yearnings of your spouse. And when you join a group studying the *Serving Love* workbook, you will learn how to understand and meet your spouse's needs within a circle of encouraging friends. They can help you find ways to meet those needs day after day, week after week. The workbook includes eight group sessions, three weekly activities, and ideas for a date night with your spouse. Easy-to-follow leader's guide included.

40 UNFORGETTABLE DATES WITH YOUR MATE
ISBN 0-8423-6106-5

When's the last time you and your spouse went on an unforgettable date? Saying "I do" certainly doesn't mean you're finished working at your marriage. Nobody ever put a tank of gas in a car and expected it to run for years. But lots of couples are running on emotional fumes of long-ago dates. Truth is, if you're not dating your spouse, your relationship is not growing. Bring the zing back into your marriage with *40 Unforgettable Dates with Your Mate,* a book that gives husbands and wives ideas on how they can meet the five love needs of their spouse. Wives, get the inside scoop on your husband. Men, discover what your wife finds irresistible. Gary and Barb Rosberg show you how, step-by-step, in fun and creative dates.

GUARD YOUR HEART
ISBN 0-8423-5732-7

GUARDING LOVE (workbook)
ISBN 0-8423-7344-6

We all need to guard our hearts and marriages. It's only in a couples small group, among like-minded friends, that you can get the solid support you need to withstand attacks on your marriage. In *Guard Your Heart,* Gary and Barb Rosberg outline the unique dangers and temptations husbands and wives face.

In the *Guarding Love* workbook, the Rosbergs give you the tools to show your small group how to hold each other accountable to guarding their marriages—no matter the cost.

Do you know of a marriage in your church or neighborhood that is vulnerable to attack? Start a small group for that couple with the *Guarding Love* workbook as a resource. Or invite that couple to a small group that is reading and applying this book and workbook. The workbook includes eight exciting group sessions and an easy-to-follow leader's guide.

**HEALING THE HURT
IN YOUR MARRIAGE**
ISBN 1-58997-104-3 **Available Spring 2004**

In *Healing the Hurt in Your Marriage,* Gary and Barb Rosberg show you how to forgive past hurt in your marriage and close the loop on unresolved conflict. Restore an honest, whole relationship with your spouse. You probably know a dozen marriages that are deteriorating because one spouse is holding a grudge or because the husband and wife have never resolved their conflict, hurt, or anger. And most marriages have past hurts that are hindering the ongoing relationship. Gary and Barb show you how to break free of these past hurts and experience wholeness again. The most effective way to heal wounds is within the circle of encouraging believers who understand, know, and sympathize with you in the common struggles in marriage.

RENEWING YOUR LOVE: DEVOTIONS FOR COUPLES
ISBN 0-8423-7346-2

Have the demands of everyday life pressed in on your marriage? Has your to-do list become more important than your relationship with your spouse? Is the TV the center of your home rather than the love you and your spouse share? This devotional from America's Family Coaches, Gary and Barb Rosberg, will help you and your spouse focus on your marriage, your relationship, and the love of your life. Let Gary and Barb guide you through thirty days of renewal and recommitment to your marriage by reviewing forgiving love, serving love, persevering love, guarding love, celebrating love, and renewing love through the lens of Scripture, reflection, prayer, and application.

Look for a persevering love book in the future from the Rosbergs and Tyndale House Publishers. This book will help you weather the storms of life without losing the passion for your spouse.

Also watch for a celebrating love book from your favorite family coaches, Gary and Barb Rosberg. This book will give you creative ideas on how to keep the fire and passion alive in your marriage.

Begin to divorce-proof your home,
your church, and your community today.

Contact your local bookstore that sells
Christian books for all of the resources of the
Divorce-Proofing America's Marriages
campaign
or
call 888-ROSBERG (888-767-2374).
or
visit our Web site at

www.divorceproof.com

Appendix B

MARRIAGE MAP
SELF-TESTS

$\mathcal{E}$ach self-test and checklist discussed in this book is included here in a format that is easy to photocopy for use by an individual couple or a small group of couples.

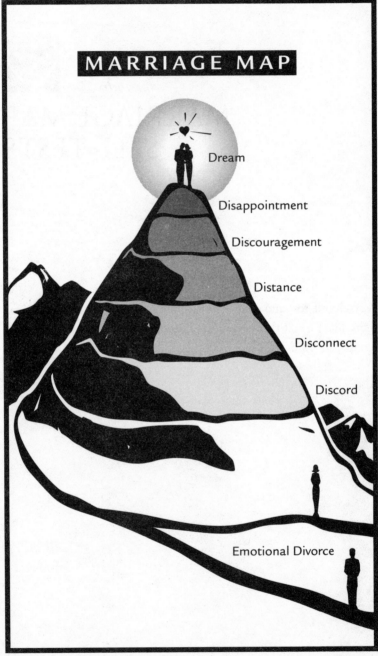

THE DREAM STOP

Compare yourself to these indicators, and check any that describe the current state of your marriage:

H   W

❑   ❑   I communicate freely with my spouse, and we keep no inappropriate secrets.

❑   ❑   I forgive my spouse when I am wronged and seek forgiveness when I offend. I am loved without strings.

❑   ❑   My spouse and I eagerly seek to discover and meet each other's needs.

❑   ❑   We have faced and conquered difficult circumstances that have undone other marriages.

❑   ❑   I consciously guard myself against threats and temptations that could pull our marriage apart.

❑   ❑   We enjoy ongoing emotional, physical, and spiritual closeness.

❑   ❑   We are committed to keeping our relationship fresh and alive "till death do us part."

THE DISAPPOINTMENT STOP

Compare yourself to these indicators, and check any that describe the current state of your marriage:

H   W

❑   ❑   I have difficulty expressing affirmation to or about my spouse.

❑   ❑   My spouse isn't the flawless person I thought I married.

❑   ❑   I feel surprised and let down when I notice an imperfection in my spouse.

❑   ❑   My spouse and I have caused each other to feel hurt and angry.

❑   ❑   My spouse and I have experienced conflict over personality differences, male-female wiring, or ways of doing things we learned from our families.

❑   ❑   I compare my spouse to other people.

❑   ❑   I have a mental list of things I wish I could change about my spouse.

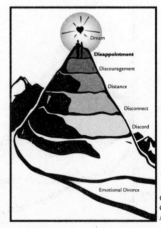

THE DISCOURAGEMENT STOP

Compare yourself to these indicators, and check any that describe the current state of your marriage:

H   W

❏   ❏   I often wonder if I am missing out on something in my marriage.

❏   ❏   I have a mental list of reasons why I am dissatisfied with my marriage.

❏   ❏   My spouse implies—or says—that I don't understand him or her or know how to meet his or her needs.

❏   ❏   My own needs are not being met in my marriage. I feel as if my spouse's friends, work, church involvement, and/or the kids are more important than I am.

❏   ❏   Even when I recognize my spouse's needs, I am not successful at meeting them.

❏   ❏   I have a difficult time expressing my needs in a way my spouse can understand and act on.

❏   ❏   I wonder if my choice of a spouse was a mistake.

THE DISTANCE STOP

Compare yourself to these indicators, and check any that describe the current state of your marriage:

    H   W

❑   ❑   I could describe our relationship as "fair to partly cloudy, with no clearing in sight."

❑   ❑   I often fill my free time with activities that don't include my spouse.

❑   ❑   I have given up most of my expectations of my spouse.

❑   ❑   I wonder if my spouse ever feels excited about being married to me.

❑   ❑   My spouse sometimes seems like a stranger to me.

❑   ❑   I keep many of my thoughts and feelings from my spouse.

❑   ❑   I worry that we might someday face a problem bigger than our resolve to stay together.

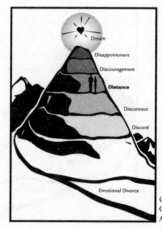

THE DISCONNECT STOP

Compare yourself to these indicators, and check any that describe the current state of your marriage:

H W

❏ ❏ I sometimes feel lonely even when I'm with my spouse.

❏ ❏ It is difficult for me to "feel" that my spouse loves me. I may know it intellectually, but I don't sense an emotional connection.

❏ ❏ When we are together, we seldom have much to say to each other.

❏ ❏ When we do talk to each other, we often misunderstand and misinterpret each other.

❏ ❏ I prefer to devote my time, energy, and money to something or someone other than my spouse.

❏ ❏ I doubt that my marriage can grow or change for the better.

❏ ❏ I don't think my spouse is very interested in who I am or what I want to do.

THE DISCORD STOP

Compare yourself to these indicators, and check any that describe the current state of your marriage:

H   W

❑   ❑   Most of my thoughts about my spouse are negative.

❑   ❑   My spouse and I verbally lash out at each other, saying things that are hurtful.

❑   ❑   I often wonder what it would be like not to be married—or to be married to a different person.

❑   ❑   I daydream or fantasize about another person who would make a better spouse.

❑   ❑   I feel as if my spouse and I are at war.

❑   ❑   True tenderness with my spouse is a faded memory. We avoid sexual intimacy.

❑   ❑   Family and close friends notice that our marriage is severely strained.

THE EMOTIONAL DIVORCE STOP

Compare yourself to these indicators, and check any that describe the current state of your marriage:

H   W

❑   ❑   I am staying married for some reason other than love for my spouse.

❑   ❑   I have given up hope that my marriage could be better.

❑   ❑   I pretend I'm okay with my marriage to keep up appearances.

❑   ❑   My first goal in my marriage is to protect myself from further pain.

❑   ❑   My spouse and I have separated or considered separating.

❑   ❑   My heart is deeply attached to someone other than my spouse, even if I am not acting on that feeling.

❑   ❑   I know I have already walked away from my marriage emotionally.

THE STATE OF OUR MARRIAGE

Review the seven stops on the marriage map as described below, then check one or two that you think most closely describe your marriage today. Realize that your spouse may have a different perspective on the state of your marriage. That being the case, Barb and I recommend that you both complete the exercise independently and then discuss your evaluation together. If it makes you feel too vulnerable to put your responses in the book, make two photocopies of the checklist and record your responses there.

H   W

DREAM

❑   ❑   We communicate freely and keep no inappropriate secrets.

❑   ❑   We forgive one another and seek forgiveness.

❑   ❑   We seek to discover and meet each other's needs.

❑   ❑   We face and conquer difficult circumstances.

❑   ❑   We guard our marriage against threats and temptations.

❑   ❑   We enjoy ongoing emotional, physical, and spiritual closeness.

❑   ❑   We are committed "till death do us part."

DISAPPOINTMENT

❑   ❑   We have difficulty affirming each other.

❑   ❑   We are surprised by each other's flaws.

❑   ❑   We feel let down by each other's imperfections.

❑   ❑   We cause each other hurt and anger.

❑   ❑   We have conflict over our differences.

❑   ❑   We compare each other to other people.

❑   ❑   We wish we could change things in each other.

H   W

DISCOURAGEMENT

❏   ❏   We often wonder if our marriage is missing something.

❏   ❏   We have reasons to be dissatisfied with our marriage.

❏   ❏   We don't understand each other or meet each other's needs.

❏   ❏   We feel unimportant to each other.

❏   ❏   We are not successful at meeting each other's needs.

❏   ❏   We have difficulty expressing our needs to each other.

❏   ❏   We wonder if we chose the wrong partner.

DISTANCE

❏   ❏   We do not see a letup in our difficulties.

❏   ❏   We do many activities alone, without each other.

❏   ❏   We have given up most expectations for each other.

❏   ❏   We feel little excitement about being married to each other.

❏   ❏   We sometimes feel and act like strangers.

❏   ❏   We keep many of our thoughts and feelings from each other.

❏   ❏   We face a problem that may eventually drive us apart.

H   W

DISCONNECT

❏   ❏   We sometimes feel lonely even when we are together.

❏   ❏   We don't feel an emotional connection to each other.

❏   ❏   We seldom have much to say to each other.

❏   ❏   We often misunderstand and misinterpret each other.

❏   ❏   We direct our attention and activities away from each other.

❏   ❏   We doubt that our marriage can change for the better.

❏   ❏   We are not very interested in each other.

DISCORD

❏   ❏   We think and act negatively toward each other.

❏   ❏   We lash out and hurt each other verbally.

❏   ❏   We wonder what it would be like if we weren't married.

❏   ❏   We wonder what it would be like to be married to someone else.

❏   ❏   We feel that we are at war.

❏   ❏   We lack tenderness and sexual intimacy.

❏   ❏   We cannot hide from others that our marriage is severely strained.

H   W

EMOTIONAL DIVORCE

❑   ❑   We are staying married for some reason other than love.

❑   ❑   We have no hope that our marriage can be better.

❑   ❑   We pretend that our marriage is okay to keep up appearances.

❑   ❑   We only want to protect ourselves from further pain.

❑   ❑   We have separated or have considered separating.

❑   ❑   We are emotionally attached to someone else.

❑   ❑   We have already walked away from our marriage emotionally.

GETTING BACK TO THE DREAM

Look at the list below, and check the loves that you feel will most effectively bring the growth your marriage needs. Then indicate in the blanks to the right which love you feel deserves the highest priority in your strategy to get back on the road to the dream. Identify your top three priorities. Complete the exercise independently, and then discuss your evaluation together. If it makes you feel too vulnerable to put your responses in the book, make two photocopies of the checklist and record your responses there.

H   W

❑   ❑   Forgiving love (priority: _____)

❑   ❑   Serving love (priority: _____)

❑   ❑   Persevering love (priority: _____)

❑   ❑   Guarding love (priority: _____)

❑   ❑   Celebrating love (priority: _____)

❑   ❑   Renewing love (priority: _____)

Appendix C

DISCOVERING YOUR TOP FIVE NEEDS

$\mathcal{T}$he findings here represent the categorical data that emerged from our survey of 700 couples in 8 cities. We gave each husband and each wife a list of 20 needs and asked them to rank them in order of importance. The lists here represent their choices.

How would you have ranked your needs? How would your spouse have ranked his or her needs? Find your top five needs, and share them with your spouse.

HUSBANDS' NEEDS	WIVES' NEEDS
1. Unconditional love and acceptance	1. Unconditional love and acceptance
2. Sexual intimacy	2. Emotional intimacy and communication
3. Companionship	3. Spiritual intimacy
4. Encouragement and affirmation	4. Encouragement and affirmation
5. Spiritual intimacy	5. Companionship
6. Trust	6. Family relationships

HUSBANDS' NEEDS	WIVES' NEEDS
7. Honesty and openness	7. Honesty and openness
8. Emotional intimacy and communication	8. Nonsexual touch
9. Family relationships	9. Security and stability
10. To be desired	10. Romance
11. Career support	11. Trust
12. To provide and protect	12. Understanding and empathy
13. Personal time	13. Sexual intimacy
14. Understanding and empathy	14. Personal time
15. Admiration	15. To be desired
16. Security and stability	16. Domestic support
17. Significance	17. To provide and protect
18. Romance	18. Significance
19. Domestic support	19. Admiration
20. Nonsexual touch	20. Career support

Notes

Chapter 2: The Marriage Map

1. Mike McManus, *"Marriage Savers* Answers 25 Tough Questions,"
   question 2, 2001; <www.marriagesavers.org/public/
   marriage_savers_answers_25_tough.htm>.
2. E. Mavis Hetherington and John Kelly, *For Better or for Worse:
   Divorce Reconsidered* (New York: Norton, 2002), 272.
3. Ibid., 262.
4. Quoted in John Trent, *My Mother's Hands* (Colorado Springs,
   Colo.: WaterBrook, 2000), 1.
5. William Doherty, "Warning Signs of a Breakup Quiz Can Assess
   Situation," *USA Today*, 21 July 2001.

Chapter 3: You Can Divorce-Proof Your Marriage

1. Robert Coombs, "Marital Status and Personal Well-Being: A
   Literature Review," *Family Relations* 40 (January 1991): 97–102.
2. Linda J. Waite, "Why Marriage Matters" (paper presented at
   Strengthening Marriage Roundtable, Washington, D.C., June 23,
   1997).
3. Mike McManus, *"Marriage Savers* Answers 25 Tough Questions,"
   question 18, 2001; <www.marriagesavers.org/public/
   marriage_savers_answers_25_tough.htm>.
4. Ibid.
5. Ibid.
6. The list of six ways children suffer from divorce is based on Karen
   S. Peterson, "Unhappily Ever After: Children of Divorce Grow
   into Bleak Legacy," *USA Today*, 5 September 2000, which summarizes the findings in Judith Wallerstein, Julia Lewis, and Sandra
   Blakeslee, *The Unexpected Legacy of Divorce* (New York: Hyperion,
   2000).

Chapter 4: The Rocky Road of Hurt and Anger

1. Les Carter, *Good 'n' Angry* (Grand Rapids: Baker, 1983), 35.
2. Lewis B. Smedes, *Forgive and Forget* (San Francisco: Harper & Row, 1984), 133.
3. See Matthew 6:14-15.
4. C. S. Lewis, *The Problem of Pain* (New York: Macmillan, 1962), 93.

Chapter 5: Closing the Loop

1. Bill and Lynne Hybels, *Fit to Be Tied* (Grand Rapids: Zondervan, 1991), 178.
2. David A. Stoop and James Masteller, *Forgiving Our Parents, Forgiving Ourselves* (Ann Arbor, Mich.: Vine Books, 1991), 263.

Chapter 6: In Honor of Your Spouse

1. Dennis Rainey, *Lonely Husbands, Lonely Wives* (recently renamed *Staying Close*) (Dallas: Word, 1989), 31.

Chapter 7: Communicating Your Needs

1. Robertson McQuilkin, *A Promise Kept* (Wheaton, Ill.: Tyndale House, 1998), 22-23.
2. Ibid., 85.
3. Ibid., 64.
4. The five levels are adapted from John J. Powell, *Why Am I Afraid to Tell You Who I Am?* (Chicago: Argus Communications, 1969).
5. Gary and Barbara Rosberg, *The Five Love Needs of Men and Women* (Wheaton, Ill.: Tyndale House, 2000).
6. Gary and Barbara Rosberg, *40 Unforgettable Dates with Your Mate* (Wheaton, Ill.: Tyndale House, 2002).
7. Please understand that we mention these books because we truly believe they can help you, not because we want to be self-promoting.

Chapter 8: Love That Endures Tough Times

1. Glenna Whitley, "George and Laura, Love and Marriage," *Ladies' Home Journal* (February 2002): 56-58.
2. Ibid., 58.
3. Ibid., 144.
4. Ibid.

Chapter 11: Building Walls of Protection

1. All Scripture quotations in this paragraph are taken from the New International Version. Emphasis is added.

Chapter 12: Rekindle the Joy of Being Married

1. John M. Gottman and Nan Silver, *The Seven Principles of Making Marriage Work* (New York: Crown, 1999), 17.

Chapter 15: Nurturing a Lifetime Marriage

1. Karen S. Peterson, "'Hot' and 'Cool' Phases Could Predict Divorce," *USA Today,* 14 September 2000.
2. Gary Smalley, *Making Love Last Forever* (Dallas: Word, 1996).

ABOUT THE
AUTHORS

$\mathcal{D}$r. **Gary and Barbara Rosberg** are America's Family
Coaches—equipping and encouraging America's families to live
and finish life well. Having been married for nearly thirty years,
Gary and Barbara have a unique message for couples. The
Rosbergs have committed the next decade of their ministry to
divorce-proofing America's marriages. The cornerstone book
in that campaign is *Divorce-Proof Your Marriage*. Other books the
Rosbergs have written together include their best-selling *The Five
Love Needs of Men and Women, 40 Unforgettable Dates with Your Mate,
Guard Your Heart,* and *Renewing Your Love: Devotions for Couples.*

Together Gary and Barbara host a nationally syndicated, daily
radio program, *America's Family Coaches . . . LIVE!* On this live call-
in program heard in cities all across the country, they coach call-
ers on many family-related issues. The Rosbergs also host a Saturday radio program on the award-winning secular WHO Radio.

Gary and Barbara have conducted conferences on family and
relationship issues in more than one hundred cities across the
country. They are on the national speaking teams for FamilyLife

marriage conferences and FamilyLife "I Still Do" arena events for couples. Gary also has spoken to thousands of men at Promise Keepers stadium events annually since 1996 and to parents and adolescents at Focus on the Family *Life on the Edge* tours.

Gary, who earned his Ed.D. from Drake University, has been a marriage and family counselor for twenty years. He coaches CrossTrainers, a men's Bible study and accountability group of more than six hundred men.

Barbara, who earned a B.F.A. at Drake University, has written *Connecting with Your Wife* in addition to several other books with Gary. She also speaks to women, coaching and encouraging them by emphasizing their incredible value and worth.

The Rosbergs live outside Des Moines, Iowa, and are the parents of two daughters: Missy, a college student studying communications; and Sarah, who lives outside Des Moines with her husband, Scott, and their son, Mason.

For more information on the ministries of
America's Family Coaches, contact:

America's Family Coaches
2540 106th Street, Suite 101
Des Moines, Iowa 50322
1-888-ROSBERG
www.divorceproof.com

FREE! Downloadable discussion guide
for this and other Tyndale titles at
ChristianBookGuides.com